D1273105

Blood River Rising

—Courtesy Thompson Family

Paul and Hadley Thompson

Blood River Rising

The Thompson-Crismon Feud of the 1920s

Victoria Pope Hubbell, Ph.D.

To Judy,
Here's to
looking at both
sides!
Victoria Hubbell
2019

Iris Press
Oak Ridge, Tennessee

Copyright © 2016 by Victoria Pope Hubbell

All rights reserved. No portion of this book may be reproduced in any form or by any means, including electronic storage and retrieval systems, without explicit, prior written permission of the publisher, except for brief passages excerpted for review and critical purposes.

Cover Art: Copyright © 2015 by Alex Hubbell
www.alexhubbell.com

Book Design: Robert B. Cumming, Jr.

Library of Congress Cataloging-in-Publication Data

Names: Hubbell, Victoria Pope, 1955- author.
Title: Blood river rising : the Thompson-Crismon feud of the 1920s / Victoria Pope Hubbell.
Description: Oak Ridge, Tennessee : Iris Press, [2016] | Includes bibliographical references.
Identifiers: LCCN 2016031969 (print) | LCCN 2016039460 (ebook) | ISBN 9781604542349 (pbk. : alk. paper) | ISBN 9781604548112 (e-book)
Subjects: LCSH: Thompson, Grant, -1925. | Crismon, Frederick P. | Vendetta—Missouri—Case studies. | Murder—Missouri—Case studies. | Ku Klux Klan (1915-)—Missouri—Case studies.
Classification: LCC HV6452.M8 H83 2016 (print) | LCC HV6452.M8 (ebook) | DDC 364.152/30977856—dc23
LC record available at https://lccn.loc.gov/2016031969

To George, Alex, and Kate. I love you and thank you.

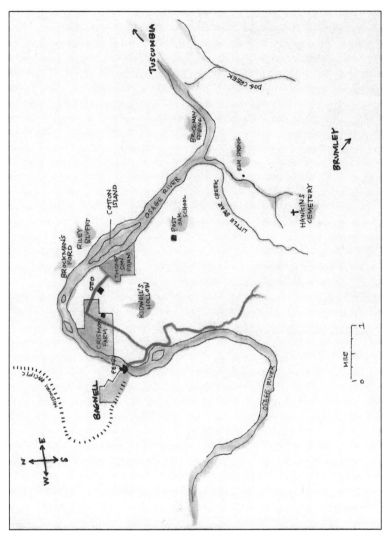

Map

CONTENTS

Hadley Thompson of Wilcox Bend; Boyhood memories; Wilcox Bend; Secret societies and the Thompson-Crismon feud; Siblings; Life on the Osage river bottom; Brotherly love; The Great War ends; Billy Sunday's revival; Hadley's visions.

Ozark and Thompson History; Decoration Day; Aunt Maggie and Plez Moore; Kleagles in Wilcox Bend; Crismon family arrives; A barn raising; Butchering; German neighbors; Witness to a whipping; Klaverns and prohibition; Vigilantism in the Ozarks; Barney gets saved.

Tom Dixon and the Klan revival of 1915; The price of friendship; Myrt produces a woods' colt; The Kleagles meet Plez Moore; Klan membership spreads; River baptisms, threshing, and nativism; KKK takes root in Wilcox Bend; Boyhood divisions; The bonds of church, lodge, and Klan; Gipsy the schoolmarm; State government moves into Wilcox Bend; Man buried alive; Frederick Crismon's leadership; Grant Thompson criticized; Klan membership meeting; Prohibition enforced; Sunday school; Hadley and Ty Sears in Bagnell.

Klan divides the community; Grant walks out on the church; Church involvement with Klan activities; Culprits kill livestock; The flood of 1923; The Thompson way; Financial slump of 1923; Klan business disrupts the schoolhouse; Confrontation begins; First Klan-related death; A big ruckus; Neighborhood jealousy; More church involvement; Another whipping; Klan adversaries; A serious shooting.

The Thompson Family*

John Christopher **Grant Thompson** (b. 1864)
was one of twelve children, including:
Margaret Virginia Magnolia "**Aunt Maggie**,"
Eleven H. Coa "**Uncle Lev**"

Grant Thompson married
1ˢᵗ wife: **Emma** Olive **Ponder** (b. 1869) who died in childbirth (1901)
and in total delivered the following seven children:

Dessie Mae (b. 1887), Harrison **Otto** (b. 1889),
Clyde Waldo (b. 1891), **John** Winslow (b. 1893),
Joanna "**Annie**" (b. 1896), James "**Jim**" Grant (b.1899),
Gie Basel (b. 1901)

Grant Thompson married
2ⁿᵈ wife: Amanda Myrtle "**Myrt**" Wornell **Thompson** (b. 1880)
[Who as a teenager had given birth to **Gipsy** Wornell]
and in total delivered the following six children:

Web G. (b. 1903), **Joe** Drake (b. 1904), **Charley** Clayton (b. 1906),
Hadley Herbert (b. 1911), **Paul** Dean (b. 1914), Karma Jean (b. 1920)

*__Bold__ denotes characters in *Blood River Rising*

The Crismon Family

Frederick Pinkney **Crismon** (b. 1880)
married
Sarah Elizabeth Shelton **Crismon** (b.1878)
who gave birth to the following three children:

Francis Marion	**Leo**	**Anita Rachel**
(b. 1905)	(b. 1907)	(b. 1909)

As well as **Logan Hickey,** a nephew of Sarah Crismon

—Courtesy Thompson Family

Joe, Hadley, and Icel Thompson

INNOCENCE (1911-1919)

Threshed and shocked corn
drying in a Missouri field

We had the first blizzard of the season last night, and after I'd gone to sleep, the fox came to me over the snow of my dreams like he always does. Head up, proud-like, every forty feet or so he stops and bends up his front leg, same as a pointer. He glides lightly through the white. His tail looks as thick as his body, and his chest and belly blend white with the snow. Four little feet take him anywhere he wants to go, but he won't go far. I know. He'll double back then cross over his tracks to confuse us all in a game I don't even remember the start of.

In my dream I'm in bed, looking out the window. The moon's a bright sun, leaving shadows like daytime, and the long fur on the fox's back shines a deep red. Feet and tail dipped in ink.

For a second, he turns his head and looks at me — looks me right in the eye. That small wise face has a mouth that looks like it's gonna smile, like we're old friends instead of old enemies. I know he's thinking, "Catch me if you can, Hadley!" Then he's off. No sound. Tail-tip flicking a wave good-bye.

I roll away from the window to my brother who's curled up next to me. Now, I often slept next to Paul or Joe, but in my dream it's always Charley with me. I'm gonna wake him up so he'll go with me. I push his shoulder and shake him, and Charley groans something. But I whisper, "Come on. Let's go fox huntin'." He smiles a bit with eyes still shut. Then so quiet nobody else in the room hears, he says, "You're on."

Next we're pushing our boots through the drifts in the woods. The tree limbs make spiderwebs of shadows on the snow, and Charley has the shotgun under his right arm. We're all full of talk and laugh. There's lots of different tracks, and we recognize them all. Wilcox Bend had all kinds of animals back then, but humans was only one of them. When we get down to the river, Charley stops and points with the barrel tip to where that prize tail of our fox has swept away the powder. Everywhere his even-spaced paw prints speckle the riverbank.

It's so quiet in my dream I can hear snow slide off the ends of cedar trees and whoosh on the shadows below. I take a deep breath, and the air is so cold it makes my chest hurt. The water whispers under the river's ice while our long coats swish against our legs. We're two happy boys out there with all we have and love.

Then a shot jumps out at us from the hills. The echo bounces off the bluffs, back and forth, until it sounds like it's all around us. Charley's shotgun comes up and he reaches, without even thinking, for the wood under the barrels. "Tck" he slides off the safety. He points the gun up at the ridge above us, and I twist around and stare, big-eyed, down the river.

*We stand there back-to-back for a bit, but we never see or hear nothin'
else. It ends there. There's only the snow and tracks under the moon and ice on
the river. I can feel the warmth of my brother's back pressed up against mine,
and I know that gun's ready to go.*

I've been having that dream for over seventy years now.

The first time I met Hadley Thompson, he said "Hello" and then nothing else for two hours.

We sat together at his kitchen table in Miller County, Missouri, where I conducted an interview with his wife, Icel (pronounced ICE-el) Thompson. I was working as a rural town historian, on a project for a nearby county. It was my job to interview elderly residents of the area, and Icel had been born in my territory.

Mrs. "Baby, you call me Icel now" Thompson was in her eighties with jet-colored hair. She was quite proud of her handmade, bright pink pantsuit. She was of solid country stock and prefaced many of her statements with, "Now, you're not going to print this, are you?"

The Thompsons lived together in a modest, one-story home painted an unusual color. It was a cheerful mix of aqua and stoplight green. I approached the house that first day wondering little more than, "What kind of people paint their house a color that ought to have its own name, but doesn't?"

After about two hours, it was time to leave. Icel's extremely quiet husband leaned forward, peered at me as though he just noticed the stranger sitting at his kitchen table, and pointed at my chest. I resisted the temptation to look where he was pointing. Then came the words I recall so clearly: "I have a tale for you." It would be years before he would be so quiet again.

Next my tape recorded his gruff voice: "It's about a man that got his head blowed off, right over there. I'll take you to the spot now. It needs to be written down, but I'm no writer." I said nothing, probably thinking, "Mister, I'm certainly not the one who's going to write it." Or perhaps it was something like, "Exactly which one of you chose the exterior paint for this house?" Anyway, I'm certain my reaction was not, "Into everyone's life drops an unexpected opportunity that shouldn't be ignored."

Mother had me at home of course, probably in the same bed where they laid my dead father. That was on the twelfth of May, nineteen hundred and eleven, in Wilcox Bend, Miller County, Missouri. I am Mother's third boy. No girls.

My father, Grant Thompson, was there to help Mother with the birth, along with a neighbor named Professor Molls. No doctor or midwife. Dad helped Mother during the birth of all four sons, and Professor Molls was there for at least two, probably all, of our births. Professor Molls suggested they name me Hadley Herbert Thompson, after the governor of Missouri. Don't know if Dad helped his first wife Emma with the birth of their seven children or not.

I remember my brother Paul's birth when Professor came to help. He stopped his buggy at the base of the hill and carried up bed sheets torn into strips. We both sat on the porch, and I watched him braid those into loops. Then they tied them to the bedposts at the end of the bed and handed Mother the looped end to pull up on. This is how they done it for me and the other three. Later, after my father buried the afterbirth, the two men stood out by the pump and washed the blood from the sheets. I remembered that scene after all those years, for that was the first and last time I saw my father do the washing.

Hadley Herbert Thompson told the story of his tumultuous childhood for seventy-six years to anyone who would listen, and by the time I met him, he was a great storyteller. Hadley could remember the number of steer and heifers grazing in his father's pasture in 1921 and the width of the river at Brockman's Ford. He felt comfortable with concrete facts and figures, yet had an artistic way of looking at the world and sometimes a poetic quality to his reminiscing. If the Olympic games had maintained competitive poetry readings as they did originally, we might be more accustomed to hearing warriors give lyrical readings. Perhaps then the notion that a Thompson could also be a poet wouldn't seem so out of character. Later I learned Hadley was part of a legacy: for over a hundred years, natives of the Ozark Mountains have been known for their storytelling.

That first visit was four hours long, three hours longer than a respectable interview should be. After Hadley started talking, however, I found it hard not to listen. Sometimes the time seemed even longer because Icel Thompson insisted on constantly brewing fresh coffee, and she bumped into the back of my chair every time she got up to pour some more.

Why did I stay? Because there's something mesmerizing about a man's voice that sounds like an aluminum skiff being dragged over gravel. It's also difficult to end an interview describing scenes from times long gone. I was also afraid he might stop talking if interrupted. If I got up, he might chastise me. There were many reasons for sitting on a hard seat so long.

Hadley was intimidating and had a way of jabbing his finger through the air when he wanted to get his point across. After that first meeting it was clear he must have been one hell of a horse trader. On other days, I stared into those blue eyes and knew he must have been a real lady killer in his day. He was both, of course. After all, he was a Thompson.

Our first interview finally ended and I resumed my day. But when I shut my eyes that night, there was Hadley sitting in front at me, sighing, laughing, shaking his head, and leaning back in his chair. There he was drawing a map for me on a piece of cardboard ripped from a box, or resting the palms of his hands on his faded corduroy trousers.

HADLEY: Ever heard of the Thompson-Crismon feud?

VICTORIA: No.

HADLEY: What do you know about Miller County?

VICTORIA: Not much.

HADLEY: Well, you know the Ku Klux Klan was here.

VICTORIA: (incredulous) Here?

HADLEY: Sure, here. What've you found out about the Klan?

VICTORIA: I've not researched it.

HADLEY: (with puzzled look and a point-blank stare) I thought you said you wrote history.

I'm going to tell you about the Thompson-Crismon feud of the early twenties, from nineteen hundred and twenty-one to nineteen and twenty-four. Some of you ain't gonna like it, some of you may. I don't know and I really don't give a damn. I'm going to make a record anyway about what I know, because folks need to know the truth.

My father moved out to God's country, the Wilcox Bend area below the town of Old Bagnell, sometime after 1900. He ran a blacksmith shop in Brumley before that. But after he married my mother, he decided to take up river bottom farming and bought 172 acres down there, about two miles downriver from Bagnell on the south side. We worked on it a long, long time. Paid for it. We farmed wheat, oats, rye, and barley. We used four horses to pull a binder that cut and tied and kicked out the crop in bundles. And corn, always. Back then corn grew taller than a man on horseback. Our fields spread out around the house like a lady's apron.

We'd a good life. Had us a good mother. Had us a good father. They took care of us pretty fair. Of course, you're going to have to understand in those days it weren't nothing like it is today. It's hard to imagine how primitive it was. We got our school lessons by kerosene lamp at night. No electricity, no plumbing. Outside toilets. For drinking water we carried buckets about one third of a mile from a spring. We did this for a long time until Dad dug a drinking well. We washed our clothes with water from the cistern. Dad built all this with the help of us kids or the neighbors.

He moved his blacksmith shop into a little cabin on the farm and except for us, and once in a while a McDowell, did the work himself. In the winter he'd do blacksmithin' for others as well. For cash if they had the money, or trade if 'n they hadn't.

We worked. We worked from daylight 'til dark. We had certain things to do and we did them. Without any questions. It was all settled there and then. There was none of this, "Oh, I don't feel good today, I'll stay in bed." We got up. Period. And I fail to see where all that work hurt us any if at all. We got our share of whippins — but as far as I recall there was none that really hurt me that bad.

If you follow the road along the upper field where the house was, and you know where to tramp down the grass and weeds, you can find the stones to the old cistern. For a long time I threw every snake I caught into that cistern. Why'd I do that? Just a stupid thing boys'll do.

All the memories of my boyhood are still fresh in my mind, seeing as how I never cut 'em loose. I leave them where I can find them any time I want. And I go back there in my mind a lot, especially now that I'm so damn old. I visit things again and again, trying to figure out why things happened the way they did.

I've come to a few conclusions about that. It had to do with the war between the North and the South. And the different groups people belonged to. I also think some of the things our government did played a part. There was aggravation by other people, but besides all that, it always comes back to things being a whole lot different then. Many things happened that we didn't think nothin' about.

Take something as simple as the ferryman's wife. Now, his name was Clyde Rogers, but I can't for the life of me remember hers. I can see her though. A big-boned woman with a face that'd stop an eight-day clock. More a watch-

dog than a wife. Whenever our neighborhood drunk, Tommy Alexander, had too much, out he'd stagger to the ferry landing, hanging on that bell pull with his sagging body, ringing, hollering and weaving until everybody on both sides of the river was awake.

Well, one night, I guess Rogers's wife got fed up with old Tommy's she-nanigans. Here she come barefoot out of her house, wearing nothing but a nightdress and an over-and-under. They say she gave him one last chance to shut up before she leveled both barrels at him from across the river. Wore a hat full of holes from that day on, and we had a good laugh every time we laid eyes on him. Didn't stop his drunkenness none. There weren't no arrests, Tommy never filed charges or sued, or nothing like that. We just went about our business, and he never rang that bell again.

None of that is how it is today, and the changes started with the end of The Great War.

A few months after the Thompson interview, I spent some time at the State Historical Library compiling my small portion of Missouri history. I visited the newspaper library, which contains papers from around the state on microfiche. I researched *The Reveille* (the newspaper from the county I was supposed to be researching) until I came to the year 1924.

I was hired to do a job, but memories of Hadley intruded: "What have you heard about Wilcox Bend? What do you know about the Thompson-Crismon feud?" On a whim, I changed over to the newspaper *The Miller County Autogram*. The reel was dated 1917 through 1925. I threaded the film into the machine, and the first page that flashed on the screen in front of me had a notation of Hadley's father, John Grant Thompson:

> J.G. Thompson, one of our prosperous down the river farmers, made another sale of a pair of extra good 2 year old mules to W.A. Thornsberry of Bagnell. This makes 2 pair of these good stretchy young mules Mr. Thompson has recently sold for a good price.

I read on, again spending more time with the Thompsons than I should have. John Grant Thompson was often in the newspaper, as were his grown sons from his first marriage, Clyde and Otto. It was protocol in Ozark communities for the papers to be little more than an elaborate calendar of community events, as well as a Who's Who of the area.

Ne'er-do-wells were seldom mentioned. The Grant Thompson family, however, was frequently described.

What can I tell you about my brothers? Nobody could tell us apart, for one.

After the shootings started, the papers always had the wrong Thompson here and the wrong Thompson there. But my brothers sure did love me. Just after they stopped beating the hell outta me. I don't know why we fought all the time — we just did.

It was nineteen hundred and eighteen. The end of The Great War. The War to End all Wars. The Last War. It had lots of names. Now, I don't remember Jim leaving for the war, but I sure do recall when we heard he was coming home. Jim, John, and Otto, all brothers from Dad's first wife. They were Ponders, you know. Jim was supposed to be coming home, and Dad was nervous about it all. Think it was a happy time? No. That couldn't be more wrong. For some folks it was the worst time in their lives.

Just stop and think now for a minute what it was like. Many of the boys made it through the fighting, as terrible as that was, only to be slapped down by the Spanish Flu. So their kin goes to meet the train, only young Howie ain't steppin' down onto that platform with the rest of the soldiers. Where's their boy? Come to find out, Howie's in an influenza ward back in Syracuse. Or a morgue. We lost as many to influenza as to the Germans.

Sometimes only a few days later, the family's off again to meet the train, but this time they pick up Howie in a box. Folks met the train, expecting to be able to throw their arms around 'im. They've got it all planned out. Gonna go home, wring the neck of a fine, fat chicken and start baking a cake. What did they get instead? Two somber servicemen with sad faces, quick to grab Mother under her arms as she collapses, just as quick to tell Father what a fine solder his boy was. Just two strangers instead of the boy they loved; two men for escorting them down to the lonely coffin traveling in the last car. Communications being what they were, sometimes the wire wasn't received until they got back home with their dead.

At my age now, I can see what a big day this was for my Dad, wondering how it's going to turn out for our family. Then? I was nothin' but a stupid kid. All I saw was another morning to get away with something.

We ate before daybreak. Dad said, "Charley and Joe, (my two older brothers) you come work with me. Barnie, (that was my nickname) you get all the eggs and those three speckled hens and take them to the store in Tuscumbia. Just have Mr. Gaylord put the scrip on our account."

So the older boys went out with him straight away while little brother Paul stayed at the house to help Mother and John. I was about seven and Paul about four. I got the hens and eggs from the hen house, put the eggs in a basket and the hens in coups, then floated in a skiff down river to the general store in Tuscumbia. It was a fine and sunny day. Not too warm.

I did the first part of the errand well enough, except for feeling compelled to slip a few eggs into the front of my coveralls. It was on the way home that the plan fell apart. I'd a swell time swimming, then cooking my stolen treats. Set 'em between hot rocks from a fire and they cook just like they was boiled. I spent a good part of the morning flat on my back, staring up at the sky, pondering important things. I was working hard, and meanwhile brothers Charley and Joe was busy at the barn no doubt taking note of my contributions.

Paul was of a like mind that day. He'd gone behind the house to toss out some dishwater and somehow noticed that if he stood on a crate, he could piss farther than usual. I'm not sure how this knowledge came about, but young boys have a knack for discovery. When I finally ambled on home, he called to me, and I went over to that part of the yard. "Have a pissing contest with me, Barney. I'll out-piss you."

The contest was on, but first we had to drink as much water as possible so we'd have plenty to contest with. All this took a good, long time, time we was supposed to be putting into our work.

Finally, Dad and them walked back up to the house to get cleaned up. Charley was a'glarin at me as he walked up the hill. Charley was five years older than me and tougher than boot leather. I could see him clenching his fists as he walked.

"Barney," he called to me, and he spat. We all said Charley was born with a quid of tobacco in his mouth. He loved the stuff. It was obvious Charley in particular was disappointed in my endeavors that morning, but he didn't say nothin'. He just chewed, spat, and glared.

Just a few weeks before, Charley and I were doing some grinding for the livestock. We had an old horse, Goldie, and that horse went 'round and 'round on a pole attached to the mill in the middle. Somehow, Charley got his hand down in that grinder, mashing up his hand pretty bad. After that Charley always had a queer-looking thumb on that side, and that day it was still bandaged.

But my big brother didn't need both thumbs to let me know what he thought of me. The minute he got into our room he started in on me, punches flying. Somehow we ended up on the bed and was really getting into it. He sat on me, which hurt like hell because of that bucket of water I drank, and I worried I'd wet the bed and get beat to death both.

Charley held me down with the elbow from his bad side and was letting me have it with his good hand. I tried to punch him as hard as I could, until he grabbed my hair and shoved my head into the rods of the iron headboard. He pulled two of them apart and crammed my head in there. Like I said, that boy was strong! Well, I hollered bloody murder until Mother heard me and came in there to get me out, and she made Charley help her. But Charley didn't get whipped that day. Mother didn't whip you.

Both the Thompson decisiveness and personal strength were evident even during our first meeting. Not only were these personality traits seen throughout the Thompson family, it soon became evident they were fairly typical for Wilcox Bend natives. The area's seclusion likely helped produce such strong-willed, rugged individualists.

The Ozark Mountains extend into five states to create one of the older mountain ranges in the United States. Eons before Grant Thompson arrived in the area, the Osage River carved out its trough on a journey to meet the Missouri River. By the mid 1800s there was a place, just a bit northeast of the railroad town of Bagnell, where the river reached out and then pulled back against itself like a bent arm. About seventy-five years before Hadley existed, locals named the land the river held in its crook Wilcox Bend.

Miller County settled slowly and steadily after 1815, and for the next one hundred years, a trinity of weather, seasons, and the river ordained the lives of the people. River bottom farming was communal farming. Mother Nature played the fiddle and called the steps, and the group moved in the same figures year in and year out. A farmer hardly shifted before the seasons called the pattern. A new family came and the others moved one space over to make room. A partner stumbled and the others stepped to his place without skipping a beat. All worked to the pace set by the river and the weather.

Throughout the early 1900s, the Osage cloistered about twenty families in Wilcox Bend. One of them, the Thompsons, was an extended family of mostly boys. If a man was in the mood to pick a fight, it was best to avoid choosing a Thompson for there were always more Thompsons nearby. If a fight did break out, as they often did at the revivals, meetings and dances, a Thompson was a welcome man to have at your side. Tough and confident, good or suspect, everybody knew the Thompsons.

Grant Thompson and his first wife Emma had many children, and they played minor parts in the feud that developed after the Crismon family moved into the area. But it was Emma's maiden name Ponder that was the most surprising contributor to the problems. One hundred years after she died, people who never met Emma told me, "She were a Ponder, you know." At first I, like any other stranger, had no idea of this significance. Then Hadley explained that being a Ponder meant Grant's children from his first marriage were German on their mother's side, a fact noted by some neighbors during the anti-German years surrounding World War I. Historical texts highlighted the Ponder significance, recording old man Ponder as the most well-known Civil War participant from Miller County. He had fought for the Union.

When it was time to meet Jim's train, all of Dad's second family went. That was my family growing up: Joe, Charley, Barney (that was me, Hadley) and Paul, all living in the same four rooms until the day I left home. John was from Dad's first family and he had some problems, but was an angel from heaven in our family. John folded his clothes in perfect squares and stacked them under his cot in the hallway outside my parent's room. He was content with that spot.

Now Joe was anxious to have the time that morning to get cleaned up. He really wanted to look smart because we was going to be at three different train stations and he speculated he might get to slide up to a girl or two. John was washing out at the pump when Joe got a nosebleed. The blood started to drip on his only good shirt. He tried to shove John outta the way, but John knew it was his turn at the pump and in his mind, fair was fair, blood or no blood. He stood his ground. Because of the way he talked he said, "Doe, die Dod," and that was, "No, by God." Give it up, Joe.

Mother insisted Joe drink vinegar in water to cure the nosebleed. No doctors to speak of, people just did what they could and passed around the cures. Well, between wrestling with his bloody shirt and John, and choking down that vinegar and water, Joe provided great entertainment. Finally, all seven of us, five in the wagon and two on horseback, were ready to head down the road toward the Bagnell Ferry.

Joe drove the team. *Driving a team and wagon might look easy to you. Simple if you know what the hell you're doing. But I'm here to tell you, in most teams, you have one horse trying to overtake the other, or a lazy one, determined to have his mate do the work, and the driver now, he has to balance those 3,000 pounds of moving determination. But old Joe, he could thread a needle with that team.*

Dad said Joe drove with his mouth as much as his hands. He'd call out, "There you go, easy now. Git up Nell. Git up Ned. Atta boy. Hold up. Hey there, up you go." Dad's theory was Joe talked so much the animals wore themselves out listening, and they did it his way just so he'd shut up.

Then that road down to the ferry landing. If it was dry, it was nothing but a trail of grey dust, flung up as we trotted, only to land on horse, rider, and brush. If a man started out riding with clean white face and hands, in a blue work shirt, setting smartly on a dappled mare, before long he weren't nothin' but gray in gray, on gray.

Leaving our farm, first it was brother Otto's place. Otto was from Dad's first family like Jim and John, and he lived close to us with his girls and wife. As we rode by, there was a space where the trees parted and we could catch a glimpse of the silent green rows in his field stretching away from us. Way off it looked like they met — arrows pointing to the river.

Then the road traveled on down past Professor Molls's house, Blankenship's and a few others, down almost three miles. A road with no name. We never named the roads, but every bend, bluff, eddy, and shoal of the river we did. And I used to know them all. Then there sat Kidwell's up on the hill to the left, and the road turned away to run down toward the ferry landing. Ring the bell and wait for the boat to come across. Pay the man a dime for the team and a nickel for each boy on horseback. Wait for the train to chug in. Watch it turn at the roundabout. It was quite a luxury getting to go.

Over in Bagnell, we weren't just three miles up river, we was a million miles away. We'd a few coins from helping Dad in the blacksmith shop and ran to spend them before we heard the train coming through Mead's Flats to Bagnell.

The Bagnell stop was just a spur for the Missouri Pacific Railroad, so the engine had to be turned around at the round house. That day was the first time I got to see that. Boy, it was really a sight. Steam shooting out above the team of men and mules. Nothing but the finest Missouri mules, beautiful in their proud, homely way. They say Missouri mules helped win both the Civil War and The Great War, and I believe it.

Can't you just see those huge mallets swinging to fall within an inch of the hand that held a bar, a wedge, a steel brace? And the railroad men. Loud, friendly Germans and one Colored, all missing a finger or two from the job, calling out to each other above the roar of the machines. Look now, there we are, standing on a boardwalk, the four of us lined up, sucking on candy or an ice cream cone, watching in amazement.

Then it was time to hand the conductor our tickets, jump on the train and run to find our seats. It all scared Paul and he clenched his little fists onto Mother's skirts, too frightened to take that first huge step onto the train. Dad said, "Come now, Colonel. This ain't nothin' to a big man like you." Then he swung him up and onto the steps. Joe found him a seat across from a woman and her daughter and prayed the vinegar done its trick. Charley and I sat together and cheered when we heard, "All aboard!" Charley was the best brother a guy could have. All of them were, really.

Jim didn't come home in a box. He jumped down from his train thinner and paler than before, but with a smile on his face, and a nine-millimeter German Luger with a four inch barrel to show Dad. Everything else Jim owned was stuffed into the army duffel he slung into the back of the wagon. Dad hugged him straight on, then backed off, shook him a bit by the shoulders, and hugged him again. Both had tears in their eyes.

Jim kissed Mother on both cheeks and danced a jig with John, his brother from Dad's first family, right there in front of God and everyone. We couldn't wait to hear Jim's stories. He gave his army trench coat to us boys, and I liked to wear it out fox hunting.

But Jim wouldn't tell the stories we wanted to hear: we wanted to listen to how they killed the Germans and won the war. Instead, I remember Jim saying what was unbelievable to me at the time: he thought of the farm so much, every night when he tried to go to sleep he shut his eyes and imagined every last thing about the dust and dirt and mud that made up our lives. The creak of the rocker on the front porch, the dinner bell, the hens fussing and this damn rooster we had for a while that'd crow in the middle of the night. Otto's kids and their homemade dolls. Our favorite sycamore tree. A dog named Black Bastard. All of Europe in front of him and what he do? He looked back in his mind's eye to see a piece of Missouri nobody ever heard of.

I didn't understand it then, but sure enough, one day there I was on a ship with men from all over the country, sailing to the ends of the earth. You know what I thought about? Everything behind me. And I wrote Jim and told him I couldn't go to sleep at night but first I'd feel Paul or Charley kicking me over to my side of the bed. I'd lie there and listen until I could hear the sound of their breathing. Only then could I fall asleep.

On the way home, Dad pulled out a rolled-up piece of paper from his breast pocket and handed it to Jim. It was the deed to a farm, a bit west of ours. A welcome home present.

Almost a year to the day after I first met Hadley and Icel, I telephoned the Thompson home again.

VICTORIA: I've thought about you and Icel often.

HADLEY: We've thought about you.

VICTORIA: I'd like to come see you again.

HADLEY: Come on then. Any time.

Then he hung up.

Again I drove across the Osage Bridge, continued on down the highway toward Mead's Flats, and when I turned off the main road I wondered simultaneously exactly why I was going back and if the correct road was County Road W or V. I needn't have worried. Soon that same amazing color, that happy blue-green found neither in nature nor paint stores, heralded me from behind the trees.

Hadley was waiting for me at the door. I looked up at him as he held the screen door open and thought he didn't look one day older than the last time I saw him. The same clear blue eyes and lopsided smile. Maybe even the same plaid shirt and baggy trousers. While I may have questioned why I was there, to Hadley it was obvious. From the moment he answered the door, he was eager to get to work. He'd decided for both of us I would write his memoir. Once again, I listened to his tales filled with surprising details, forgotten ways, and old-fashioned sayings. His part was to tell me what I needed to know, and what I needed to do. He decided my part would be to research until all his memories had explanations.

It was as though I never left. Icel poured coffee as strong as sin, and we all sat down at the kitchen table. Once again I questioned that there was a Ku Klux Klan group in the area.

VICTORIA: Are you sure the KKK was really here? There were never many African-Americans in this county.

HADLEY: (with firm shake of head) The Klan weren't never about race. It were always about power and greed.

On the whole, Saturdays weren't special. Oh, sometimes we'd have a dance or play party, but most times we got a trip to the smokehouse for a bath and that was about it. There was one Saturday I've always remembered though. Jim had been home for a while now, and we all went to go see Billy Sunday. As a boy I remembered that day for all its excitement, but now I see it also as the last year our dear Professor Molls lived next to us.

We rode the ferry over to Bagnell real early in the morning. Did our business like usual, bought supplies, took corn to the mill. Visited. They'd put up a huge tent in an empty field down by the river, and when the sun slipped behind the hills, it was finally time for the show. Mother felt the chill of the river breeze, so she told me to go run fetch her shawl from the wagon. I got the shawl all right, but like a foal finally let loose from the birthing stall, I had to stop to sample everything on my own along the way.

Everybody in the area was there. Threshing was over, but it was still too early to get ready for winter. This was always the time of year when the revivals came to Bagnell, and everybody knew Billy Sunday was the biggest celebrity we'd get to see. That wasn't really true of course; I got to see General Patton.

Anyway, Reverend Sunday was pushing for prohibition and even those who didn't care for whatever he was preaching went to see him if they had the chance. We'd no movies or television; preachers and salesmen were our entertainment.

There was Model T's, wagons, horses, and mules waiting under every tree. There was an ox chained with a nose ring, which was a very old-fashioned thing to see, because one old timer from down along Dog Creek used him to pull. That old guy still ground his meal in a stump like my grandpap did. A real hillbilly!

A gypsy wagon was there, with roasted chicken and rabbit legs for sale. Dad wouldn't let us give money for gypsy food. "They snitch chickens and poach rabbits. A gypsy'll rob you blind if you so much as blink."

But their food tasted sweet and spicy and better than ours, so I used my two pennies to buy both a chicken and a rabbit's leg. I ate most of it standing there, staring at them whilst they stared back at me.

A no-toothed gypsy woman was curled up in a bent-reed chair, her back round like its wheels. She was poking her cane at dogs sniffing around their wagon. Three men in striped baggy pants stood lined up behind her, like they was triplets, arms folded across their chests, chewing, spitting, smoking, watching. Gypsies was always watching. Any other day they'd try to snag me to bet on a shell game, but even they didn't dare gamble outside a revival tent.

I saw another wagon, and this one had painted wooden sides and top like a house on wheels. A real pretty lady started to climb down. She slid one leg along the side and saw me staring at her. She stopped, all glitter and bangles. Fingernails painted red and long, thick hair that wasn't pinned up. Looking right at me. Wouldn't my brother Joe wish he was there watching her instead of me?

She started playing with the buttons on her front a bit, smiling at me all the while. Her fingertips slowly brushed against her blouse and in a flash I was looking at her brown, bare breasts. I know my heart quit on me right there, but somehow I bolted toward that revival tent like the devil was chasing me instead of her laugh.

A man with store-bought pants was standing by the tent flap. He had red braces to hold up those pants. I never knew men wore such a thing. He called out and waved me inside, me holding a shawl and a half-eaten rabbit leg. So in I went.

That tent was crammed full with every kind of person you'd imagine ever living in Miller County. Everybody was cleaned up and smelling of lavender and lilac water. I saw a bunch of town boys my age, hair slicked back with witch hazel tonic trying to look like their older brothers. They was sharp and paid no heed to the country bumpkin taking note of all they did. There were chairs and boxes for women and older folks to sit on, benches made out of planks and kegs. The men were at the back, to accommodate them that needed to duck under the tent to spit. The little ones sat Indian style on the ground around a center platform. They rolled and wrestled about like puppies until Auntie wacked 'em upright.

I got shoved up against two men and one of them said plain as day, "Brother Kenneth's a son-of-a-bitch and his wife's a lazy ass," and it shocked me, hearing the brother and the son-of-a-bitch in the same sentence and all. A person shouldn't talk about somebody in their church like that.

It was pretty clear I wasn't going to make it over to my family with us all squeezed in like we was, and Mother wasn't going to get her wrap until it was over. Then a man sprang up the crates stacked in the middle, and we knew it was Billy Sunday. He wasn't especially big, but he was husky and hard, built like a tie hacker. Shirt sleeves rolled up, he spread his arms wide above his head. "Welcome Friends!" filled the air. Everyone cheered and clapped. He wore red braces over his white shirt (like all the other men helping to put on the show) and cut his hair real short above a nice-enough-looking face. He started the usual way, asking us to bow our heads. We was all humble Christian soldiers and so on, and even though he had his eyes shut and his head bowed in prayer, his voice rose and flew around that tent until every spot of air seemed filled with the sound of it.

"Oh Lord, as we join in the ranks of Christian salvation, I ask you..." He went on like that for a bit, until he ended with an even louder, "Amen!"

"AMEN!" roared the crowd back at him.

There he stood, standing like a lightning rod before us. I can see Reverend Sunday slowly raising his eyes, looking into all the souls under that canvas. He saw me with that rabbit bone, a sign of weakness against gypsy temptations. He knew it was a sad day when a mother couldn't trust a son to do one little thing she asked. Sunday clasped his hands behind his back and started to stroll slowly around the makeshift platform. Above him the lanterns glowed warmly. Nobody moved. Even the kids were quiet. Not a breath. Not a whisper.

Then he started in on us. Oh the evils of drink! The taverns of Hell! Loud and crisp, he talked right to every person in that crowd, pointing, whirling, falling down on his knees then up with a jump, shouting, crying, laughing.

Still and all, my mind started to wander a bit, because what he was saying really didn't fit our lives too much. We never bought drink and had no saloons in Wilcox Bend. About every family I knew made their own. Plum wine, home brew, corn whiskey, stump water, and white lightning. Some just for medicinal reasons, but everybody knew the recipe for some kind of drink, each as individual as their mother's cornbread recipe.

But the rest of the crowd was really taking it in. Sunday pounced in front of Uncle Lev and his pals from the Bank of Brumley. They was wearing fine suits, silk ties, pocket watches, sitting tight together on a bench like blackbirds on a wire, bobbing with every word he said. I think carefully now and wonder, did I see a little bulge in the vest pockets of those men? The outline of a flask or a pistol? It was usually one or the other, or both.

Then the reverend strode over to the women. Mother and the other ladies looked thunderstruck, staring up at him in Sabbath hats. Behind them those from the Bagnell White House showed off their tight blouses and rouged lips. Like I said, everybody was there, even women my mother wouldn't let us stare at on the street. Yet all of them had one thing in common that day. They dabbed their eyes with lace handkerchiefs and gazed up at him, smiling.

Groups from the Anti-Saloon League and Women's Christian Temperance Union were crying, really howling out loud and shaking their gourds. The sound of the rattling joined with the sound of Billy's preaching. Streamers were flying. Men shouted "Amen!" and "Tell it Brother Billy!" In the back,

Tommy Alexander and his buddies were pushing in a train, tripping out of the tent on their way back to the Bagnell tavern.

Sunday hollered over the ruckus, "What key will unlock the door to Hell?"

"Whiskey!" came the chant, "Whis-key! Whis-key! Whis-key!"

But then, I never got to hear his last words. A woman under a brim of feathers swooned, folks fell around her and the men in red braces reappeared, this time shoving baskets fixed on long poles in front of each person. People put money into holes in the tops and everyone was smiling, nodding and patting their friend on the back agreeing it was some mighty fine preachin'. A basket came to me and I dug out the rabbit bone and slipped it into the hole where it fell with a convincing clatter of coins. Then off I sprinted to catch up with my family.

Now that, that was some Saturday night!

One day Hadley took the two of us down to the river, standing here and there, telling me what had happened so many years ago or what business had been on the opposite bank. He pointed to where the trees had been and how the river had changed. He kept the scenes from his childhood in his mind's eye, and soon I could see them as clearly as if I had stumbled down the dirt path myself. Look there, there's the south side of the ferry landing on the way to Bagnell, in a place where trees and brush are cleared away. The river's so narrow there, over on the Bagnell side it's easy to read "Boots's Boats" written with white paint on a ragged piece of grey lumber.

Back on my side of the river the ground is even and flat, and the water laps night and day, along the edge. A gentle sound. Folks are waiting for the ferryboat running on cables across the Osage, and they're visiting and getting along just fine, because river bottom farmers always get along. They notice how calm and friendly the water looks. Maybe they're thinking how that same river washed away people and livestock every year since 1840, because it's hard to judge the current out in the middle. How's a person supposed to tell when it's dangerous and when it's not? The ferry man knows, and the locals of course.

The people waiting patiently look up now, because they hear somebody else coming down the path. Hear him before they see him. It's a busy day at the landing: a peaceful, but active, typical day along the Osage, in Miller County, Missouri. That's all there is to the first picture in my mind.

Then the second scene takes over, like a photograph tossed onto a table, completely covering the picture beneath it. Still the same ferry landing, same side of the river, but now it's winter. Most everything is white including the frozen water. At the river's edge lies a man, legs bent under him, eyes staring up at the sky, a hole above his right eye with bits of brain scattered on the river bank like pebbles on the ground, because the back of his head is blown away. Patches of red blood splatter the beautiful white snow. The man's sons are there, and they can't believe what they're seeing.

That's not all. There's another body lying on the snow. He's young, much too young. He's been shot too, but this one's still alive.

The first time Hadley told me the story, it took him nearly two hours to get to the crux of the tale, to the bodies lying on the bank. When he finally did, it shocked me. I didn't understand why events happened as they did. Much of it made no sense. Hadley didn't have all the answers either: "I know what I saw and I know what I heard, but I don't know what it meant," he said.

Since he was thirteen, Hadley had wondered about the time between those two pictures. The progression from idyllic river valley to a riverbank covered in blood had captivated Hadley his entire life. Few wanted to hear about the subject any more, much less talk about it. Because the answers to Hadley's questions involved two prominent and respected families, as well as the murder of a man and one not much more than a boy, most people just wanted to forget this small slice of local history. Why did residents cast off traditions that had been established with the founding of the county? Like a tick on a hound dog, Hadley wouldn't let go until he got answers he wanted.

ADVENTURE (1920-1921)

Grant
Thompson

—Courtesy Thompson Family

Plez
Moore

—Courtesy Thompson Family

Hadley may not have known Billy Sunday played professional baseball for eight seasons when he speculated Sunday looked as though he was a tie hacker. Tie hackers were men who cut railroad ties to sell to the railroads. From 1880 until 1920, Missouri counties along the Osage River produced as many railroad ties as any place in the nation. The Bureau of Labor Statistics stated that in 1913 Bagnell shipped more railroad ties than any other place in Missouri. Cutting ties was always a good way to supplement the income of most families. Just as important, it was a good way to get real money, as the railroads paid in cash, instead of using dogs, horses, written scrip, or other methods of payment typical for the area.

Heavily wooded forests provided the wood, and the Osage provided cheap transportation. Men made rafts from the ties and floated them downriver to their takeout points. Then the rafts were disassembled so the ties could be delivered to their new owners.

Because hand-hewn ties like the ones produced in Wilcox Bend weighed over two hundred pounds, full-time tie hackers were strong, well-built men. Most everyone cut ties at some time, and even youngsters helped older brothers and fathers. But the men who worked in the forests throughout the coldest months and into the hottest days, drawing cross axes through trunks to fell the trees, constructing the ties with a broad axe and then finally hauling the finished products to the river, those men were the admired professional athletes of the area. Like most of Hadley's seemingly irrelevant details, tie hackers were important to the story. As the popularity of the automobile increased, the railroad companies stopped expanding. Soon there was little need for new ties.

There was more for me to learn about than just bygone ways. Understanding the Thompson family's complex constellation was an ongoing research problem. During our second meeting Hadley went over all his siblings, whole and half, and then introduced his father's family, as well as Uncle Eleven (called "Lev") and Cousin Happy. Cousin Happy was easy to remember. He was the bootlegger and in my mind this made sense; he was surrounded by liquor so he was happy. But Uncle Lev was more difficult because even though Grant's parents did have eleven children (there were eventually twelve), Lev was born number five. The rationale behind naming one's fifth child Eleven remains elusive.

As though the familial overload of two different families with such a mess of children wasn't confusing enough, there were aunts, uncles, and grandpas who really weren't aunts, uncles, and grandpas. In the Ozarks, an older man, related or not, could be referred to as "Uncle" if one felt affection and respect toward him. The same goes for "aunt," "grandpa," "grandma," and "cousin." So Cousin Happy may not actually have been a blood cousin. (He was.)

In Ozark tradition, names often evolved. "Old Man So and So" would begin as somebody older and unrelated to the speaker. But if Old Man So and So pulled a sputtering kid out of the well and then came in for cornbread, he might be renamed Uncle So and So, still no relation. Since everyone in Wilcox Bend knew the family history of everybody else in Wilcox Bend, these terms were only confusing to people from "off."

It quickly became evident there were many differences between us, but the greatest was that I was from "off." "Off" meant not a product of the Ozark Mountains. To Ozark natives, this also meant off-base, half-a-bubble-off level, and the unwilling recipient of practical jokes. For instance, Hadley told me they found his older brother Charley in a stump. Not knowing that "stump" was the Ozark equivalent of "stork," I believed Hadley's older brother was actually discovered out in the woods. Kinda like some people leave babies on doorsteps. Hadley loved to remind me (and anyone standing nearby) of that joke with a hearty laugh and a slap to his knee.

During my fifth visit to the Thompson's, Hadley left the room to get a picture to help explain the family tree. This time it was Icel who sat quietly and only listened, until she heard Hadley opening drawers in the living room. Then she leaned over and almost hissed, "I don't want him diggin' up that old story. It'll just get him all riled up. It's long over and done with. His mother pleaded with them all to let it go, and if she were still here he wouldn't be bringin' it up. A few years ago we was in town and I was awaitin' for him in the truck." Icel glanced over her shoulder, before continuing.

"Out he comes all in a tither and says, 'That Crismon boy's in there. Get me that hammer. He's in there.' Then Hadley started digging around on the floor of the truck for the hammer, which I knew was under my purse." Icel pursed her lips and nodded at me.

At this point the thumps and bumps from the next room ceased. Icel straightened away from me and looked at the calendar nailed to the wall. Hadley came back into the kitchen and passed through on his way to the bedrooms. We heard more drawers being opened and shut. Icel and I leaned back together and she whispered,

"That Crismon boy! Even if it was him, he'd be about Hadley's age." Hadley returned to the kitchen. This time we both straightened and tried to look as though we weren't talking about him.

"Icel? Where is that picture of everyone at the wedding?" Although he was slightly stooped, Hadley was still a good-sized man. His bark was intimidating.

"Well baby, look in that album in the dining room." The minute his backside disappeared through the door we both tilted our heads toward the other.

"How old is your husband?" I whispered.

"Eighty-six."

A bellow from the other room: "This is Greg's album. Where's the one with my Navy pictures in them?"

"Try over by the T.V., baby," she responded sweetly.

I whispered again, "Were you there when the feud happened? Did you know about it back then?"

"Oh yes. Everybody did. Mother wouldn't let me have anything to do with any of the Thompson boys. I couldn't go out with him until she passed on. The Thompsons was all handsome and they could be a bit wild, but they was good boys. Each and ever one of 'em. Everybody knew the Thompsons. But baby, you don't want to write this all down. Just play along with him. That's the best thing to do."

No pictures were found that day and the interview ended on a rough note. I made the mistake of telling Hadley, "This really is a great story, you know."

Blue eyes squinted at me with distrust. Then my tape recorded the sound of a strong, broad palm slapping the table, and the sound of a dented aluminum boat being dragged across a sandy shoal.

"It weren't no story!"

They used to call it Decoration Day, not Memorial Day, you know. It was the last holiday until threshing, and we expected everyone to leave dogs, grudges, and worries, pack up their best food, and come. We spent the day at the cemetery, cleaning up and decorating the graves. That doesn't sound like much, but we looked forward to it the whole month of May. Everybody was there, many we hadn't seen since butchering the fall before. Best part though, there was lots of food. We was always hungry back then.

Decoration Day was the start of something new. No more shoes. The first wildflowers. Gooseberries in cobblers, both tart and sweet on our tongues. The end of planting and the start of summer and the start of so much work too. New piglets, new calves, foals. The garden coming up and the fields planted in perfect rows. Think it's strange we celebrated all that in the graveyard?

We worked on the Thompson graves first, but then everybody straightened and cleaned the other graves, relatives or no. Charley, the brother five years older than me, prided himself on being the best worker. The girls were already starting to notice his strength, and this drove old Joe crazy. Both my brothers had eyes like an Oklahoma sky.

After the work was done, we'd eat. There'd be a wagon, unhitched, and while the men and children worked, the women took down its sides and covered the bottom with a pretty cloth. Finally — all that food got spread out. The women were very competitive, but it wasn't Christian to let on they were. We men just stoked that fire for all it was worth so's they'd bring their best and try to outdo the other. I don't know how we learned how to do this, but even the young ones did a fine job at it:

"This chicken yours, Auntie Sue? You raise all them chickens yourself?" or "Why Miz Williams, I can taste your sweet potato pie from two years past." You wouldn't believe the things we did just for food.

Most of our neighbors were there: the McDowells, Blankenships, Hawkins, Plemmens, Walls, and all the Thompsons. Most never had nothin' to do with the Klan. There were other people living in the area, like the hill folk and the river men, but they weren't much a part of this. Dad's first family was there. I can't name the order they was born in, but they was Clyde, Jim, Otto, John, Annie and Dessie. And my half sister Gipsy. It was the only day of the year all us Thompsons got together.

We had one aunt, Aunt Maggie, who was always there from Brumley, and she was the only one of Dad's sisters we saw every year. (He came from a family of twelve, you know.) She believed it her duty to make sure we knew about our other aunts and told us boys tales about them. Dad didn't have much patience with her mission, but Mother enjoyed her. Mother was pretty happy anytime she got to see another woman.

And there was one more person we always saw there. He was a kind of idol for all the kids, or at least the boys. His name was Plez.

Plez Moore was a dandy. Thinking back over my time here, not just in Wilcox Bend, but my whole life, there are a few people like him who stand out. They just don't seem to fit, because there's nobody quite like them. You speculate how they turned out like they did and how they could be brave enough to live different from everyone else.

Harry Truman was like that for me. Give 'em Hell, Harry. Nobody quite like him. And General Patton. Ever get to hear his voice? Kind of a high squeaky thing. Not what you'd expect from such a great general. Plez Moore was another one. He wasn't a great man like Truman or Patton, but there weren't nobody like him and never will be, I'm sure.

All the ladies liked Plez, and he liked them just as well. He was the only man brave enough to hang around the tables with the women before we ate on Decoration Day. I can hear them shriek with laughter to this day, even the sternest old wart, when they'd gather 'round him, hens to a rooster, and listen to him tell a story or two. He'd stride up to a group, hold a straight arm in front of him, palm out like a traffic cop, and say, "Stop whatever you're doing!" Then he'd gossip and carry on with the women, describing what the ladies were wearing in Kansas City or Tulsa, or some funny story:

"You know Miz Ferris threw out Lloyd last Sunday? Yes mammy, she did. Been sleepin' in the barn loft a week now. Why? Well, he come home drunk late one night, and she'd barred the door. He knocked, she called out, 'That you Mr. Ferris?' and he hollered at that door, 'T'is ma'am. You might as well let me sleep in your bed, 'cause if I go home now, that old wife o' mine ain't gonna let me in anyway!'"

And a rooster Plez surely was. Always had him a purebred, black horse, and they cantered in and out of our lives with the outcomes of his poker games. A gelding for a few years, then a stallion or mare, some better than others depending how his luck with the cards held out, but always black. Fine leather tack. Pay us a nickel to clean and oil it when he came. We never saw Plez in coveralls, never saw him kicking the dirt out of his cuffs. Sleek black hair like his horse's mane, thick and wavy, skin like a bronze doll, and smooth hands that probably never touched an axe or shovel. I can remember watching those slim fingers dance on the piano keys during play parties in winter.

There were other men of such a type, and you'd see them once and again in Bagnell, but the local folk were cold to them and stared at best, or at worst took the poor suckers for a ride. So you're thinking the men didn't like Plez much, him being as fancy as he was. T'weren't so. Out of that saddlebag of his (black leather with PM tooled into it) he'd pull cigars and Tennessee whiskey to pass around before settling in with the men talking machinery and livestock.

"Stop whatever you're doing!" Out came the flask. A fine silver flask with a stag etched on the front. And when his coat pulled back and his hand reached

in we might glimpse the butt of a pistol. I asked once why Dad liked Plez, him being nothin' like us. Dad said he didn't know exactly. Then he added, "He does things sometimes I wisht I could do." I think it was like that for a lot of the men. Their lives were harnessed to their plows, always waiting to see what the river was going to do. When they listened to Plez, all that was different.

He paid attention to us kids, too. He'd help carry water for us and pull a quarter outta our ears and give it to some lucky son-of-a-gun. He'd tie our legs together for the three-legged race and shoot his pistol for the start.

And then, just when we got used to him being around, one morning we'd get up and he was gone. Never said goodbye. Rumor was Plez had a stash of gold hidden in a cave someplace in the hills and he came whenever he needed money. None of us knew how he lived, but in those days you didn't ask such things and certainly not if you were a kid. There was a phrase, "A dandy ain't nothing but a high-classed bum." That could be true. But we boys sure loved it when our dandy came around.

Every year on Decoration Day it was the same. After we ate, Mother and Dad strolled up and down the rows of tombstones together. My mother was a little, bitty gal and her long skirts brushed the grass around the stones when she walked. She did not approve of skirts that showed the ankle. At each and every grave they stopped, read the stone, murmured little things about the person buried there, maybe how they died, if'n they gave piano lessons, how they liked their ham, salted or sugar cured. Even if Mother and Dad never met the person, they'd repeat what their parents said, and what their grand-paps said, during all the Decoration Days before. Us kids thought it a big joke, them going on and on talking to those old stones and staring at the writing like something new was going to show up that year.

Of course, there was also a lot of talk about bloodlines, and nobody could talk bloodlines like Plez Moore. Some men memorize baseball facts; Plez memorized families. Growing up I thought Plez claimed kin to us in some way. I don't know where I got that, but really, quite a few folks treated him like family. My oldest sister Dessie Mae even named her boy after him.

Plez liked to stay with Aunt Maggie in Brumley, which made sense to me at the time since her husband died and she'd a spare room and all. When he stayed over with us it was always in the summer so he could sleep in the granary. You can't blame him for not wanting to share a room with four boys or sleep out in the hall with John.

Aunt Maggie loved to talk about the family and argued fiercely with Plez when his talk of bloodlines strayed into Thompson territory. For a while she had a little dog at her heels with an amusing way of lifting its leg on the minister of the Baptist Church in Brumley. When the minister was standing outside the church in the sunlight, shaking hands with parishioners and nodding at their every word, that little thing saw his opportunity. The dog was so small the man didn't notice the christening of his cuffs every Sunday, and Aunt Maggie felt it better to pretend nothing happened. I believe she seen it though.

Aunt Maggie thought the Thompson family tree an important subject, but she had only a handful of stories, which we heard with some frequency. Still, there was a warm and inviting way about our aunt, who never preached at us or pointed out dirty hands or loud manners. She smelled of vanilla, made a prize-winning stale bread pudding with raisons soaked in plum brandy, and every time she wanted to tell us the same three stories during Decoration Day, we sat on the ground on the hem of her skirts and listened.

One of Maggie's stories was about Dad's baby sister, Aunt Grace. She was a bit of a wild thing and quite a beauty. She liked to spend a lot of time with Pa (my grandpa Thompson) and he allowed her to sit with him and the men when she was a girl. I'm sure she was the only girl who did this, and it probably created quite a scandal. Aunt Maggie said Pa let her take a turn at the old stone jug when it passed by and taught her to ride astride, which was a no-no in those days. Anyway, one day she rode into Brumley on horseback and was seen leaving in the buggy of a drummer who was passing through. She was about seventeen when she ran away and never seen by a Thompson again. Later someone traced her to St. Louis, where they said she died giving birth. Nobody ever knew what happened to the baby.

When I got older, this whole tradition at the cemetery became more than just a good time, it became a real comfort to me, because I figured that by the time I was planted there, I'd know everybody around me real good. To this day, point to a dip in the ground, even with only a flagstone marker, and I'll tell you who's buried there, how they died, and who dug the grave for them. And how they liked their ham.

Soon I visited the Thompsons about once a month and usually taped the interviews. After we'd met a few times, I asked Hadley, "How do you think I should write this?"

"What do you mean? You write it like it happened," he said in a tone that let me know what a stupid question I had asked.

"I meant, should it be as fact or fiction?"

"Fact," he almost shouted. "It's all fact."

I tried to explain proper use of quotation marks and citations for a nonfiction book. Hadley had little interest in this and only shrugged. But I showed him the transcript for the section about his birth, and then how later he had corrected himself after he talked to his older brother Joe who had reminded him that Professor Molls brought the bed sheets over. I tried to explain that I would need to note this information was added at a later time and through another individual. He just shrugged.

So I wrote the pieces in his voice, even though most required editing. When Hadley read the compositions I gave him, he said, "Victoria, it was like you was there."

In between visits I'd research. About nine months into this process, I sat down at the familiar kitchen table with Hadley. Icel was at the sink. I asked Hadley a question. He paused, waited almost a minute, and then said,

"No, it's too much to go into. I don't think I want to talk about that."

I said, "All right. Let's talk about something else then. I'm still confused about the Thompson genealogy. Let's start with you and your brothers."

"No, I mean I don't think I want to do this at all." He didn't speak in a short-tempered way, just a matter-of-fact, "I've changed my mind" way.

Then Icel said, "Now Hadley, don't do her like that. I hate those kinda deals." By now she was on my side. She loved company and felt it was helpful for Hadley to talk about his childhood. But he just sat there and didn't say anything while I looked at my notebook. Surprised, awkward, still from off.

I said, "Well, I guess I'll be heading out." I gathered my things and left. Days passed. No word. I stared at the piles of notes, books, and tapes I'd already compiled.

Even today, life in the Ozarks moves slowly, winding around the moment, going off on tangents. People stop and watch the sun go down. In the fall it's deer season. Construction work trickles to a standstill. Workers at the grocery store plan their shifts so everybody has a chance to go hunting. Housewives pray their disposals won't back up, because if they do, they'll stay that way for a while.

In March, the high school principal, the nurse next door, everybody combs the woods for morel mushrooms. That year I joined them. I also went turkey hunting. Turkey hunting is good way to learn about waiting.

And then there is the fishing. Fishing takes a lot of patience, because fish may be the most stubborn creatures in existence. Besides a Thompson, of course. One skill every Ozark native learns is how to be patient. Grant Thompson and his neighbors had to wait on Mother Nature. Life made Hadley wait for seventy years to have his story written. Hadley made me wait for a few months. Waiting is not that big of an issue in the Ozarks. Waiting, some would contend, can be a good lesson.

"Patience is a virtue," Mrs. Thompson told her sons. "All things come to those who wait." I waited. But not patiently.

Finally, I realized I needed to put the notes in a burn barrel and torch them or contact Hadley again. "Fish or cut bait," the locals say. In a brave moment I decided to fish. I called the Thompsons. Icel answered the phone.

"You come on, baby. I'll make cobbler."

I gathered up pens, recorder, tapes and extra batteries, threw everything in my car including my dogs, drove over the bridge, turned once as I neared Mead's Flats, again at the funny bluish-green house, parked under a shade tree, and knocked.

"Hello, baby. You come right in. Why look, Hadley, Victoria's here."

He stood. Big smile, pulled out my chair. "Hello, stranger. Icel made cobbler."

"Here's your coffee, Victoria. You like it black, don't you?" That day, she was in a lavender pantsuit.

I sat, took a bite of peach cobbler and a sip of coffee. Icel only made cobbler in the summer when she could find fresh Missouri peaches. I looked up at her and said, "Icel, your cobbler could pull a person from a cement grave." She beamed. Hadley nodded, ate his cobber and began to talk. I turned on the tape recorder and thought about what I learned during that time. I'd learned that a lot of folks' problems could be solved by some good, homemade cobbler and coffee as black as a coal bin at midnight.

About nineteen and twenty, nineteen and twenty-one, we started getting a lot of newcomers in Wilcox Bend. But I'm just going to tell you about three: The Klan, the Leids, and the Crismons.

Now, people may tell you the KKK was about race. I'll tell you now, and I've said it ever since that time: the KKK weren't never about race. I don't give a rat's ass for books that says it was about a man's blood, really, because I've seen 'em all change the rules for whatever suited at the time. I was there. I've watched enough meetings to know what I'm talking about. They just wanted to have somebody to hate. But yes, the Klan claimed it was about bloodlines at first.

What you have to realize, and what all the relatives of folks around here don't want to admit, is for a time, eighty percent of the people in this area was Ku Klux Klan. That's one thing I want people to know. Almost all of them. Dad was not Klan and this played a part in the killings. Blankenships wasn't Klan, McDowells neither. And there were some others of course.

It started with the Kleagles. They were the ones who went into the neighborhood getting new members. It seems to me the Kleagles came into the area at about the same time the Crismons did, within a year at least, because I had three years of schooling by that time, two by Miss Annie and one by Miss Gipsy. When they came to Wilcox Bend, I don't remember them using the name Ku Klux Klan. I remember them calling it the "100% American Lodge." Very soon the problem arose, of course, that Dad, Otto, Clyde, and Jim was all supposed to join up and become members.

That day, Dad, Otto, Charley, me, and Paul, we were working off the poll tax on our road. Now, leaving our farm, we first went past a giant sycamore and down on the other side of the ridge, and then were at the end of the field. Our road went under some trees for a bit, maybe fifty yards, until we were out of our farm on our way to Otto's and our neighbor, Professor Molls. And that road there, after our farm ended, it was county road and they charged a poll tax to maintain the road. Well now, every year after planting was done, we'd go and work off the poll tax instead of paying in cash money, because Dad never paid money when he could trade work or goods. That was just the way old timers did it back then. Try not to spend cash. Want to know the first time I saw a man with folding money? During a Klan meeting.

So there we were. It was afternoon. We started after dinner, cut a swath through the brush on each side of the road, hacked up roots and sprouts in the dirt, and took out rocks with a hoe. Paul and me, we hauled stuff off and threw the rocks into the timber as our part. Of course, we was none too efficient trying to see who could hit this tree or that tree and so on. Dad or Otto always swung the sickle. It was as sharp as a razor. Charley used the hoe.

So we worked enough to have a nice layer of sweat and dust on us, when the cattle looked up and stopped chewing, and the birdsong changed a bit. Now, that's a funny thing about that time. I don't know how we knew the things we did — how we knew there was a stranger in the neighborhood. In *those days, folks didn't come into Wilcox Bend unlessen they had business. I can remember all the times strangers came, and there were less than ten that I recall. If a stranger appeared it meant somebody was in trouble: you or them. Otto said, "Dad, somebody's coming."*

All Dad said was, "That so." He just kept swinging that sickle. Swish — swish — swish. Could've sung a song to it. We still didn't see or hear nothing. Then sure enough, here come two horses, two men. Taking their own sweet time at a flat-footed walk, smiling from under their hats. Paul and I stood there and stared, mouths hanging open. What were they doing, just riding up like that on our home ground? This was our dirt.

I looked at the sickles in the hands of Dad and them and knew what weapons they were. One good swish and they could hobble a horse and make dough out of a wrist or ankle. Of course, a sickle weren't much against a gun.

"You boys need some help with that work?" Dad still didn't even look up. Just swish — swish — swish. We went back to working on the rocks, but out of the corner of our eyes we had to look at those men. I saw them many times after that. Got to know their looks real good. They usually wore clean white shirts under their red braces. They'd been part of the Billy Sunday crew, I guess, because of those braces. Maybe he gave them to everyone who worked the revival. I don't know. But after that, whenever we saw those two, that's what they was wearing.

One man liked to crop his hair short and the other left it long. The long-haired one was younger and during all the meetings we saw him at later, when we watched from our spot on the crest of the ridge, we never did see him smile much. Maybe that was because he had the biggest damned set of teeth you ever laid eyes on. Mule's teeth. That was his name from then on. The one with the short hair grinned all the time, even later when he took the switches from Les Leids and said, "Let the lesson begin." But that day, they was both looking real friendly and Dad was not.

"Grant Thompson?" All smiles.

Swish — swish — swish.

"These must be some of your fine boys. We just came from Eldon, where some of the Mason members have spoken highly of your family. I believe you have brothers Eleven Thompson and James Thompson who are Masons? And a nephew Dr. Preston Thompson?"

Swish — swish — swish.

"We heard your fine sons Clyde and Otto are upstanding citizens with farms of their own. Will Jim be joining you, now that he's back from the war?

So glad to hear he suffered no injury or disease. Must be the good strong blood of the Thompson family that pulled him through." Mr. Shorthair did the talking.

Swish — swish — swish. Old Mule's Teeth didn't know much about horses. His horse just stood there, head down, eyes closed, but he hung on to those reins for dear life like he was sure that horse was going to jump over the nearest bluff from a dead stop.

"Yes sir, the good strong blood passed down from your southern-loving mother, a woman who loved her country, maybe as much as she loved her children?"

Swish — swish — swish.

"There's some that say the confederacy needs to rise again, because the strength of this country comes only from men with blood such as the Thompsons. I can see that just looking at these handsome boys. Smart too, I hear."

Now, how he knew that with us standing there with mouths open like catfish I don't know.

"Would this be Otto, Joe, Hadley and Paul, or Joe, Charley, Jim and Hadley?"

Finally Dad said something, though he didn't look up and never stopped swinging that sickle. "We don't take kindly to strangers not lettin' their business be known." Swish — swish — swish.

They still sat there, grinning like a pair of jackasses eatin' cockleburs. Creased pants. Shiny shoes. Not a speck of dirt. Later Dad said, "Their white robes can't cover the dirt underneath." But that day he didn't say nothin'.

"Well now, Grant, you don't mind if I call you Grant do you? Because I can tell we're of like minds. Grant, we're starting a new lodge in the neighborhood, and we're askin' only the finest folks. Now, I know what you're thinking, that you don't belong to no lodges. But this one's different. This one practices Klanishness. Let me explain what this means." Mr. Shorthair pointed and gestured all the while he talked.

Dad worked his way up to almost the horse's front feet before he turned to go on down the other side of the road. Just turned his back on them and walked away to where he'd left off. They should have taken that cue because everybody knows what that means. But the Kleagle kept talking. Dad started working his way up toward them again on the north side of the road. Swish — swish — swish. The cows went back to chewing. Charley and Otto never did stop working and didn't let on who they was. I don't know what the heck Paul and me was doing, just staring I suppose.

"In our lodge, a man takes an oath toward Klanishness that he will do business with only his fellow Klan members and they will do business with

him. So you would have all your fellow members beating down the door of your blacksmith shop. And that blacksmith in Bagnell, I hear he's a Catholic, well now, I can guarantee ya they won't be taking their business to him."

Swish — swish — swish.

"We're having our first meeting Thursday evening next, after sunset, in Kidwell's Hollow. Looking forward to seeing you and any of your sons. They're all welcome."

Finally Dad said something. "You'd best move those horses. I'm not as good an aim with this blade as I used to be."

So they smiled some more, tipped their hats, turned their horses, and left. Dad said, "Boys," which was all the reminder we was gonna get. Those men, they'd never met us, but they came the closest to getting us all straight as anyone. How'd they do that?

On the way home Otto said how he'd heard about the lodge as well, and it was a modern lodge. Unlike the old ones, where men were separated by profession, this one accepted men in all professions. Also, they had a section for the women. Folks were impressed by that. All so up-to-date.

Now maybe I've already mentioned it, but Dad was a Republican. Period. If he could've been baptized both Baptist and Republican, he would've. And there were men who were Democrats. Period. And when their kids could vote, they knew they would vote like their pa. When the vote for women came about, my dad never considered any man's wife or daughter would vote different than the man of the house. But as far as I know, before Fred Crismon moved in, all democrats lived across the river from us. That's right.

All our neighbors were Republicans, excepting for one by the name of Les Leids.

Les was a little squirt of a man and he wore a big hat all the time. You know what they say about that: big hat, no cattle. I find it hard to believe he did all he bragged about. Maybe he did. I don't know. He slicked his hair straight back and wore a little bit of a beard on his chin, and when we saw him on the street we boys went, "Ba-a-a-a" like goats. Nobody much took him serious before things started changing.

Les didn't belong to a church, but he belonged to a number of lodges. I heard a story once that someone was trying to convince him to join a church and get baptized. They asked him, "Ain't you worried about the hereafter?"

He showed 'em the lodge pin on his lapel and said, "You see this pin? It's all I need to get me in. I'll just show this at the pearly gates."

Mrs. Leids always imagined herself to be a head above anyone else and had little to do with our mother, who was stooped, didn't have fine clothes, and had one bad eye. Mrs. Leids wore store-bought dresses from Jefferson City.

If you saw her out in a wagon you saw a hat with flowers or feathers, even though other ladies wore sunbonnets. They'd two children, Suzzie and Buster. I tell you about the Leids now, because we come to find out Les was behind much of what started to happen in nineteen hundred and twenty-two.

We all worked together and depended on one another, nothing like the way it is now. In spite of this, there were lines being drawn underneath. Couldn't see them but you knew they was there. The territories, the boundaries. There weren't backyard fences and signs and roads like there are now. We kids roamed the woods like they belonged to us all. The livestock often did the same. But there were divisions we knew about. Kids had their places, women stayed in theirs, and even the men had their limits. And if you crossed over your line, somebody was going to call you on it.

When I was growing up, the grandpaps of my friends fought on both the Confederate and the Union sides. Still and all, we knew these things about everyone else's family. Do you know that about your friends? Do you know what side of the war their ancestors fought on? We did. I could recite them to this day. And you didn't trust those as much who'd fought against your kin. Just the way it was in Wilcox Bend.

The Klan in our parts hated folks for many different reasons. They hated that Abe Lincoln and his Republicans had stood up for the Coloreds. And they hated the German-Americans. We didn't know this about the Klan at first, and they didn't know Otto, Jim, Annie, Dessie and John was Ponders, and therefore German.

I'm sure Klan members had German in their blood. I know they did. There were so many Germans in Missouri, but many didn't claim that about their kin during that time. It just so happened everybody knew about German blood in the Thompsons.

Sometime between hell and breakfast, I managed to get the Thompson family tree finished and straight in my mind. Hadley's insistence that the Klan was in the area was an unpleasant thought, and I questioned memories from so long ago. There were many lodges in the area, as well as traveling salesmen and con artists constantly on the move. Perhaps he simply misinterpreted events. I avoided the topic with him.

Instead, I began to familiarize myself with the location of the old Thompson farm as well as the sites of various altercations surrounding the feud. In the 1800s, dense underbrush and soil consisting of rocks held together with spit and a handful of clay made the wooded areas a challenge to settlers. Although more like rolling hills compared to other mountain ranges, the Ozarks still presented tremendous obstacles. The timbered areas were so thick they forced the first pioneers to follow animal trails when they traveled. To those journeying into the area after 1820, the Osage River Valley was a gracious reprieve from highlands that refused to welcome settlers. Soon river bottom farmers were enjoying the richest tillable soil in the county.

The first time I hiked through the old Thompson farm I was mesmerized. Was it more beautiful than any other Missouri farmland? I don't know. I walked directly to the barn, where the years of weather had worn away the cement foundation. I saw the stock of a rifle showing through. Along with the hidden gun was a tobacco pipe, like the kind young Charley liked, both buried in the foundation. Hadley often talked about this barn built by the boys without the help of their father. He said those items were put there as just silliness. Others stated they were buried evidence. It did seem strange to me the Thompsons would throw something like a gun away when they saved and reused everything else.

I strolled into the center of the structure and looked up. I'm not sure how long I stood like that, but it was at least as long as I once admired the Sistine Chapel. The wooden supports lacing through the loft held the roof symmetrical and straight. I knew this was wood that wasn't simply ordered from a lumber mill. The boys had carefully chosen each type of wood for the job it would do. Hickory for straightness, oak for strength, ash for durability. They made sure it was properly cured and dried. Without the benefit of elaborate blueprints and sophisticated machinery, they had built the barn with their bare hands.

The barn was erected in the autumn of 1925 when Grant Thompson could not give any advice or help. Seventy-five years later I tried to find fault with its construction and could not. Grant Thompson sure did a great job teaching his boys, and despite their boyhood antics, they had learned.

I used to could go straight where Old Man Leids stashed his whiskey. Knew those woods and river like they was my own house, and after a storm I'd notice every little twig out of place. Leids would fill quart jars with stump water and bury them in a sandy shoal so the river rushed over their lids. Ba-a-a-a. Thought he was real smart, hiding them and keeping them cool at the same time. He'd sell 'em for thirty cents and it didn't make him much never mind

how old his buyers was. Of course, we kids knew what he was doing, since we prowled around taking note of everything. So we'd snatch a sip or two, dunk to fill the jar up, squeeze it back where we found it and wait a minute. I tell you what, that stuff would take the chill outta the mountains. Don't know if anyone knew what we was up to, but nobody ever called us on it.

For a long time we'd only Professor Molls as our neighbor, and between our farm and his was a ridge. A sycamore with a perfect fan shape set up on that ridge. I could draw it out for you now, because each dark winter morning during chores, I glanced up at that tree every few minutes and memorized its ash-colored trunk and long delicate branches to last all my days since. It was right there in the spot where dawn showed the first pink. When Dad caught me staring at it he'd holler, "Barney, keep your eyes on your work!" Don't know why they called me Barney.

But I kept looking over that way because when the dawn took up its color that tree looked like two hands, covered in coal and bound together at the wrists, fingertips spread out, reaching toward the sky. And the minute that black outline became a shadow cast against the light of sunrise, Mother rang the breakfast bell. There ain't a more welcome sound to a boy doing chores before sunrise than that. I can hear it now, "Clang, clang, clang!" It called through the waking sounds of Mother Nature like a fox horn.

As soon as Paul was big enough to come tagging along outside, maybe four or five, Dad started us doing something we did for years afterwards, and it became something we had to do every New Year's Day for good luck. Paul, me, Charley, and Joe stretched our arms around the trunk to see if our fingertips touched our brothers'. They say a tree like that grows for a hundred years, lives a hundred years and takes a hundred years to die. The last time we all tried to touch was January first, nineteen hundred and twenty-four, and we still couldn't reach. That tree was the gateway to our farm.

On down the road was Professor Molls's house. He was like a grandfather to us, and a father to Dad. Us kids bird-dogged him every chance we got, and he put up with us following along at his heels. He was round and friendly, with a respectable word for everyone. Rough-hewn river men called out, "Hey Prof!" and waved their hats as they floated by. Fancy town ladies, who ignored river types, nodded in their reserved sort of way, and curled up the ends of their lips ever so slightly when they said, "Afternoon, Professor" to him as well. To smile outright would've signaled more, since Professor was a single man and all. It never occurred to me before the trouble started that anyone wouldn't like him.

If there'd been a Mrs. Molls (and I believe there once had been) she would've been at the bedside to help our mother give birth, instead of her hus-

band. But until my brother Otto's wife and Mrs. Crismon moved to Wilcox Bend, Mother was the only woman around.

Professor was a short man who wore a vest and jacket on most days. He smelled of horehound drops, pipe tobacco, and cedar. He was what they call a "gentleman farmer." Professor did the things he liked to do with farming and didn't do the things he didn't like to do. He'd a few Banty hens (but don't know as how he ever wrung a neck) and a dairy cow and two beautiful drafts.

Oh, those horses. Finest in the county and probably the state. Noah and Moses. Slow to startle, gentle and strong, hooves the size of dinner plates. Lead Noah and Moses followed, but Moses wouldn't go without Noah.

One winter when I was about six years old, we had deep snows. For two months the roads were covered, and most nights a white dusting freshened up what melted or blew away. Dad traded for a sled, the men hitched up Noah and Moses, and we took those horses all over. Warmed our hands on their sides by watching our fingers disappear in their winter coats. Fur as thick as bear skins.

Sometimes it was Professor and us boys, sometimes Mother, Dad, Professor and sometimes all of us in that sled. Weight made the horses no matter; they just worked harder because they loved to pull. We'd lead 'em into the barn, and the minute they heard the jingle of a harness pulled off the peg, they'd snort, paw, and toss their manes, eager to get on with it. Noah had to be hitched on the left with Moses to his right, and then we boys climbed over ourselves to get into that sled. Professor snapped the reins on their backs, and from the instant they lunged forward against the leather, their work was as one.

Some days Professor came to take only Mother and Dad for a ride, so us boys stood and watched from the front porch until they crested the ridge and passed our giant sycamore on their way down the road. Then we'd wait a bit longer, breathing in the cold and listening to the sleigh bells jingling until the silence returned.

Professor was the only Catholic I knew growing up.

By the time I was born, Hadley had already fought in World War II and retired from the Navy with over thirty-five years of service. He had become a well-educated man, mostly self-taught. Hadley tried to write the story of his boyhood on a few occasions, but gave up and looked instead for someone to write it for him.

I often stared at him across that kitchen table, listening to his stories about rural Missouri and eventually the feud, and wondered two things. The first was always if all the seemingly irrelevant details he described were actually necessary to the story. Well, yes, he was usually correct there. The second idea was more bothersome to me. What if I discovered the Thompsons were the real villains in this story? What if the Thompson boys had started killing livestock and harassing locals all those years ago?

Many people I interviewed told me how respected the Crismons were. Years later Frederick Crismon's grandson verified this by providing me with copies of his grandfather's Justice of the Peace commission papers between the years of 1910 and 1922.

I never told Hadley my fears. I wonder now if he knew what I was thinking, because he so often repeated this advice: "Never be afraid of the truth."

Nowadays people'll build a fire any old way, just to get it going you know. But my older brother John always made a fire the way it should be done. Sparks and ash wouldn't dare fly outta one of John's fires. He cut the wood and seasoned it to build the fires in the kitchen and smoke house. He built fires in the washhouse too, on Mondays, because that was washday. Excepting he knew Sunday was his day off, and if you tried to get him to do something that day, he'd just say, "Doe, die Dod!" And that was it. Son, you just better give it up.

John was the oldest boy in the house, but I don't mean oldest in his head. He was a big help to Mother. I have no idea how women lived back then. Just washing clothes in a washing machine is a job today, yet Mother did it all by hand. He stayed by her side until death split them apart.

When John was three years old, somebody gave him an old tin horn. He was playing with it one day and got that mouthpiece off and sucked it down in his throat and started to choke to death. My sister Annie ran and grabbed a pair of tongs Dad had in his shop, with long handles for blacksmithing. She went down in there and brung up that mouthpiece. Saved John's life, but robbed him of oxygen so long it hurt his mind.

It was the job of us kids to carry drinking water in metal syrup buckets from our spring. That was hard water. After Dad and us made the concrete cistern, the rainwater drained off the house into gutters and ended up there. It was as unsanitary as you can get but was soft water for washing clothes. Mother used washboards with the lye soap we made. Even years later when we got her a washing machine she still washed on Mondays.

Dad built the house for Mother, which wouldn't look like much at all today, but back then it was pretty nice. It had five rooms. A parlor, with an organ for Mother, a dining room and a kitchen. There were two bedrooms, one for us kids and one for Mother and Dad. The kitchen had a back door toward the outbuildings, and the dining room had a pot-bellied stove for heating the house. The house is gone now, but thinking back to that old place, I can see it and even start to hear it, too.

Like the door of Mother's stove. I can hear that damn thing today. Heavy cast iron. The minute Dad's toes touched the floorboards, John jumped out of bed and trotted over to that stove. Then he'd carefully lay in the kindling from the wood box to get the morning fire going. Creak…the little door opened, squeak…it shut. John got cranky if we so much as picked up a piece of wood. "Don-Don do it," he'd say and snatch the wood from our hands. Didn't matter how he opened that thick, black door, slow or fast, it called out, "The day's long started, and you're late for chores!" The sizzle of lard in a hot skillet, the bubbling of water boiling, the grinder working on the coffee beans, each and every morning I heard those sounds.

For a while Dad had a certain hound dog, a blue tick that loved to scratch in the dirt. He was out of the bitch Damsel Blue, a prize winning dog in Sedalia. Anywhere that dog went, he never settled in 'cept he'd first scratch, scratch, scratch, long enough to hollow out a spot for hisself. He just loved to dig was part of it. About once a year in an afternoon he'd dig 'til he disappeared under the hen house. We'd see him doing it, but pretend we didn't because we loved what come next. Before long there it was — squawking, screeching hens, fluttering and flying into each other as they burst through the doorway. Then Mother, sailing out the kitchen door in a cloud of dust, feet barely touching the stoop, hollering, "Boys!" with lungs she got from taking care of five boys under one roof. We knew better than to let dogs tease her chickens like that.

The Crismons moved in when I was about nine. We'd already rushed down to Brockman's Ford once that spring, dropped our tools in the dirt before we run to the bank. Word came a couple traveling through was being washed away by high water. Their horses with them. But we were too late and never saw 'em. It was nobody from around here.

Brockman's Ford was a low spot in the hills where mist liked to settle. If we were floating downstream in the early morning we might come around the last bend and suddenly there'd be no bank, no sky, just black water, and only for three feet in front of the skiff. Then in a blink you couldn't even see your toes. Fog as thick as a blanket. Even on a fine day we learned all there was to know about the river at Brockman's Ford.

Now living there we could tell exactly what the river was doing by watching the sycamore roots along the bank. Three feet of roots showing in the dead of summer was typical. You could ford at many places when it was that shallow, even by foot if you didn't mind getting wet. A foot or two of roots meant it was deep enough to run the tie rafts, and still okay to ford at Brockman's on horseback. No roots showing? Boy, you best stay home unless you knew exactly where to take your horse along the shallow path underwater that went from shore to shore. That was the ford. Us boys and the fox knew that way.

Until the trouble started we were very lucky our farm was right between Brockman's and the Bagnell Ferry. Some people were land locked when the river was up, but us Thompsons always had a way out. But when everything took over, that wasn't so true anymore. And I think that's one of the reasons Dad acted like he did. He was backed into a corner.

By this time Professor Molls was gone. He thought he was getting too old to be going back and forth like he done for years. He left Noah and Moses in pasture next to the house, harnesses still in the barn, and got someone to look after them. I think a Blankenship. Professor still came to visit a few times a year, especially during threshing and sorghum pressing. His farm sold to a man we'd hardly met, when before you know, it was up for sale again. I don't know how many acres was in that farm, but most of it was in bottom land. It had a pretty good bottom in it. Good soil. Professor built the house that's still there today.

When the Crismons were just looking at the place, before they moved in, Dad met Fred Crismon and got acquainted with him and found out Crismon was going to pay $19,000 for the farm. I guess Dad knew how much Professor paid for the farm, or maybe what it sold for the first time, because he said, "Fred, don't pay $19,000 for the farm. I believe I can get it for $16,000." Of course, that'd be a hell of a bargain today, but that's the way it was then. I don't know how Dad was going to do this, unless somehow through Uncle Lev's bank. But anyway, Crismon went ahead and bought the farm, paid $19,000 for it.

Now came talk that the Crismons was coming our way, but broke an axle and were stuck at Brockman's Ford. We went down there again, this time in the wagon, with tools, spare wheels and axles, enough to get them patched up and on their way if we could. Mother came too, a basket of food on her lap, and we were all excited to greet the new neighbors. Mother'd been having a tough time of it that spring. She'd had our sister, Karma Jean Thompson, in April. But I never saw my sister alive. Dad put in the garden for Mother that year but she didn't seem quite recovered. I recall her saying, "I hope the new people have a daughter."

And they did. There was Fred and Sarah Crismon, one daughter, Anita, and the two sons, Leo and Francis, and that was nineteen hundred and twen-

ty, I do believe. Later, a nephew of Sarah's came to live with them, too. They were a redheaded bunch. Leo was about Charley's age, thirteen or so, and they became good friends that summer. Francis was a few years older, about fifteen, about a year younger than Joe. Anita was just about two years older than me, so about eleven or so? I think that's correct.

Fred Crismon, the father, was a big, raw-boned person, red face, red hair. Hair was very thin. I remember that day and how he bent down and shook our hands and repeated our names to get them all straight. He was nice to us boys and quiet mannered. I remember Mrs. Crismon as a short, sandy-haired person. I think she had a few freckles. Our mother was shy and tended not to go out of her way to meet others, but Mrs. Crismon was more sociable. She popped around, meeting us all, and later liked having play parties and Bible studies at her home. Finally there was some female company for Mother.

So that first day down at the ford we helped them out, shared a bit of dinner on the river bank and then followed them back to their new place. Along the way we saw Noah and Moses, standing in spring grass so lush and tall it swallowed up their enormous hooves and wove itself into the feathers covering their hocks. Jet-black manes and tails perfectly matched. They raised their huge heads as we rode by, mouths dripping with green, and we all agreed they were a fine and beautiful sight. Come to find out, Leo especially loved horses.

This same spring there were other new people moving into the area. My brother Jim put in crops at his new farm. It was an exciting time. New dogs chasing the wagon when we drove by, new livestock ambling into Mother's garden — and after we herded them back to their home, a bite of cornbread, tasting just a bit different from Mother's, was our reward. We boys welcomed the changes.

For years the Crismon family eluded me. But finally I found the grandson of Frederick Pinkney Crismon, the man Hadley referred to as Mr. Crismon. He was Leo Crismon's son. This grandson, also named Fred Crismon, was a man in his sixties, an avid historian, and fellow writer. In our initial discussions, he related a great deal of helpful information about the Crismon family. On 8 March 2008, he wrote:

> As far as I know, the Crismons were strict teetotalers. There was a small bottle half full of whiskey in their house in Iberia, which was there for 'medicinal reasons'.... Incidentally, the level in that bottle was about the same for 8 or 10 years. And I surreptitiously tasted it once.

On the subject of bloodlines, he shared a document that his father Leo Crismon wrote in the 1960s:

> My father [Frederick Pinkney] has left a precious heritage... He was an heir to that which was best in the German people, a love for freedom. The Crismons were among the more noble Germans who left the old German empire... 1740-1786 or earlier.... He was in the Philippines 17 months... he enlisted Sept. 25, 1899 and was discharged on June 30, 1901.

When Frederick P. Crismon returned to Miller County he married Sarah Elizabeth Shelton, and the wedding was performed by a Christian (Campbellite) minister. In the same document, his son Leo writes, "My father was converted after he reached manhood. I saw him baptized in the Little Maries Creek in 1913 or 1914 by Rev. Charles Sooter, of the Christian Church...." Leo also recounted a story of his father who, when placed under ether for an operation, sang a Christian hymn.

Leo's chronicle continues: "Evidence of the Public [sic] spirit of my father is shown in the fact that he was elected Justice of the Peace...." This act was the result of a general election in 1910, and he served for four years. Then again in 1915, he was elected to serve until 1918. Further evidence of public responsibility is suggested when Leo states, "I remember hearing him take part in a speaking program at the Bert Stevenson place in the interest of the Red Cross, or the sale of war bonds during World War I. He liked to sing in public and have singings in the home."

Now a lot of folks who aren't from Missouri think since the state was divided during the Civil War it meant those in the north were Union, and those in the south, Confederate. T'weren't so. Counties were divided; families were divided. And it didn't matter which side of the state you stood on. During the war, even the county seat Tuscumbia was divided. The confederate flag flew on the north side of the ferry and the union flag flew on the other. On our side. Part of it had to do with where the Germans in our area lived, who were all for the union to the best of my knowledge. One family, the Tellmans, were special friends of ours.

Mr. Tellman was a foxhunting friend of my father's and Mrs. Tellman was the only woman with courage enough to attend butchering. She was as generous as the river, but I was a bit afraid of her. Her name was Missouri, Mrs. Missouri Tellman. She made German blood sausages.

Butchering was the formal end of the growing season and the beginning of winter and like all the other times we got together, it was a festive occasion. Our butchering spot was a spring down along Little Bear Creek, and we met there when the weather was cool with each man bringing a hog or two. Any spring would suit for the fresh water, but we chose that particular one because next to it was an old oak. Its limbs grew sideways, eight or ten feet off the ground, horizontal, and they spread out like that in all directions before they reached upward. Those oak branches were perfect for throwing a rope over, and strong enough for hoisting up four hundred pound hogs.

A McDowell or two would also be there to help, and we'd all give them a part of the meat for pay, like we'd also do at the mill or if somebody helped at threshing. There were all sorts of McDowells in the area and some of them had a pretty tough time of it. This old guy, Arthur McDowell, didn't have much. I think the only dirt he owned was under his fingernails. He often helped Dad and Professor Molls and was a good, steady worker when he had the mind to work. But then he'd disappear into the hills and be unavailable until one morning, here he'd come, walking down the road in them coveralls, lunch pail in hand, and ready to do whatever. Dad often saved a string of chores for the morning Arthur McDowell appeared. "That'll wait for McDowell," he'd say. Even today, I say to myself sometimes, "That'll wait for McDowell" about something that needs attending to but I haven't the mind to do it.

Butchering was no easy task. First, we'd flip the hog and sit on it while we lashed a rope to the back feet. There ain't anything nastier than a hog bite, but they can't turn their heads sideways, so if we held onto their shoulders good and tight we'd be okay. Then in one motion we'd release the animal while our buddies jerked the rope back, and Mr. Hog was hoisted high above the ground. Kicking, snorting, trying with all his strength to get free — he never did.

Then the knife across its throat, and Mrs. Tellman was there with a bucket to catch the warm blood as it poured like a faucet from the squealing, jerking body. She'd build a fire under a wash bucket filled with beer, blood, and herbs and then all day long as the men cut, she'd guard her pot while we threw the scraps from the carcass into the simmering bloody mix.

I can see her standing there now, thick-legged and sturdy as the tree trunk next to her, wearing three aprons over her coarse dress, stirring and stirring. Later Mr. Tellman would help her strain the mixture, squeeze the meat into casings and tie them off. Then every family who contributed pork into her vat of secrets received, like magic, a string of the delicate and delicious presents. By the end of the day there were sausages for everyone. Mother always counted on us bringing them home for supper that night.

When Mr. Tellman came out to hunt, if we were lucky, he would bring Mrs. Missouri Tellman's sausages she'd cured in brine. His contributions to those midnight hunts were as good as anyone's; we always ate Tellman's food. Chicory coffee so strong you could arm wrestle it and lose, Indian squash with sorghum cooked over the fire, and always, Missouri's packages from butchering day. It was inconceivable to us that folk like the Tellmans would ever be considered suspect and hated.

Most of my memories of Dad have to do with the farm and things like threshing, butchering and planting, but I got to see a whole other side when he walked away from the plow. I went fox hunting with Dad and his friends whenever they'd let me, and some of my favorite memories are of those old fox hunts. They'd go out in an evening and often spend the night out there as well, a far piece from home. If it was a clear, moonlit night they'd hunt all night. If not, they'd just shoot the breeze, sleep a bit, and wait until morning to start up again. I'd curl up on a coat or a pile of leaves by the fire to sleep and listen to the men talk. If they thought I was asleep sometimes I got to hear something I shouldn't.

I thought a lot about how to explain fox hunting, because it wasn't like the hunting we did to eat. It was a social occasion. We rarely got a fox, him being faster and smarter than us. Usually the dogs gave out before they caught up with him, but sometimes we got lucky.

One October when I was ten, I was out on one of those all-night hunts. Charley was out in the timber with Dad. The dogs were baying from the darkness, running purely on the fox's scent. Charley stared at the woods in front of him but could see only darkness. No street lights. No glare from a nearby city. And no flash of red or pointed nose. Then out of the black the fox ran right across Charley's path. He got over his surprise in time to get a shot off and we all said Foxy ran himself into that bullet. Charley was a damn good shot as a kid and he got him a fifty-dollar fox tail that day. I won't tell you how many fox hides I came home with even though I went on a hell of a lot of hunts. Let's just say when the hide buyer came through it was usually Charley and Joe that had something to sell.

The hunters was a bit of an elite group, and they was tight. The only group tighter was the railroad men, or maybe horse traders. They had their own language and signals. Old Grandpa Thompson, the one they called "Pa," hunted with the bell, the shot, and the horn. We only used the shot and the horn to tell each other what was going on.

Hunting was a time to get out and do something with your pals. Dad had his foxhunting friends, and they all had their special dogs and their special routine when they got together. You want to know what they was really chasing? Their freedom. That's all. Later, I came to realize maybe others didn't like this group just because they weren't a part of it.

Besides fox hunting and taking a drink now and again, Dad loved to listen to stories. Now, one thing about that time, the men loved to tell stories, and there was a whole tradition about it. Singing was like that too. Some men were kind of like the professional storytellers for the neighborhood. Dad didn't do much story telling, but he liked to listen and one of the few times he'd lay aside his work was for a good story.

He didn't belong to any of the lodges in Bagnell, Brumley or Eldon like many of the men did. Us boys heard the other men talking about lodge meetings, and when Professor Molls brought by newspapers we'd see the printed notices. But that was about it. So we were very curious about them, with the symbols and handshakes and all.

I'm not blaming us going to the Klan meetings on Dad, because he didn't have anything directly to do with it. But I will say that going out in the woods day and night with him like we did made us very unafraid. It wasn't quite as wild as Aunt Maggie's days, although there was a great deal of wrong that could happen out there. However, we just knew trouble was never going to catch up to us. The hunter never imagines he's going to be hunted. So before long, we decided we was grown up enough to go prowling around at night.

First, we'd lie on our backs, two, maybe three to a bed. Turning blue in the dark trying not to breathe hard enough to make any noise. When my father's snores rolled down the hall to our room, we knew it was as safe as it was gonna get, because when we heard that freight train coming from our parents' room, it meant brother John wasn't as likely to hear us from his place next to their door.

I'm sure Mother tried to teach us the virtue of patience, but it was Old Joe, our oldest brother, who really showed us what the word meant. Patience for us boys meant waiting for just the right moment and then either creeping like a cat or running like hell.

I usually slept next to Charley or Paul, and we'd lie there, eyes wide open in the dark, waiting for Joe to give us the high sign. Then we'd slide off the bed, snatch up our trousers, and squeeze our skinny bodies out the window. Off we'd go, running along the path in the woods, so scared and excited we'd have to stop and pee while our brothers laughed. Even though Dad let us go 'coon hunting at night, it was a boat load more fun trying to get away with something. We snuck out for all manner of reasons. We just loved knowin' we was getting away with something.

When we got wind grown men were having lodge meetings out there under the stars, and not in a building in Eldon or Bagnell or Brumley like they usually did, well, how could we refuse that? All in all we went to fifteen or twenty of those meetings, enough that I could tell you all you want to know about that bunch of coyotes — and I will.

Close now, we'd fall to our bellies and crawl up the hillside, having quite a game of it. Near the crest we'd wait, face pressed against the dirt. Laughing, hands clamped on our own mouths so we wouldn't make a sound, waiting for them to come. We were only kids, but we thought the meetings were silly at first. They was supposed to be a big secret, but we'd hear about them just hanging around, pretending not to listen. In the beginning, the group hadn't taken over the schoolhouse yet and always met outside.

We knew they were coming by the smell. Even before the snorts of the horses or the low, quiet talk, the sweet, sticky smell of kerosene came through on the breeze. There'd be a bonfire set up, and out of the back of a wagon came torches made of rags soaked in kerosene. Usually there was a wooden cross in the back as well, about as tall as I was. All the rags was wrapped around it and tied with baling wire. And there were the two who came down the road to the farm, trying to get Dad to join the group. They was just like before, one bossy with short hair doin' all the talking, smiling all the while. The other one with them big front teeth.

Usually nothing much happened besides a lot of talking and singing of hymns and patriotic songs and all. They didn't always light the cross, just during special sessions. For a very long time, Shorthair and Mule's Teeth was there leading the meetings. And I do believe Shorthair was as mean a man as they come. So during that first meeting, all of a sudden he motions, and here come two more leading a third. They'd bound their quarry's wrists behind his waist and blindfolded him. It was Ty Sears, a man we knew about but didn't have contact with. He lived somewhere along the north bank of the Osage near Bagnell.

Shorthair was standing, a switch in one hand. Then he held it underneath his arm to light a cigarette. He took a few drags off that, just looking at Ty standing there with his eyes covered. It must have been terrifying for that man, bound like a pig for slaughter, blindfolded, just waiting. But he just had a "you son of a bitch" look on his face, even with the blindfold. He was bigger than any of the men there, so I have no idea how they caught him and got him there.

Shorthair threw the cigarette down and snubbed it out with his toe. He was just takin' his time. He picked some tobacco specks off his lower lip. Then he put on a hood he'd jammed in his back pocket and out came everybody else's as well. Now all their faces were covered. Shorthair took ahold of that switch and the other two men pushed Ty Sears down on his knees and took off his blindfold. He was facing us, but then he turned and looked back at them all. Eyes full of hate. Shorthair just stood there, all calm and cool-like under his hood. Then he pulled back and started to whip that huge back in front of him, saying something to Ty all the time we couldn't hear.

What I remember thinking is it didn't look like it hurt that much because Ty's face stayed hard and still. His back, however, seemed to belong to somebody else. It jumped and twitched every time the switch lashed across it, leaving black strips we could see even through the darkness. But the face was separate from all that and looked like it could have belonged to one of the men watching. Just blank and staring.

We got outta there all right and ran on home and maybe because we were just stupid kids and didn't realize what it really meant and all, never told nobody about what we'd seen. I know that is hard to believe. We didn't think that you don't give a man a licking like you do a kid and that whipping a naked back is much different than a slap with a belt across the rear. We knew nothing about laws or the Klan and its history. We just knew we'd be up on that ridge again the next time we could sneak out.

Soon after that, our nighttime trips had to involve more than eavesdropping on a meeting, or Old Joe wouldn't come with us. He preferred nighttime excursions with girls involved, and even on trips to Bagnell he'd turn into the dry goods store as soon as he'd done what Dad asked. Then out he'd come, just as fast, his pockets stuffed with hair ribbons for some girl. So our trips often started at some gal's house with Joe throwing stones at her window until she popped her head out.

"Joe Thompson! Pa'll skin you!"

Then there's Joe, holding up a hair ribbon to tempt her, or maybe just using a compliment for bait. Sometimes the girls came out and Joe stole a kiss or two, but his endeavors never got too far because it just wasn't right for us to let them alone. He'd hide us in the brush, but before long we'd have to sing out,

Now boys, keep away from the girls, I say
And give 'em plenty of room
You'll find when you're wed she'll beat you 'till you're dead
With the bald-headed end of the broom.

That usually ended Joe's fun, but we sure had a lot of our own. When toilets got moved inside I wondered, what excuse did young gals give their fathers when they wanted to sneak out?

What kind of man was Grant Thompson? Hadley said his father was a tough man. Actually, everybody said he was a tough man. "He wasn't one to back down." "He was as high-tempered as a meat axe." "All them Thompsons got a temper on them." Even ever-loyal wife Myrtle Thompson said on more than one occasion, "He could be ugly when he was in a mind."

According to family genealogy, Grant got his toughness from his father, John Christopher Thompson. By all accounts, the marriage of Grant's parents was not a happy one. It didn't help that the two couldn't agree on something as monumental as on which side of the war to fight. When John C. went to fight for the Union, Sarah, a southern sympathizer, loaded five kids in a wagon and drove her team over two hundred miles to Miller County. She hid the family gold in the bottom of a nail keg, which she filled up with soap. Bandits stole items from the young family throughout the trip, but never found the gold.

Husband John C. later joined his family, though he often left for extended periods, returning with no warning and refusing to say where he had been. Once he took the youngest child, Hadley's father, with him for two years. Despite these disruptions, the couple managed to have twelve children, although John C. was never very nice to them.

Grant's brother, Eleven C. Thompson (Uncle Lev) used at least some of the gold smuggled north in the keg during the war to start the Bank of Brumley. He eventually owned a mercantile company as well and was a successful businessman his entire life. Later, the Crismons would reference this success, saying it gave Hadley's family unfair advantages.

For the Thompsons, something stated frequently in history books was intimately played out within their family. The Civil War didn't just split the country; it split states, neighborhoods and even the Thompsons. Over a hundred years later in 1969, while studying Missouri politics during the progressive area, historian J.D. Muraskin noted, "Because Missouri experienced a civil war within a civil war, the trauma of this experience ran deeper than in many other states." Many other historians have concluded that this situation also produced men and women used to fighting.

Clearly the Thompsons could be a source of irritation to the strait-laced and order-loving Frederick Crismon. Leo later recalled,

> Even though Grant Thompson was a nominal member of the Elm Springs Baptist Church and even though it was the days of prohibition, he often got drunk (on moonshine whiskey) and it was only on such occasions that he had courage enough to attempt any threats. Although it has been so many years ago that I cannot remember events in exact chronological order, I remember his stopping and sitting on his horse with a shotgun across the horse's shoulders, pointing toward our house. He was well out of range of any gun which he knew we had.

But according to Hadley, Frederick Crismon was a "big-wig" with the local KKK chapter. This statement, as with others, required additional verification. Not surprisingly, it's difficult to get people to confess their family's involvement in the Klan, even though it was so many years ago, yet this was clearly necessary for the research. Often Hadley would point me down the correct gravel road, and then armed with a loaf of homemade bread as a gift and our two hunting dogs who were always useful to start conversation, off I went. "Don't let them know which side you're on" was the only advice I got. Asking relative strangers to confess intimacies about their families and ancestors did not come easily.

I soon learned a tendency that surprised me, and that was the embarrassment families felt when recalling that the Klan had once targeted them. I expected descendants to hesitate to tell me they'd found evidence of their ancestors joining, not the other way around.

When others started confirming the existence of a Ku Klux Klan chapter, it became evident that the KKK had moved into this all-white community. I just didn't know why and neither did anyone else. By this time I was also convinced that the Thompsons would either fight them off or die trying. They were not a family to be told what to do, nor were they one to give in.

Les Leids was at the meetings from the beginning as far as we could tell. With all the glad-handing and "Ain't we great?" kind of talk, he fit right in. I don't

think Les ever went by a group of men before he'd have to shake a hand or pat somebody on the back. Ba-a-a-a. Liked for everyone to think he was the finest fellow there with lots of friends.

The night I'm going to tell you about now was right around or just after Crismon moved in. We'd got to our spot a little early. It was a perfect night for scampering around and all four of us, Joe, Charley, me, and Paul, were out. No moon. Still air. Bats reeling against the light of the lanterns the men hung in the trees. Les and two others, Pud Downs and Inky O'Brien, were setting everything up and making quite a show of it.

Inky, fat as a tomato, walked with his feet pointing east and west even if that belly of his was going north. What did Pud look like? He was a big fella. Hair nothin' but a mess of cowlicks. There was no mistaking the three of them, no matter if they had on hoods and gowns. Pud and Inky worked at Leids' mill in Tuscumbia and stuck to Les like beggar lice.

"Wap!" All of a sudden Charley flattens me out with a palm across the back of my head, holding me down, face in the mud. Of course my first reaction is to fight the son-of-a-gun back, but he whispers "Shhhhh" so I lay there and wait, just thinking what I'm going to do to him if he's fooling with me.

Sure enough, here come somebody down the path we've made, the one we was sure nobody knew about. "We're sunk," I'm thinking. None of us is moving. We're just eight bare feet, sticking out of worn coverall legs, lined up like kernels on a cob. I know any minute I'm going to be hearing or feeling something bad.

"Hey there!" Leids hollers up, and somebody behind me calls back. Nobody breathes. Charley's still got his palm on the back of my head and my face's in the dirt, and I figure I'm either going to suffocate in a minute or two or be killed by a stranger.

But Paul, well, he's so young he don't have the sense to be afraid, and besides, he can outrun anybody we've ever come across. He sneaks a little peek at the man who is only twenty or thirty feet away. There's Mr. Shorthair, suckin' on a flask, taking a breath, and then downing some more.

Then Shorthair pulls out a stick of sassafras root and chews on it a bit. To take the smell away, you know. He calls out, "Les! Shine that lantern over there. I think I see something." Well at that point, don't you know we about died right there. But it's okay because he's pointing away from us. Les's eyes follow that outstretched arm, then he strides over that way.

Like a miracle from heaven sent to protect stupid boys, they is all looking at the other side of the ravine, away from us. Shorthair corks his flask and slips it into a hollow of a tree trunk. He tosses the sassafras aside, wipes his hands on his trousers, and starts on down to the rest of them. He just didn't want them to see him drinking none.

The liquor in the flask must've done the trick, because when it was time for the speech, Shorthair really went to town that night:

"Remember history!   During the Middle Ages, the Roman Catholic Church sought control of the world, but it was the English who were the heroes." He tried his damnedest to be just like Billy Sunday, with his moves and all. But he wasn't as believable as Billy.

"The English, the ancestors of everyone here, died defending this sacred gift to you. And what was that gift? Our country. Are you men? Will you stand against the alien tide and defend the English way of life?"

He was on a roll, I'll tell you what. We didn't see any burning cross — it all looked like a bore, so we left. But not before taking the flask from the tree. We ran down that path toward the river and right into Old Man Sons.

"Well, hello boys." His smoke pit was going like usual with a string of pretty fish dancing over the fire. I said I'd be back in the morning to fish with him, and he motioned with his chin to the fish smoking line and said to tell Mother he would send smoked fish for dinner. Then Joe tossed him the flask we'd found. It sailed over his fire, flickered and glimmered in the firelight before it landed in his rough, old hands. He smiled. Long yellow teeth. Kind of scary looking with his long white hair sticking out so, but oh, how we loved him.

Sons never asked questions. Just winked, nodded, and said, "Thank you kindly. I was just thinkin' it might be getting a bit cool tonight. You boys be careful out here." Another wink, a hearty swig. "Never corner nothin' meaner than yerself." He gave a nod. We took off to home.

For families who lived in the Ozarks for generations, the vigilantism the Klan started to propose in the 1920s was not a new concept, but a revival of an old idea. After the Civil War, the population in the Ozark hills surged. As people moved into the area, horse thefts and highway robbery also became more prevalent. The rugged countryside and poor roads, combined with the many caves and waterways, made it easy for criminals to elude the county sheriff.

There had always been gambling, drinking, fights, and houses of ill repute throughout the countryside. There was also a more pious, church-going sect (and some who enjoyed keeping a foot in each camp) for initially there was plenty of space to simply avoid each other. But by the late 1870s, a group of the more staid, country folk became convinced that the livelier entertainment establishments supported criminals whose most obvious crimes were harassing travelers and stealing horses. Records also noted some of the squabbles were related to the Civil War: neighbors were more likely to turn in an establishment if its proprietor fought on an opposing side during the war.

Lawmen raided the establishments, but warnings of the raids often traveled faster than a sheriff on horseback. Even if the culprits didn't disappear and an arrest was made, the criminal's friends would swear his innocence to the traveling judge.

By 1886, a group of citizens were dissatisfied with the protection and policing. They called a meeting at Bald Jess, one of the higher, timberless peaks in Taney County, Missouri. Such peaks were called "balds" or "knobs." Legend states this was the beginning of the Bald Knobbers. It was a time when the idea of taking the law into one's own hands was condoned.

Bald Knobbers rode on horseback, held their meetings and made their raids at night. Their victims were usually proprietors, who were tied to trees and flogged with horsewhips, from where they could watch liquor barrels emptying in the dirt, buildings burning, and gambling paraphernalia being ruined. Some wore masks.

At first the regulators were organized as a league to assist the sheriff and other law enforcement officers. In the absence of police they carried out justice as they saw fit. A man pledged himself, under oath and penalty of death, not to divulge any plans, or to refuse orders. After the initial meeting on Bald Jess, citizens went back to their own neighborhoods and called similar meetings. Although greatly sensationalized, their numbers remained in the hundreds.

The plan worked. The countryside was cleaned up, most Bald Knobbers returned to their homes and farms, and the organization was officially disbanded in 1889. But certain individuals seemed to develop a taste for the raids and continued to harass others on their own. Tales of their escapades filled the newspapers as those of their criminal predecessors had done previously, but more importantly to this story, children grew up hearing their Grandpap tell the stories of his days with the Bald Knobbers. The name Ku Klux Klan may have been a name unfamiliar to Wilcox Bend natives, but there was nothing new about vigilantism.

My mother, Myrtle Wornell Thompson, had the misfortune of getting pregnant while she was a teenager. You couldn't have done anything to a family that was more degrading. My mother had to bear both the sentiment of the people as well her father's reputation, for her father, James Maston Wornell, was deacon of the First Christian Church of Brumley for forty years and a Civil War veteran from the Union side. Grandpa Wornell had a mercantile business as well as a pension from the war of fifty dollars a month. That was a lot of money back then. Pretty much made him king of Brumley, Missouri.

Every Sunday morning, Maston Wornell was right there in the front row on the left hand side. Everybody knew that was his spot. That was his church. His wife and family lined up with him, and on winter mornings the light streamed in through the tall windows covering him and his family, and the spot they sat in was warm and sunny. Everybody else sat behind Maston Wornell, looking at his broad, strong shoulders and noticing his wife's new hat every Easter.

My mother wouldn't name the baby's father. It was customary to send the pregnant mothers away in situations like this. Not talk about it. She'd go visit relatives for six months in another town. But not Maston Wornell. He saw to it that none of his family was leaving that front pew. No, they sat there Sunday after Sunday and Myrt got bigger and bigger. Soon she had to reach around to push herself up from the back of the pew when it was time to stand for the reading of the Gospel. Soon winter came and her coat didn't button over her belly. But every Sunday they're there. And everybody knows.

Did they ask Maston Wornell to resign as deacon? To leave the church? That I do not know. But I know he did not.

When Mother gave birth to Gipsy, it was Maston who carried little Gipsy through those thick, wooden doors. Maston was the one who marched to the altar, cradling that baby in his huge arms, presenting her to the minister for baptism. Nobody's going to turn down Maston Wornell. Grandpa Maston is the one Gipsy grew up sitting next to in that front pew. And when it came time for my dad and mother to be married, they made plans to leave Gipsy behind and move out along the river. Dad picked out a farm along the Osage and Uncle Lev's bank lent him the money.

Gipsy stayed with Mother's sister and her Grandpa Wornell. And lately, I've been thinking about it and wondering if that was a kind of trade off. Mother found a man to marry her, but she had to leave her baby to be raised by her sister and father. So my folks got married, and first came Joe Drake in 1904. As long as I can remember, Dad called him Old Joe. Next they got Charley Clayton, two years later. Then me after about five years; I told you he

*called me Barney. Then three years after that, Paul Dean, the Colonel. And
what ended up happening is those kids from his first family raised us. Dessie,
Otto, Clyde, Jim, John, Annie and Gipsy were always there for Joe, Charley,
Paul and me.*

*My half-sister Gipsy grew up to be a little thimble of a gal, who wore
her hair down and pulled back when she wasn't teaching. When she walked
to school in the mornings it was at a fast clip, determined, a notebook pressed
against her chest. But after school she tarried a bit, because she'd find a stone
in the road, and hurry it along with her foot, kicking at it while she walked. I
always liked this about her because I did the same thing.*

*Now, there are some people who'll give you another opinion about the
whole thing and about the character of my mother. There's also some who'll say
my dad was a drunkard. He was not a drunkard. Sometimes he'd take a drink
of whiskey in the morning, whiskey he made himself. We got the old still to this
day. But I think he married my mother to raise his kids. I don't know this; I
just surmised it.*

At the age of twenty-two, Grant Thompson married his first wife Emma,
the one who was a Ponder, you know. Nine months and a handshake
later, Emma gave birth to Dessie Mae in 1887. Sometime before 1900,
about the time Maston Wornell was emerging as a community leader
in Brumley, and Frederick Crismon was serving his country, Grant was
playing poker and found himself in a small disagreement over the outcome of the game. The dispute was settled in a gentlemanly way. Grant
Thompson left with the tip of a knife blade imbedded in his head, which
rested there until the day he died. Apparently Grant didn't spend all
his time gambling, for five other children followed until 1901 when Gie
(pronounced Guy) Basil came along. Emma was now thirty-two and her
husband Grant was thirty-seven.

There were complications with Gie Basil's birth. No official birth
records were found, consistent with the absence of a physician at the
birth. However, family records state that ten days after the birth, Emma
died on 13 July 1901. Family members and neighbors prepared both the
body and the grave, keeping with local custom. Emma's sister took the
baby and tried to save him, but he died thirty days later and the family
buried him next to his mother. Later, Grant's second wife Myrtle helped
tend her grave on Decoration Day. They were first cousins.

If Grant had joined the local Klavern, both the drinking he refused to hide and his "marrying cousins" (the rumors distorted the facts to sound as though he was marrying his own first cousin) might have been overlooked. But he didn't, and they became issues that upset members of the Wilcox Bend Ku Klux Klan. The group was having a hard time harassing German-Americans, due to the large number of citizens from German descent. Nor was it easy to bother minority ethnic groups due to the miniscule number of Blacks, Jews, and Catholics. Instead, the group focused on "morals charges."

Some didn't go to church at all. Not so different from today. It was policy in our family to go to church, if at all possible. We went to the Elm Spring Church, because we hadn't one in our neighborhood, but it was a far piece down the road. We had to get up at 4:00, get the horses fed and have breakfast ourselves, then get them hitched up. Then it took about three hours to go what would have been only five miles if we rode straight through the timber. Of course, we couldn't with Mother and the wagon.

Wilcox Bend didn't have a church proper for the longest time. But once in a while a preacher came through so we met at Post Oak School, which was much more convenient. These were called circuit preachers, and they traveled throughout the counties, sometimes on foot, and sometimes preaching at three churches in one day. Everyone that wanted to go, did. Didn't make no matter what you were: Baptist, Methodist, Church of Christ, whatever.

How did we know which Sundays to go to the schoolhouse? We had a system as efficient as anything I saw in the Navy. This is how it worked. We passed a neighbor on Tuesday, who mentioned that his wife's sister was avisiting since Monday, and brung news a circuit rider in Iberia Sunday past was headed our way next. Then we packed this news up and took it with us when we rode into Bagnell. We handed it over to the folks at the mill along with the grain, and when our neighbor went upstream on Wednesday he picked up the news, brought it home and gave it to his wife along with the sack of ground meal. On Thursday, she tucked the news in with her fresh eggs, and the widow woman, living in the woods out back, knew both would be delivered to her in time to make it to Post Oak School by Sunday. If we was all to bring food to share, Tommy Alexander was there too.

After we got to the schoolhouse, we visited outside and waited for Preacher to come, and then we ate. More often than not, it was Preacher Simon P.

Cox. There was one particular Sunday at that schoolhouse my brothers teased me about my whole life. They called it, "The Day Barney Got Saved."

It was a muggy, steamy day. Probably July, but I can't remember exactly. Preacher trotted up in his buggy, the withers of his horse glistening with sweat. He used a governess's cart. As often as not his daughter sat beside him on that narrow seat. We took up a collection for him, shared the food, and then it was time to go into the building.

I expected cool darkness to be traded for hot sunshine, but I was out of luck there. Almost all the folks in Wilcox Bend filled up that little room, pushed the windows all the way up, and some of the men was left standing, leaning up against the wall at the back or perched on the windowsills. I prayed for a puff of breeze, but I guess God was busy watching Preacher Cox and forgot about us boys needing air.

Now, I'm here to tell you, no man ever worked harder at scaring the devil out of you or putting the fear of God into you than Simon P. Cox. He had a certain pattern and was faithful to it every time he preached. He wore a black hat with a wide, hard rim that he whipped off the second he strode through the door. The men left their hats on pegs along the back. Cox hung his there too, rolled up his shirtsleeves on his way to the front, then kneeled and prayed in silence at the mourner's bench. He'd have his back to us and we'd get really quiet, waiting. Then, he'd unfold his huge hands, push himself up, turn around real slow, take a deep breath, and start in on us.

Preacher stretched out those long legs of his as he went up and down the aisles — his big old boots on the plank floor drumming the beat for his preaching. His hair started out combed and straight in the beginning, but after a while he'd run his hands through it so many times it got to looking all wild looking, like he lived in the woods.

First time Cox raised up his fingers spread wide and shouted to the roof, us boys stared up there to see what he was looking at. He'd go on like that for a while, then stop, come back to earth, point his arm out stiff, finger pointed as straight as a hickory branch, and holler at someone, "Brother? You hear me Brother? Do ya know what I'm talkin' about?" And you, didn't matter who you was, boy, you better answer nice and loud. We kids figured out if he came to us, we had to do more than nod. Because he'd keep after you, or come back later if you didn't make it clear you were serious. It was his job to be sure we was all saved from our sins.

Now that particular day, the day I remember so plain, my brother Joe went to sit with the oldest kids in the front pew. Preacher didn't bother those up there where he could keep an eye on them. Brother Charley, being just that much older and wiser, figured out to take a seat in the middle of our bench.

Plenty of buffer there. I was on the end, along the aisle. Next to me was Paul, not in school yet, with his face buried in Mother's lap.

I know Preacher figured I was old enough that he should commence to worrying about my soul. I see that now, some seventy-so years later. But all I knew that day was Cox was slowly coming my way and I had to work fast to get out of his. First thing I did was give Paul a good elbow in the side so he'd sit up straight and hear me.

"Come on, swap places with me," I whispered into my chest.

"Nuh-uh."

I started tempting him with all sorts of bribes: my fishing rod for a week, doing his chores, things like that. But you know what that little skunk did? Just buried his head back into Mother's skirts. No matter what I said, all I got was a headshake "No!" Too late. Those dusty gray boots was parked next to mine and I knew I was in for it. Preacher slapped a claw on my shoulder and I'm sure the devil jumped out of me right then. Words crashed in my ears like thunder,

"Little Brother, do you have something you need to tell Jesus?" I couldn't even breathe I was so scared. "Little Brother, do you know your divine father in heaven?"

I was shaking, trying to muster up everything I could in order to holler out so he'd leave me alone. A little croak came from somewhere that was supposed to convince him the answer was yes. But even God Himself couldn't hear me.

Simon Cox never gave up. He had a live one now. His voice boomed again,

"What'd you say, boy? We're asking you now, how well do you know our Lord? Do you confess your sins to Jesus and accept Him as your Savior?"

All I wanted was for Preacher to just go on and leave me unsaved. There was a bunch of silly girls sitting in front of me, giggling behind their fans, and Paul was making little snorting noises in Mother's lap. She leaned forward, touched me on the knee, and said something I couldn't hear.

All this time Preacher was hollering at me in front of everyone. My face was on fire. My heart raced. I had to get out of there. I jumped up, tripped over my feet or his, fell to my knees, and suddenly it came to me what I needed to do. I raised my arms open like Preacher's and hollered up as loud as I could, "I can see the light! I can see the light!" This time, everybody in Miller County heard me.

I didn't know what else to say. I didn't want to lie in church and there was some sunlight coming in through the cracks in the eaves. Somebody started singing "Onward Christian Soldiers" and everybody joined in while Cox's rough hand reached down from heaven to muss my hair, and then, praise God, he charged after the next sinner. I had been saved.

That day, we traded so many sacks of chickens, walnuts and hams for our salvation, Joe and I followed Preacher back to his cabin in the woods to help carry it all. So we each took what we could on our horses, the chicken coups riding in the buggy with Cox, and Joe spent the whole time twisting around in his saddle making faces at me and saying things like, "Hey Barney, ain't that some light up there?"

And yet, even as a boy I knew I was on a road following a man I could trust. The chickens' naked heads bobbed to the clip-clop of his skinny horse who knew the path with its eyes shut. Soon all of them, beast, fowl, and man were dozing as they rolled through the familiar and predictable woods. Is that why none of us saw any of the changes coming? Had our eyes closed to it all?

As much as I tried not to listen, Preacher Cox taught me many things, and the one that's done me well my whole life is, "Tell the truth. The truth shall set you free." I have to tell you, whenever I hear the phrase "the hands of God," I can see those huge hands of Simon Cox, fingers like sausages, spread out and reaching to heaven.

ALLIES (1921-1922)

Leo and Anita
Crismon

Frederick and Sarah Crismon

Francis Crismon

—Courtesy Thompson Family

As the research progressed, Hadley and I often looked at various information spread out on the Thompson kitchen table. Sometimes he agreed with it; sometimes what he read succeeded in sending him into a frenzy of finger jabs and head shakings. Sometimes he read interviews from other people and then stared at me with those blue eyes, before pronouncing them dumber than a bag of nails and me just as bad for listening. Sometimes Icel set us all straight. But the house never lost its vibrant color, the coffee was always as black as death, and it seemed I never had as much energy as Hadley. There's something to be said for growing up on a farm.

In the years before Hadley's birth, Grant Thompson was a busy man, minding the affairs of blacksmithing, farming, and fathering in the Missouri town of Brumley. With his first wife dead, he was alone raising six children. Certainly, with a blacksmith shop to run and the oldest child only fourteen years old, Grant Thompson's hands were full.

A few states to the east, Tom Dixon was just as busy serving as the minister of New York's Twenty-Third Street Baptist Church and writing books. Many of his sermons and all of his books warned of "creeping Negroidism" and urged his fellow white Americans to protect themselves, their religion, their families, and their country against the bad influence of the Negro in America. Dixon and Thompson never met, but Dixon's racist views contributed to the flood of events that eventually ruined a way of life Grant Thompson assumed would continue forever.

The Klan's activities after the Civil War and throughout the 1960s are well known. Many people in Missouri owned slaves before the Civil War, generally one or two. The usual assumption is the smaller the percentage of African Americans in an area, the fewer vigilante groups. Research by experts on the Ku Klux Klan explains why this assumption is wrong and why Hadley was correct when he stated the Klan "weren't never about race."

Since just after the Civil War, the Klan's long and varied history included different purposes. For a short time in the beginning, it was a harmless fraternity of pranksters raiding friends and relatives. But for over a hundred years since that time, the Ku Klux Klan has been a bona fide hate organization that every few decades changed its mind about which group of people they wished to harass. First the newly freed slaves, the Abe-olitionists, and the Black Republicans bore their wrath. By the end of the nineteenth century, things cooled off and the Klan wasn't much of a force.

Then at the start of the twentieth century, Reverend Dixon joined an already vocal group of racists and certain ideas began to gain widespread appeal. These statements included, "For a thick-lipped, flatnosed, spindle-shanked negro, exuding his nauseating animal odour, to shout in derision over the hearths and homes of white men and women is an atrocity too monstrous for belief."

All the teachings were exclusionary: ideas about how one group was far superior and others deserved only to be thrown out of whatever town, city, county, or country they inhabited. These were the kind of ideas men like Les Leids clung to — like the teeth of a trap on a hound dog's leg. Les had never enjoyed the community honor and respect he thought he deserved and joining the new group proved a pivotal move for him.

Grant Thompson may have heard about the immigrants arriving at the rate of 2,000 a day. The newcomers came from different countries than the generations before them, and although white, their new customs and languages upset many living in the eastern United States. For a segment of the population, this strain manifested itself in fear and prejudice. But considering Grant's busy personal life, it's doubtful he placed much attention on these kinds of national events.

After a wedding on 13 June 1902, Grant's neighbors noted he was now on his second go-around. Myrtle left her wood's colt Gipsy in Brumley while she went with her new husband to take up river bottom farming. Instead of her own daughter, one of Grant's children came to live with them. For all intents and purposes Myrtle adopted the seven-year-old John, who already had speech and cognitive problems from his choking accident. John was never allowed to go to school with other children his age.

There is little mention of the huge immigration or other national trends in either the *Miller County Autogram* or the *Eldon Advertiser*. Even for those who read newspapers from larger towns, most never suspected the impact these changes would have on their lives in small rural communities like Miller County, Missouri. Despite the radical changes in the larger cities, for a time, life went on as usual in rural America.

We say the Ozarks have two snows. Once in winter, and then again in the spring when the dogwoods bloom. We really didn't notice these trees any other time of the year because they hide in the shade of the others. But April is their

time. It's a beautiful sight — the hills all covered with the stark white set against the new green. And after the dogwood snow, you'll never get another snow until the following winter. The dogwoods mean spring is here to stay and summer not far behind.

That spring, nineteen hundred and twenty-one, rain was slight and the Osage pulled well away from its banks. The old-timers said the river was as low as they'd ever seen and this was worrisome to them. The bullfrogs loved it and their bellowing took over the night. We went frog gigging a couple times a week and Mother rolled those fat legs in cornmeal and sorghum then fried them. We would eat those things three times a day if she let us. I doubt I could stomach one now, but we sure loved them as boys.

Dad was careful to mark the normal course of the river when he laid out the corn in rows. The new rich land was tempting, but wasn't worth the loss of grain if the river came up late. After the seedlings started to appear, he took a sack of corn and told us to go and hand plant kernels in all the spots none had germinated.

A few weeks after that was Decoration Day again. That year it was just darn hot by May thirtieth. We were at the cemetery, just like usual. I went to fetch water from the spring and as I came back up to the crest overlooking the cemetery, I could see the difference between the two groups, men and women. They were night and day.

There were the men, all browns, grays and black. Serious-like, standing or sitting, talking about important things.

But over by the women, it looked like someone tossed a huge handful of wildflowers under the umbrella of the trees. White, yellow, purple and red: daisy, sunflower, spiderwort and trillium. They nodded and laughed in their colorful sunbonnets while the breeze lifted their bright aprons. Then more color was spread out as they covered the beds of the wagons and the grass with their quilts. Sarah Crismon was there, red hair shining in the sun, her figure a testimony to her good cooking.

Mrs. Crismon was kin to somebody from Brumley so they came along to help and socialize. I don't think many people missed a Decoration Day even if it was too far to go to their family graveyard. I do believe Crismons came to our cemetery from that year through nineteen hundred and twenty-three.

The men soon took off their coats and started to work, and right then Charley elbowed me because he saw Old Shorthair and his long-haired friend, Mule's teeth. While we were waiting for the food to get set out, Fred Crismon and the two Kleagles moved over toward Dad and some others, so we boys figured this was our invitation to eavesdrop.

Fred said, "Grant, I think you've met my two friends here, Mr. So and So and Mr. Such and Such."

"No," said Dad, "Never seen 'em." This might have been the truth because I'm not sure Dad ever did look up from the sprouts when he was working on the road that day.

Mr. Shorthair was smiling as smug as a cat in a corner, and his buddy was trying to act confident. He really thought he was somebody, when they weren't nothin' but a pair of phony salesmen. I feel sorry for their kin now and wonder if they know what their grandpaps did.

So Shorthair, Mule's Teeth, and Crismon proceeded to work on Dad about the American thing and Dad says to Fred, kinda rude, "I don't think it's my business to convince men to join or quit their lodges, and I don't think it's their business to do the same to me. I wouldn't give any man ten dollars for the privilege of being in his company, for any reason." Then he said something about our mother needing help and went over to the women, which my father never, ever did. Charley and I thought that part hilarious, Dad over with the women looking like he had no idea what he was supposed to be doing. Of course, Plez had already swaggered up and said, "Stop whatever you're doing!" So Dad didn't look out of place to anyone else. Just two brown spots over there in the middle of the color.

But then we heard what the others said after Dad left. They stared after him and mumbled "the little spick this" and "the little spick that" with a spit between each insult. We'd no idea what they were talking about. Didn't hear "spick" again until I was in the service.

After dinner we spread out under the trees in the cool grass and chewed on gossip, the men leaning back with their hats over their eyes, pretending not to listen to the chatter and gossip of the women. Kids was supposed to be quiet, so the littlest could take naps with their heads on Mother or Dad's lap, but I wasn't too successful with that. It was much harder to ask me to be quiet than to clean up the graveyard.

Then the time was almost over. Quilts were folded up and the sides fastened back on the wagons. Time for one last round of horseshoes. Aunt Maggie announced, "Time for an exhibition!" and swooped through the graves gathering children like a hen scuttles after her chicks. She had very long hair, hair that flew out from her small head as she ran and laughed. It was loose that day. We all went to the back of the cemetery and down the hill toward the creek.

Down in a small hollow was Plez, twirling his gun like a baton, and Aunt Maggie lined us up on a ridge behind him. He came up toward us, and as she held up her skirts with one hand, Plez helped her pick her way over the

*rocky side of the hill to a small mound, where he carefully placed her, a statue
on a pedestal. Then he left her there, smiling at us, while he returned to his spot
a good twenty yards to her east. We squirmed. What'd they have in store for us?*

 *Plez turned again to her, took out his gun, the sun catching its smooth
pearl handle, and nodded. Aunt Maggie balanced something on her thumb,
turned so her side was toward Plez and flipped a coin into the air. Bang! He
shot it. And then another went up. Bang! Again, Bang! Eight out of ten
times from twenty yards he shot that coin into the clouds and we all whooped
and clapped each time. Eight cents blown to smithereens, just for our amuse-
ment.*

 *Then for the last of the demonstration he turned away from us all, drew
a bead on something sitting on a branch, clear up the hill alongside of the
cemetery where the men had gathered to promote their new lodge. There was
something out on a limb there, a black spot I figured was a crow. Plez stretched
out his arm perfectly straight. We held our breaths.*

 *Bang! The spot became a hat that sailed into the air, along with our cries
and claps. Then a shout, "Hey! You son-of-a-bitch you!" The women turned
and frowned. We heard Grandpa Blankenship say, "Young man!" Not at Plez,
but at poor Mr. Mule's Teeth whose hat was now complete with air conditioning. "Sorry, old man," hollered Plez in his direction, looking embarrassed and
solemn. "Afraid your hat got in the way of my target." But I saw his grin when
brushed some dust off the smooth pearl handle before it slipped into the holster.
You know, 'ole Plez didn't miss much.*

 *Then the two men strode across the yard toward each other, one smiling a
perfect smile of white teeth and one with no smile, eyes aflame. Plez reached
in his pocket and pulled out some folding money. "Buy yourself a new hat,
neighbor," he said in his easy way, the way a man might say, "Look there, the
cow's eatin' at the clover." Mule's Teeth knocked the money onto the ground and
leaned down to brush the grass off his hat instead. He weren't gonna take no
money from a lousy spick.*

 *Finally it was time to go home. I assume Plez went to Aunt Maggie's,
because he didn't come home with us. When he was fixing to go, I held his horse
for him. Not that he needed it. He always trained his horses to stop dead the
minute he let go of the reins. I just wanted to help him, like the way a man will
hold out his arm to a pretty woman when she takes a step, whether she needs
it or not.*

 *And what did he look like, sitting on his horse like that? Smooth. That's
the only word to describe Plez Moore. Smooth hands, smooth coat of the gelding, smooth black leather and then, right as I let go of the reins and he turned*

to canter off, a smooth smile down at me. Then this, "Well, Hadley, I figured every horse's ass needed one."

A hole, you know.

Everywhere, times were changing fast. Throughout the country, automobiles were catching on. Although there were fewer than half a million in 1910, by 1920 there would be eight million. In 1912 Woodrow Wilson was elected. He was the last president to take a horse-drawn carriage to his inauguration.

It's debatable if there has been another time in our American history with more changes than the years between 1900 and 1920. Amendment Sixteen gave the federal government the power to levy an income tax of one percent. The next amendment placed the power to elect senators directly into the hands of the people. But one thing nobody could have predicted is that a film would have a greater immediate effect than two constitutional amendments.

The film *Birth of a Nation* was based on one of Tom Dixon's books. It portrayed the KKK as the noblest of American institutions, comprised of heroes who salvaged the nation's culture and rescued the maidenhood of southern ladies after the Civil War. Because it was a silent movie, the audience read the written descriptor "historical facsimile." Millions of viewers believed the film a depiction of actual events. Another frame in the film quoted President Woodrow Wilson as a supporter of their theme.

What exactly was the theme? Good over evil. And the plot? America was on the verge of chaos due to newly freed slaves and radical Republicans until the Ku Klux Klan saved the day. Good triumphed when the Klan saved the country's culture. For many viewers, *Birth of a Nation* was their first film and some didn't understand it was a staged event. For those who saw it before 1920, it was likely the most memorable film they saw in their lifetime.

When D. W. Griffith directed his African-American actors to gargle with hydrogen peroxide so they'd froth at the mouth, they complied. This, along with instructions to try to drag their knuckles on the ground when they ran, produced the effect the director wanted. In the years following 1915, some of the twenty-five million viewers were so moved by the scenes of the ape-men gathering to lynch innocent whites and chasing after beautiful women (like Lillian Gish) to rape, they cried, believing their ancestors from the Union side had fought on the wrong side of the war.

At the end of the film, the slim, handsome southern gentlemen (who always treated their slaves with the utmost respect) were finally able to take back the country from rampaging ex-slaves. But they wouldn't have been able to accomplish this feat if it weren't for the help of the Ku Klux Klan. Even their own well-loved slaves agreed the evil ape-men needed stopping. According to the film, the Klan was a hero to all respectable persons, black or white.

One of Mark Twain's quotations, "Truth is stranger than fiction, because fiction is obligated to stick to possibilities and truth isn't," certainly seems to describe this time in history. After such a convincing portrayal, many called for a Klan revival and they got it. From the 10,000 people on the rosters of the KKK in the early 1900s estimates started to soar. The resultant wealth was close to a half a billion dollars when compared to 2015 equivalents. America was still reeling from the loss of life due to Germans in World War I and the Spanish Influenza. Income from farming was on the decline. Many farms had lost their heirs in the war. People felt the need to band together to stand against change. By 1925, close to five percent of the population had joined the Klan, and their rosters boasted between four to five million.

Whenever the Farmer's Almanac and the oldest man that anyone still listened to said it was time to plant, we did. But long before this, a great deal of discussion took place about how the river was coming up, if the oak leaves were really as big as squirrel ears, or if the yellow finches had come through yet. For such a solitary group, farmers can be as long-winded as politicians.

Of course, there was always those that did the opposite of everyone else. For a while a man lived down by Les Leids who got his mule out to plow while the ground was as hard as rock. It was a yearly bet to see who was the most stubborn: him, the mule, or the ground. And if Old Man Vaughn planted at all he was about a month late it seemed. But it was best to plant together.

I still like spring, though it will never be quite like it was back then. First came the bad — spring cleaning. Then there was the good part, like catching bullfrog tadpoles in the cold mud. That's how we boys liked to welcome spring. It was always too early to go barefoot and our toes quickly numbed from the cold. We believed leaving our shoes in the bottom of the wardrobe would make the summer come that much sooner.

Then there were the baptisms. Time to start anew and all that. And here come Simon Cox, announcing he was baptizing down at the river. At Brockman's Ford usually. Those were glorious times and everybody went to watch. Kids and even some grownups pulled themselves up tree limbs so they'd have a good enough view. I can see them perched up there now, waiting for the big event like turkey vultures watching a scene below. Down along the riverbank, men waited in white shirts and women wore white as well. I'll confess, we liked to see the girls get wet in those white dresses.

In order to fully lay claim on all of God's blessings, Cox said you had to be totally submerged in the river. So Preacher stood out there, waist deep in the water, reading from the Bible he held in one hand, his other on the shoulder of the sinner before him. Then the question, "Do you?" and the "Yes, Preacher." Now, Cox was a strong man and it was all he could do to keep his Bible dry during this next part. Because he didn't have an associate pastor or none of that. Over the back of his right arm bent the poor sinner, until he lay down flat on the river.

"Relax in the arms of the Lord!" Cox called out, and then the sinner disappeared, with only his faith in Simon Cox's strength to bring him up again. Down he went and up popped a saint, sputtering, wiping the water from his eyes, and bearing a great deal of resemblance to the person who'd disappeared. I watched Tommy Alexander get baptized more times than I could count. I think he hopped into sainthood each spring, and we'd get to see him doing the drunken dance of the sinner a month later. Once, after he come up for air, someone cried out, "How's the water, Tommy?" And he yelled back, "As warm as my mammy!" Then from the trees, "Dunk him again, Preacher. He's still a liar!"

Finally I remember the hymns, always about the river:

As I went down to the river to pray, studying about that good old way
And who shall wear the robe and crown, good Lord, show me the way.
Oh mothers let's go down, come on down, don't you want to go down?
Oh mothers let's go down, down to the river to pray.

So that spring, nineteen and twenty-one, Crismon made plans to plow up all the bottomland and put it in corn. Dad went to him, "Fred, don't plow up every foot of that river bottom. I've lived here quite a while, about twenty years, and this river has a habit of getting up every so many years and washing all your top soil away if it's been plowed. You won't have much of a farm left after a couple of times of this." But Fred was like that. He should've listened to Dad, but it was just like when he bought the farm for $19,000 when

Dad could've helped get it for less. Crismon used every livin' inch for corn and soon had just about as pretty a corn crop as you've ever seen.

That summer was very hot, but with enough rain, so all the crops up and down the Osage were as good as anyone could ask. Folks was all in a good mood, but cautious you know, because farmers are always kinda holdin' their breath, not wanting to say too much and jinx the future. We fished and hunted with Leo Crismon all summer and our mother quilted with Mrs. Crismon and Anita. Dad said if the weather held, he was going to buy us a car. A nineteen and seventeen Ford touring car for sale in Brumley. A man's wife had died, and the owner thought the car bad luck.

Dad wasn't too superstitious, but he didn't tempt luck either, as he liked to tell us. But Crismon didn't approve of that manner of thinking because such things weren't in the Bible. Seemed like everybody hung sheets over the mirrors if a body was laid out in the house, and Crismon very much disapproved of things like that.

We'd about a thousand traditions like that. "Don't put that hat on the bed, it'll bring bad luck. Be sure and wipe the dust from your shoes after a coffin passes you if you want to live another ten years. If you wake up at midnight, someone you know is gonna die." I wonder if when Dad said, "Always save one-third back when you plant," Crismon thought that was just superstition as well, because why else wouldn't he take such good advice?

Crismon made plans to buy a tractor and we all knew about it because salesmen from off came and talked to him. Really, you can't imagine how exciting those first tractors were. We'd all stand around in silence, waiting. Then the smoke started to blow, then a rumbling and when that tractor finally jumped forward we'd all jump too, then clap and pat our pal on the back. Crismon was king, I'm telling you. All the other men were watching to see how the whole thing panned out, wondering if they'd get a tractor too some day. All but Dad of course, because never in a million years would he give up horses. And then as it is with all summers when you're a boy, before we knew it, both August and threshing time had arrived.

Leo Crismon's written account of the early years on their farm along the Osage differs somewhat. After selling their previous farm to a cousin, Clergy Crismon, the family moved to Wilcox Bend:

> We then moved in three or four wagons, perhaps with some cattle which were driven. Also the Maxwell car was driven along, by Francis,

I believe. [The car proved unsatisfactory and was traded for a mule from Dell Popplewell, Dessie Mae Thompson's husband.]

Years later Mother said that she thought our many misfortunes and tragedies which happened to us, the Vineyards and others were due to our having moved to the Osage River farm on a Friday, the thirteenth.

The price paid was $20,000. Father entered into the life of this community as he had into others where he had lived. He was interested in the Post Oak School nearby, since my sister, Anita, was still in grade school.... My father was appointed Justice of the Peace of Glaize Township, by the County Court in Miller County, Dec. 19, 1922, to serve for four years.

Because community singings had proved so successful in [our other community], my father opened up his home for singings and encouraged the neighbors to do the same. We often attended services at the Bagnell Baptist Church and at the Elm Springs Church on Little Bear Creek where both the Baptists and the Christians held services, although the building belonged to the Baptists.... Services were being held regularly at Post Oak, that is Sunday school, largely due to the interest of my own family, however, Baptist literature was used.

In order to cultivate the Osage River farm it was necessary to purchase a considerable amount of new equipment.... Although the Osage River land was fertile, it had not been properly taken care of. Even the river bottomland which overflowed annually had been planted in corn for so long that it was insect infested and in need of lime, and other results of lack of crop rotation were evident. It took a few years to realize this fully, as the corn crops especially for a few years were very poor. This fact, with frequent floods which destroyed crops, and the low prices from 1920 to 1924, resulted in very little income from the place.

But this time it was different. The harvest of nineteen and twenty-one was the first year I was to be in the company of the men during threshing. Always before John, Paul, and me helped Mother and the women cook and serve meals for the workers. That was fine with me, because the other boys and girls my age were there. But that summer it occurred to Dad I might be old enough to help in the fields. I surely thought I was grown up; I was ten, so of course I knew everything. For weeks beforehand I pondered which place, house or field, Dad would have me go. I hadn't the gall to ask. Then at supper the night before he said, "You go with Joe and Charley in the morning." I don't know if I slept at

all that night, but I do know I'd already squirmed into my trousers by the time I heard the creak of Mother's cast iron stove door.

We started earlier and worked longer during threshing. For wheat or barley, a thresher was rented from a man who charged by the day, so we all worked on each farm during every bit of daylight to get our money's worth. Corn we cut by hand, but we still did the same. We always got along during threshing. Jim and Otto came over for breakfast and after we ate, when it was still dark, John shoved a wad of something wrapped in newspaper into the front of my coveralls. It was half his biscuit from breakfast. John was twenty-seven that August, but never did get to go out with the men.

They were starting at the first farm below Bagnell, Kidwells, and we trotted our horses up there together. Dad, Joe, Charley, me, Jim, and Otto. Dad questioned my older brothers about their farms along the way. The river was running low and lazy, and the birds had already stopped their morning songs for the most part. Seemed like Mother Nature knew what a scorcher of a day to expect. This was perfect threshing weather. Rain had been shy for a week or two, the ground nice and firm, and the crops dried out and ready for the taking. Men from other families were already there, waiting in the shade of the three post oaks near the river. One of those trees they said was the oldest in Miller County.

I remember Preacher Cox giving us a sermon one time about why God always made it so unbearably hot during harvest, but I can't remember the reason. I only know if you have a field to harvest, or vegetables to can, it's bound to be a fiery day without a lick of breeze.

I watched the younger men and older boys shrug off their shirts and drape them over tree limbs. When I saw those backs I got a bit anxious and my heart beat a bit faster because it hit me, you know, what was I gonna do out there? Down in those fields, men harvested by hand. If they sliced hard enough with a corn knife, the stalks fell over their shoulders and onto the ground in one swipe. But corn stalks are solid and hard with leaves that cut like a knife, too. And they don't fall so easy. Most men needed to take a few hearty hacks at them, and soon shoulders, neck, and back ached. They can straighten up for a minute, but there are stalks after stalks that have to be cut ankle high from the ground and they can't take forever doing it. You and your neighbors got to thresh the whole river bottom.

It hurt worse if you didn't have a shirt on. But if you kept the shirt, the sweat ran together with the dust and critters from the cornfield, and soon your whole uppers itched and stung. So you'd off the shirt and take the whipping, mostly because this was the way men always did it.

If you'd threshed corn before, you knew to start working without your shirt during spring's first warm days. Then your skin would tan and thicken as the muscles grew stronger every day. Slowly your chest became broader and your mother fussed when you struggled into your Sunday shirt, because the buttons at the throat pulled open. But by the time threshing season came, if you'd worked in the fields with the other men, you'd grown strong with the corn and your back and arms told the whole world you weren't just a kid.

Those were the backs I stared at.

Then there was ole Barney. Me with only bony elbows and a backbone a person could count the bumps on from thirty paces, what kind of help would I be? In all my dreams about joining the men during threshing, I never considered what I might actually have to do. Now, seeing them start to work with their knowledge and strength, I felt a bead of sweat tickling me under my arms. I kept my shirt on like the old men.

Before I could get any more worked up about my predicament, I smelled horehound and cedar. A familiar arm across my shoulders. Professor Molls never missed threshing.

"Hadley Herbert, yours is the most important job here. Look at those men." He pointed to the group starting to organize themselves at the edge of the field. I felt the tattle-tale sweat in my armpits again. "That line still moves if one man stops. Now your job's different. Without your job none of them can work." What was he talking about? Like I wasn't nervous enough as it was. He handed me a wooden water bucket and a dipper.

"You're the coal for the steam engine, because if the men don't have water, it'll all come to a stop." Then he told me to first water the horses and with a friendly wink I was on my own.

Soon I carried a steady stream of water back and forth from the spring. Maybe it wasn't really the most important job out there, but it was surely the most popular. I can hear the men working in a rhythm, swinging their knives at the base of the stalks to the beat of whatever song they was singing:

> *I was out in the country one beautiful night*
> *And spied a fair maiden, my heart's delight.*
> *She was handsome and true, warm-hearted and fair*
> *A widow's own daughter, a widow's own heir.*

In the early morning the men drank one dipper at each turn. When they got hotter, one dipper was for them and another went into their hat before going back on their head. Most had been a water boy when they were younger and remembered their blisters as much as they welcomed the drink. They were careful not to spill any water or sweat into the bucket.

All but one.

It was Francis Crismon's first year out there too. He was quite a bit older than me, about sixteen. But that day he did something I never forgot. Every time I came to him he took a drink and then handed the dipper back to me. Next, with both hands he took that bucket, dumped the whole thing over his head, grinned at me, slapped his hat back on and that was it. No thank you, how-dee-do, nothing. He did that every time, and I'd have to go all the way back to the spring and start over. Course, that stunt weren't so unusual between boys. We'd just laugh if our buddy was chased into the river by ground wasps, and those things can kill you.

Along towards noon everyone was pretty spent, and it was easy to see the working had slowed. The biscuit John gave me was long gone. Then, what's that? Here come the sound of creaking wood and dirt ground beneath wagon wheels, harnessed together with the sound of women laughing and the snorts of horses. We heard talking and giggling. So the pace sped up, the men's singing got louder and it seemed nobody was tired at all:

> *Oh swing that gal, that purty little gal,*
> *The gal I left behind me.*
> *She's purty in the face an' slim around the waist,*
> *The gal I left behind me.*

Women had that effect in a cornfield. Now came their response, which always sounded so sweet after listening to our own rough voices all morning:

> *When I was single I dressed in silk so fine,*
> *But now I am married an' I wear rags all the time.*
> *Lord, I wisht I was a single gal again!*

Soon Professor Molls called a halt to the work, and the men went down to the river to clean up. Shirts were found and slipped into. Excepting Joe, who was always last for putting a shirt on if there was a girl within a mile. Then after Preacher Cox lifted up our food and labors to the heavens, we finally got to eat, and eat some more, until there was nothing left. Then came what I remember more than anything else, like recalling Dad washing Paul's blood out of the sheets. On the way back to the field Charley did something out of the ordinary: he stuck up for me.

"Go around the other way, Barney. By the time you get to Francis, there won't be enough water left in the bucket to worry about when he dumps it." That's just what I did.

Good luck comes in threes and that's exactly what we had that year. The weather was perfect for growing, the river didn't flood, and the price of corn was high. Dad bought the car and we had a swell time learning to drive it. Though the day Otto showed me, he couldn't get it out of reverse, so we drove around the barnyard in backward jolts all afternoon, our heads bobbing fore and aft like proud roosters.

When Hadley talked about his father saving one third back, this was a tenet with which even farmers from off would have agreed. The farm's total resources should never be sunk into one crop any more than all of one's eggs should go in the same basket. But if a farmer didn't have enough capital and had to make a return on all his land, he often felt there was no choice. During those years, Frederick Crismon may have been tempted to try to get as much as he could for reasons we might never know.

After the 1915 Klan revival, recruiting was on a roll and KKK organizers were getting rich from the hefty $10 a person initiation fee, equal to over $100 a hundred years later. Klan leaders quickly saw the financial advantage of rallying people around some preconceived fear to get wallets to open up. Certainly there were people, like Hadley's Mr. Shorthair, who seemed to relish hate and violence. But in Wilcox Bend it's hard to believe that was the case for most. Fear, ignorance, and greed seem to have been the main culprits.

Suddenly people who had been working and living together for a century began noticing differences in their neighbors. In 1916, *The Passing of the Great Race* was published, Madison Grant's response to America's twelve million new immigrants since 1900. He warned that America risked "polluting her Anglo-Saxon heritage by admitting those inferior but sensual aliens." Though not every American agreed with the rise of nativism, the philosophy received a great deal of attention from many sources: the pulpit, books, literary journals, newspapers, and now the cinema. Nationally, exclusionary influences continued to proliferate, but historical texts from Miller County rarely noted a problem with ethnicity until the 1920s.

Throughout the country, drummers for the Klan convinced men to attend introductory meetings. If the recruit joined, the Kleagle got two dollars of the initiation fee, equal to $25 in 2015. It must have seemed well worth the two Kleagle's time to make the lonely ride to the Thompson's the day the boys were working off the poll tax, but not because they were really worried about foreigners taking over Wilcox Bend. Here was a man with four grown sons and four more who would soon be old enough. Here was the possibility to make between eight to sixteen dollars.

Shorthair and Mule's Teeth appeared to have stayed in the area for slightly over a year. They taught men like Les Leids the basic vocabulary: Kloran was the KKK bible, Kligrapp was the recording secretary for the Klavern, and Klonvocation was a Klan convention. After the Klavern was established, the real work began. It was time to police the neighborhood. Slowly, new dictates took the place of those established in the previous century. Many people I interviewed noted, "If you weren't for 'em, they took it you was against 'em."

We were more concerned with where the other boys lived than how they lived. There was none of this keeping up with the Jones' thing. We all had a whole lot of nothing, and I mean nothing. I had a brother and sister dead at birth. Once in a while we had a crop. Once in a while we didn't. Until the Klan came, the biggest thing that happened in Wilcox Bend was when somebody turned over the outside toilets at school.

We had to watch out that we didn't go across the river without any of our people or we'd get beat up. It wasn't our neighborhood. And if they was dumb enough to come to Wilcox Bend, same thing. We'd have to show them they were on our home ground. If you was going down the river in a boat, boy, make sure you get out on the same side you got in, or you best be stopping at a town.

That winter, two of Dad's dogs, Nick and Diner, was hot on the trail of a fox and the chase lasted the entire night. There were patches on snow shining in the moonlight, but no ice on the river and no wind either. A beautiful winter night just made for a fox hunt. By the next morning, Diner had given out and come home, but Nick was still on the scent.

Dad could tell Nick was having a hell of a time with the trail by his baying and all. So he said, "Barney, why don't you get in the boat and go across the river and help Nick out." So I took a johnboat from the bank, rowed to the other side, and left the boat on the bank. Right off I came across this old guy checking his traps. He'd hardly looked up before he said, "Haul your sorry ass outta here boy." Well, I knew I could run faster than him so I paid him no heed and kept following Nick's tracks and calling. Then I saw the dog in a clearing.

Well, all of a sudden this other farmer come outta nowheres and asked me who I was and where I was from, and you know, he didn't look friendly at all. I noticed right off he had a pitchfork, prongs up, in his hand. That was kinda like carrying a loaded gun with the safety off. Carry a pitchfork prongs down, because it's better to jab a toe than to lose an eye. Prongs up? You're fixin' to use it real soon.

So anyway, I started to call the dog off the trail when this old boy reached for the collar of my shirt. I wriggled outta that situation real fast by sacrificing my shirt. I bolted for the boat and kept calling Nick so he'd swim out and meet me. Poor dog, he was so tired the river just sucked him under by the side of the boat. He came up again and I reached down, hauled him in over the side by the scruff of his neck. That old guy would've killed him at worst or stolen him at best. I got home okay with the dog, but without a shirt. Mother wasn't pleased. But she let Nick lay by the fire inside the rest of the day, he was shivering so.

Even within Wilcox Bend we had little gangs, and we liked to go after one another when we didn't have enough to do. But we did it fair. We gave our knife to someone else to hold while we fought and we fought one to one. I had my share of bloody noses. Some I asked for, some I didn't.

There was one time I remember, when the situation could've gotten a lot bloodier than it did. I went to a meeting at the Elm Spring Church. It was in the evening so I thought surely some of my little gang would be there. I hoped to see a girl, Hilda Brandt. I was probably all of twelve years old, but listening to Joe and Charley must have given me a touch of girl fever.

I got to the church before the sun started to set. The old building looked especially fine in the afternoon sun. Someone had brought over their horses with a binder mower behind them and cleaned away all the weeds and grass from around the church. I saw pretty quickly I was alone without my pals and of course, Hilda hadn't shown up either.

I went inside anyway, where the meetin' was, and sat on my pew and listened to the sermon. Or tried to. It was near the end of summer, all the windows was flung wide open, and I was alongside the west wall. The sun kept blinding me. I shifted and squirmed to get outta the way, but it followed me. Then I realized somebody had a mirror outside and was flashing it in my eyes. Kind of a come-on you know, doing it on purpose.

Well, I couldn't just ignore that, could I? I ducked out there to the side of the church, and darn if there weren't a group of them outside the window.

Five of 'em. Duncan Atkisson, Dolf Riley, some others, and they were daring me to fight. Said I'd stolen a watch so they come lookin' for me. They was just bored and looking for something to do. I thought, "I'm really going to get it now. This ain't gonna be any kind of fun."

I had a knife on me. We always carried a pocketknife in those days — I handed my knife to Alfred Cox, the preacher's son who was standing there, because he never took sides. I handed him my knife on quite a few occasions during those years. Isn't that just the beauty of life? Here's Simon and his daughter inside leading the prayers and outside the son is keeping watch over the weapons.

I said, "Who's the son-of-a-bitch flashing that light in my face? Just step up."

And Virgil Huddleston said, "Maybe you mean me?"

Then me, "Well, if you done it I mean you." With that he hit me right square in the face. I went down like a tin duck at the county fair. He got on top of me and was beating me up pretty good. I was swinging at anything I could get close to and finally managed to get back on my feet. I took a few quick steps back, still facing them before I realized they was all really struggling. Virgil was crying out and hobbling around. I thought, "I guess I really threw some good punches. I must be getting stronger than I used to be."

Then I decided I shouldn't tempt luck, so I turned and ran like hell. Made it out of there and never looked back. Yea, I sure showed them!

I'll tell you the truth about what really happened. Remember how I said they'd mowed the field next to the church? They'd left a few acres of green stubble. Some of those stalks were spears as thick as your thumb. I wore shoes on account I was going to impress Hilda, but they'd gone barefoot. That was one of my more successful encounters with boys from the other side.

During my time with the Thompsons, Hadley often told Icel to get her purse, he'd get his hat, and we took what he called field trips. Hadley liked for me to drive, and he'd sit next to me. The hat I remember was a baseball cap with the name of his Navy ship embroidered on it. He'd talk the whole time, and Icel would sit in the back, content to listen and stare out the window.

We'd try to stop at the Eager Beaver Restaurant in Eldon or Camp Bagnell Restaurant in Bagnell on our way to or from our destination. The Thompsons always spoke to somebody they knew, a paper napkin always inspired Hadley to diagram a bridge or sketch a map, and the coffee was never strong enough for Icel. Sometimes we interviewed relatives and visited the Hawkins Cemetery or the river landings on the north and south sides. There was a great deal of pointing and gesturing.

While Hadley was explaining the land of his boyhood, my research continued. I visited historical libraries throughout the state, read old newspapers, and interviewed anyone who would talk to me. It was soon apparent his memories and ideas about the Klan were accurate. By the early 1920s, neighbors who were previously friends were being pitted against each other based on their choice of Klan affiliation.

For the ten years between 1915 and 1925, Klan leaders cloaked their intentions with respectability. The Klan claimed to be nothing more than an organization for strengthening America. Their meetings were advertised in the newspapers in many towns. I found an advertisement in the *Eldon Advertiser* announcing a Klan meeting at a church. Fliers in Jefferson City, Missouri announced their marches. And although historians differ on the degree of involvement, many note both President Wilson and President Harding had communication with the group. With five percent of the voting public a part of the Klan, they were hard to ignore.

When people justly complained of threats and lashings, these acts were blamed on "night riders," and Klan leaders disavowed any involvement. Night riders were supposedly people bent on destroying the Klan's fine reputation by posing in Klan attire and committing atrocities. Of course, night riders were nothing more than Klansmen carrying out their darker missions, often with the help of a good dose of the alcohol they claimed to have rejected.

Kleagles were faced with a difficult mission. How to recruit prospective Klansmen in an unfamiliar town? Their answer was to seek others already familiar with the neighborhoods. It was not unusual for local lodges and churches to supply Kleagles with membership ledgers because the Klansman came with donations for the church. After all, the Klan was nothing more than the "All American Lodge." Why shouldn't legitimate groups want to help them? According to newspapers, cemetery inscriptions, and interviews, belonging to two lodges was customary for men at that time. Belonging to three was not unusual. For a man in his economic and social situation, Grant's rejection of lodges was not the norm.

The Klan began rallying men using scapegoat tactics, distortion of history, and out-and-out lies. In referring to children born with attributes from both white and African American parents, the Klan preferred to ignore all the times slave women were victims of white male sexual dominance. Instead, the Klan said mixed blood offspring were a result of white women giving birth after being raped by African Americans.

Then the Klan moved to the Jew. First, they proclaimed Jesus was not a Jew, and that this was only a rumor started by Jews to make their blood seem more acceptable to law-abiding, God-fearing Christians. Because formally educated ministers were a rarity in many rural areas, folks taught themselves from the Bible. Some fell for the lie that a Jewish Jesus was indeed a myth.

What about the institutions depended upon to provide accurate information? Schools, as a start? Some schoolteachers, like Otto, attended schools such as the two-year Iberia Teacher's Academy. But more often teachers were sixteen or seventeen, with no formal training. At least two teachers from the area were fourteen. Teachers may have been good models of reading, writing, and ciphering for the times, but their knowledge base of world events often lacked.

There were no radios in Wilcox Bend. The two local newspapers in operation at the time were filled mostly with reports of the comings and goings of the county's notable citizens. The only book in the Thompson house besides the Bible might be a schoolbook brought home on loan. Wilcox Bend's ignorance of outside events was as startling as it was understandable.

All of these situations were typical for many homes. Lucky for Klan organizers during those times, there were many such secluded pockets in rural America. Leaders could tell the crowds almost anything and be believed. The idea of inferior blood was always a favorite topic of the Klan, and soon all Asians, Native American Indians and people from India were included in the early twentieth century Klan's list of favorite people to hate. And then, the war in Europe proved to be the best recruiter Kleagles could have hoped for.

By this time in history, German-Americans, Italian-Americans, Polish-Americans and all "Hyphenated Americans" were under suspicion. While German-Americans were known for supporting the Union cause during the Civil War, they were now reluctant to fight against soldiers who might be relatives. Many Irish-Americans didn't want to fight against any country fighting the British. Although historians now know how large the American opposition to The Great War was at the time, these Hyphenated Americans were blamed as being an outspoken minority.

President Wilson was quoted as saying, "Any man who carries a hyphen about him carries a dagger that he is ready to plunge into the vitals of this Republic whenever he gets ready." Klan leaders snatched up this part of the war effort and continued to run with it long after the war had ended.

Post Oak School Number Forty-Nine was a little one-room schoolhouse with a wood floor. It was a frame building up on a hill. It had three windows on each side that opened up all the way in the summer with a heating stove for winter. Right in the middle of the classroom.

Boys and girls were usually mixed in, with the little ones sitting at their desks in the front and older ones in back. When we got to school we hung our coats on pegs in the back with our dinner buckets. Teachers were elected by the men at the end of summer, and there was always a big ruckus every year as to who was going to be teacher. There were different factions and a vote taken to decide. Dad was always involved. I guess he carried a lot of weight. Sometimes Otto would be the teacher, sometimes my sisters Annie or Gipsy.

So the year I recall was probably nineteen hundred and twenty-one, maybe twenty-two. That morning was the first day of the fourth grade for me, and it was Paul's first day of school ever, so he'd planted himself next to me like he'd grown roots. Another new boy was there besides the Crismon boy and some new girls too. Buster Leids had been waiting for some older boys to graduate, and now that they were gone he decided to take over and be top dog.

Buster thrust his face in mine and said, "What grade you supposed to be in?"

I was pretty pleased that I'd done so well so far and said, "I'm in the fourth. I got promoted."

"Well, bully for you," and he gave me a shoulder bump as he walked by. Paul was all wide-eyed, hanging on to his lunch bucket for all he was worth. I told him not to worry. We didn't fear much with brother Charley around.

Miss Gipsy (we had to call her "Miss" like the other kids when we were at school) rang the bell and in we went. Then she stood up at her desk in front of the blackboard, and I'm sure she did the same thing that first day teaching that she did every day she taught. She pulled open her top drawer, unbuttoned her tatted cuffs so they wouldn't get chalk on them, folded them neatly one atop the other, and laid them inside before rolling up her sleeves. Tiny hands went to her long hair, to twist, twist it again, then wrap it on top of her head in a big knot, and "Jab!" A long pin got stuck in there to hold it all up. And every time she jabbed, I flinched, 'cause I was certain she was going to stick herself in the head one day. She said it made her look taller to have her hair like that.

Well that day, she surely needed to look tougher than the nice person she was because Buster was really giving her the once over, and I could tell he'd already decided this tiny thing was no match for him. Miss Gipsy started calling the roll and asking kids to come up and write their name and age on the blackboard, probably to see where they were because we were all grades, you know. When she got to Buster, he squatted on the floor and bull-frog hopped, all the way up the aisle. And every time he landed he burped.

I needn't have worried about Miss Gipsy. Growing up a woods' colt in Brumley made her tougher than she looked. She looked down at Buster. A kind, soft voice. "Please get up now."

He belched again. A smirk. She asked if he heard her. He responded with the same intelligent comment. Snickers from the back of the room. Nervous awe from the little ones.

"Whoosh!" Gipsy snatched up a hickory switch laying across her desk with one hand, pulled him up by the hair with the other, and preceded to lay that switch across his backside, crack, crack, crack. Then she let go, smiled sweetly and said, "I don't allow toads in my school. Only nice boys and girls."

Oh, what a joyous day at Post Oak School Number Forty-Nine! Laughter busted through the countryside, while twenty sets of bare feet stomped on the wood floor and forty little fists pounded on desks. We made such a commotion Clyde Blankenship stopped digging potatoes a quarter mile away to listen and wonder just what kind of a noise it was.

That was all it took for the rest of us. After that, if Miss Gypsy gave a fella one of her looks, he shriveled up like a dead opossum on a sunny windowsill and what was left of him slunk back to his seat.

But Buster was tougher than us and didn't quite give in so easily. He sat and plotted the revenge of his reputation all morning. At lunch in the play yard he announced he'd take some of my lunch. He still hadn't gotten reacquainted with Charley. When I said "No" he stood up and said something like, "Maybe you don't hear so good. I'll take that lunch and maybe I'll take it from that little worm of a brother of yours as well." Well Charley heard all this, didn't say nothing, just ran up from behind, ducked and rolled hisself into the back of Buster's knees, knocking him down, and then sat on him and instructed him that if he needed anything from a Thompson in the future to just ask him, Charley Thompson. That was the first day of school. Thompsons were on the top; Leids were on the bottom.

In the wintertime at our school, Gipsy set a big stew pot on the stove, filled with water and pieces of fried, salty meat. We all brought vegetables, and she cut those up and slid them in the boiling water, letting us breathe in the steam of field onions and home-canned tomatoes as they simmered all morning. This was a heavenly torture we endured while we worked, and there wasn't anything we looked forward to more than schoolhouse stew.

I want to tell you one last thing I can see when I think about school during those years with Miss Gipsy. We're all outside during recess. Gipsy is alone on one side of the building with the bat and ball in her small, strong hands, and we're gonna play a game of Annie Over. One person hits the ball over the schoolhouse, and the kids on the other side have to try and catch it before it hits the ground.

I see Gipsy listening carefully to hear where we are on the other side of the school, but she can't see us and we can't see her. She's trotting back and forth the length of the building, and she's pulled the hem of her skirt up and tucked it into her waist. She's trying to determine where she should send the ball and we're hiding behind the schoolhouse, trying to shut up so she won't know where we's at, but you know that's impossible, because there are a lot of instructions that need to be whispered back and forth. Then, when Miss Gipsy thinks she knows just where that empty corner is, she throws up the ball, grabs a hold of the bat with both hands, jerks it back and swings hard and swift, aiming right where we ain't.

The ball shoots up, past the three tall windows, up to the roof. It flies over the peak and we start to yell and holler, because now we can see that ball sailing over and there's nobody waiting in its path. So we run, hands aflying, screaming, "Get it! Get it!" like it's a magic bird flying over the schoolhouse instead of that old gray ball. It's noon and that sun is right overhead. The ball disappears in the sun. When it reappears, it's right there so the quickest of us has to dive in order to catch it, because if we missed and it hit the ground that would be the worst thing in the world, and we might all die right then and there.

Miss Gipsy played ball with all those brothers, and they'd taught her exactly how to be sure she never missed her mark. Once we had our dirty hands on that ball, we ran around the schoolhouse to give it back to her, then back to our spot, yelling all the while about only God knows what, and by the time recess was over, Miss Gipsy had us ready to settle down again.

Even before America entered the war, she sent food to European allies. On 3 September 1917, *The Eldon Advertiser* noted "extraordinary efforts to increase the production of food stuffs, and an extensive movement to save 100,000,000 bushels of grain annually consumed in the manufacture of intoxicating liquor." The Drys, those who were pushing for total prohibition of alcohol, used that as their practical argument: good food was wasted on the production of alcohol. On 18 December 1917 a proposed ban on the manufacture, sale, transport, import and export of intoxicating liquors was formally proposed to Congress. Because grain was necessary to feed the troops and their families left at home, using it to make liquor now seemed blatantly wasteful.

The government's wartime involvement in Missouri's food production translated into something intensely personal to Hadley's father. This was the first time the government had intruded into the heretofore private arena of food production during Grant's twenty years of river bottom farming.

The involvement started with the onset of World War I, but it continued after the war ended. State agencies promoted modernization of the farm to boost productivity and provide financial assistance in low and delayed interest loans for farmers who bought tractors and other machinery, or who participated in government programs. Certificates of appreciation were given to those who complied with the farm bureau's suggestions.

The Miller County Committee on Farm Labor was initiated to help with wartime shortages. Local citizens were given jobs, or they volunteered to find surplus food to channel to troops and civilians in need. When the war ended, the committee still had people in need of help and did not want to disband. But some, and perhaps Grant Thompson fell into this group, thought this was just a ploy for people not wanting to give up their government jobs. Letters written by farmers chastised "Citizens wanting to look over the farmers' business because they didn't have enough work of their own...."

Grant felt state and federal legislatures had no business attempting any kind of regulation for what a man grew, ate, and drank. Regulatory entities had to have accurate information on what crops were being grown, how much was produced, when crops were harvested, and more in order to complete their mission. What did Grant Thompson do when a stranger appeared with a clipboard and a list of questions? He reacted much like he did when the Kleagles rode toward his farm with their ideas. He refused to change to adapt to any of the new ways. Instead, he continued sending his boys throughout the neighborhood with food to those who needed it, as had been his custom during his adult life.

Throughout the state of Missouri, prevailing war sentiment gave little leeway for individual interpretation of patriotism. Even though Grant's son Jim fought in the war, authorities questioned why men like Grant disliked being told what to do, why he was not cooperating with their modern plans, and what he was hiding.

We were in Bagnell getting supplies when we learned about a meeting coming up that night. But that weren't the most exciting news of the day. The most exciting thing that happened was Paul and I discovered the man in the hole was a fake.

The sign said, "Man buried alive!" So we went over there and a slick-look-ing character in plaid pants and a straw hat was charging a dime to look into a hole in the ground. He called out, "Come see the man who was buried alive! Yes Siree, my unfortunate friend died peacefully underground while investigating a tiff vein, trapped before he could receive a proper burial!" We had an extensive discussion, wondering if this was how we should spend our two nickels. It would be a peek at some old fink and then no candy, soda, or ice cream. But I persuaded Paul that the sweets would be there when we came back. Instead, we should take advantage of this great opportunity: looking at dead folk we'd never met. Still, it was a hard decision for us both.

I went first. Gave the man our two nickels. He reached down and pulled a cover from a piece of glass in the ground that made a window. A window over a man, eyes closed, not moving. Dressed a lot like the hawker standing next to me. Then it was Paul's turn, but Mr. Slick dropped the curtain back and said, "No. One dime for one look only."

"But it was both our nickels!"

"Only one viewing per payment." Big smile gone like last night's dream.

So Paul, who'd just been gypped outta his nickel, snatched that straw hat right off the fella's head, turned, and ran. He disappeared down that dusty street faster than a snake into a hole, and honestly, even I didn't see where he'd gone.

No chance of me doin' the same. The man held fast on to me: collateral for his hat. Then church bells started to ring for twelve o'clock noon and time seemed to stand still for a moment. We just stood there, because it's bad luck to interrupt time, and we both knew this. Everybody does. So there we were, listening to the bells and counting them in our minds.

One... two... three... I'm wondering if I should stomp on this guy's foot to get him to let go. Four... five... six... whose side is Dad going to be on if he comes out of the mill and sees all this? Seven... eight... I know whose side Mother's gonna be on. Nine... ten... where the heck did Paul run off to because by now I realize we should just give the hat back. Cut our losses and leave. Eleven... maybe Dad'll talk to the man, or maybe he'll just tell us we was stupid to pay for such a thing, that we deserved to be suckered.

Twelve. And then I see him. Not Paul, not my dad, but the man in the hole. He's walking out of the house right next to us. It's noon and it's his dinner break. I jerk one arm free and point down the street.

"That's him!" I yell, "The man in the hole. He ain't dead at all, it's him!"

Mr. Slick tries to slap his greasy old hand over my mouth to get me to shut up, but I'm not going to let that happen after all those times I wrestled free of my big brothers. Hell, I might not've been the best fighter, but I was a professional at running away. One good bite on the hand and one more sound jerk, and I'm off down that road, disappearing in the crowd along with a walking dead man, my little brother, and some shyster's hat.

I found Paul hiding down by the landing where we waited together to see what would become of the hat incident. I told him the dead man somehow got out of his tomb and that there must've been a tunnel from his hole underground to the house next to it. And while we was speculating if anyone was going to come after us, two men met one another in the alley off the corner where we were crouched. One drew letters in the dirt with his toe, AYAK then the other drew AKIA. Only after that did they talk, ignoring us like we weren't even there. It was a sign you know, to see if the other was safe to talk to. Soon the men was talking about a Klan meeting that night in Kidwell's woods. After a bit, we slipped into a group coming up from the landing, threw the hat on the porch of the dead man's house, then ran like bandits back to the wagon to wait.

That night, after everyone had gone to bed, we were off on another adventure.

If we got out of the house early enough, our best strategy was to circle around behind the group and come up on the far ridge. We would be so close we could clearly hear all that was said.

When the Kleagles were in charge, each meeting was about one separate thing. Like about the Jews one week, Catholics the next, immoral women the following. The little short-haired one loved to talk, and he was a pretty good speaker too. Mule's Teeth, the other one, didn't do much but count money, haul out the cross, and things like that.

At first, the meetings was always about religion. "God wants you to do this," and "God wants you to do that." The big deal against the Catholics was they had a foreign leader, the Pope, and since we had just come off World War I, people were really afraid of the foreign leaders. We heard a lot of, "They ain't no Americans! Don't think it's something that won't affect you, my friend, because at this very minute, in Eldon, there is a Knights of Columbus meeting going on. What do you think they're planning there at that secret meeting? We do all our work in the open, in the light of the cross."

Honestly, so many folks had a hard time of it after the war. They said we won the war, and the politicians were all hunky dory with it, but the families really suffered. To a farmer, the loss of the son might be the loss of their farm. No more farm, no more family. And this was an unexpected thing. They never figured something so far away could hurt them all the way back in Missouri like it did. It all made folks afraid.

Then the Jews. Kikes they called 'em. Now, we didn't have no Jews, but sometimes they'd get off the train on their way someplace, and I think there was a merchant for a while in Bagnell. But it took the Kleagles a while to figure this out and drop it and in the meantime they had a whole harangue about them folks.

Down in that ravine, they set logs on end and made benches by laying boards between them. They still hadn't moved into the school yet. In front was a makeshift table and a few chairs for the leaders. Men in the crowd started wearing at least the hood, if not the whole white robe. Men like Inky O'Brien were easy to tell by the way they walked. Funny thing about a man, he can change about everything but the way he walks.

What I remember about that night was the chant. Little Shorthair stood up there and shouted, "Jesus ain't a Jew!" Then the chant, "Jesus ain't a Jew, any more than me or you!" The crowd chanted after him again and again, "Jesus ain't a Jew — any more than me or you!" Raised fists punched the air. These first meetings that's mostly all there was. Speech making, chanting, and some singing. Always they sung the hymn "The Old Rugged Cross."

A day or two after that meeting there was going to be a party at Crismons, and we was pretty excited about it. The Crismons often had what we called play parties, with music and games. The preparations consisted of carrying the furniture outside to leave the parlor floor empty. For a real fancy party, we sprinkled sawdust on the floor for the dancing.

The morning of the party, the birds stopped singing their morning prayers long enough to signal a wagon coming up the road. Old Clyde Blankenship was bringing a wheel for Dad to repair. Charley and Dad took the wheel, and Dad said he'd just fix it then and bring it to the Crismons that night.

I can see the next scene clearly, and I like thinking about them altogether like that. Charley about Dad's size, walking shoulder to shoulder. They have their backs to me, and they're going down our farm road that went toward the river. Paul is tagging along behind them, rolling the wheel along the bumpy drive. The wheel skitters this way and that, jumping when it hits a bump in the road, threatening to fall over when it gets stuck in a rut. All three heading down to the blacksmith shop between the house and the river.

Charley'd decided he'd learn the trade and it was a good choice, him being as strong as he was. If you don't think there's an art to blacksmithing, just try fitting an iron hub on the rim of a wagon wheel sometime and you'll see. Charley worked hard at smithing and to become a farrier for a number of years, for in nineteen hundred and twenty-two everyone knew cars, trucks, and tractors never could replace horses.

Joe was fixin' to leave on a mission of his own. He'd already groomed his horse 'till she shone, blackened hooves and combed mane, tail, and his own hair, maybe with the same comb. Dad told him to ride over to a widow's house with a smoked ham and a tow sack of flour tied to the saddle. Joe was happy with his job because the widow lived with her daughter and small son, and Joe wanted to convince them to come to the party at Crismons.

It was like that then. You'd have a party and weren't always sure who'd show up, but it made no one much of a notice. Sometimes a river man or somebody from way up in the hills might be seen standing off from the house in the dark of the timber, listening to the music. Just leaning against a tree. Sometimes a man knew them and motioned for them to come up to the house, but sometimes you just let them be.

Anyway, we finally finished enough to satisfy Dad, scrubbed the forge's black from our faces and hands, helped Mother and all the food she'd prepared into the wagon, and we were off. Already folks was having a good time talking outside on the lawn. Joe was there in time to help the widow's daughter down from the wagon, and he took her by the waist with both hands and swirled her up and around, her feet clearing the wagon's sides with no effort, and we all got a nice glimpse of white ruffles under her skirt. That sight was really something back then.

Joe acted all innocent of course, just trying to keep her good shoes outta the dirt. He knew what he was doing. Joe was clever about things like that. The gal kept her hands on his arms for a minute, no, just a second longer than she needed to, and then we all knew she kind of liked old Joe for his brashness.

Inside the empty room the old folks set in straight-backed chairs, lined up along the edge of the room like turtles sunning themselves on a log. They'd set there all night, telling lies about what good dancers they used to be when they was young. Well now, I take that back. When they'd play a slow waltz some of 'em would shuffle to the center of the room, and we could tell they'd been good dancers in their day.

The Crismons had a piano or an organ, I can't remember which. And there was fiddling and dancing going on for hours. I'm not sure where we got all that energy, but we did. We danced all kinds: square dances, of course, and different sorts of patterns. Then somebody's niece stepped up and demonstrated whatever step was new, and because she was good looking, the young men acted like that's what they always wanted to do — learn that step. Then others gave it a try. Then they got some kids like me out there to jig dance. Simon Cox's son, Alfred, he was the best at it. He was a great dancer with a head of coal black hair he never could control despite the prayers his mother probably said over it, and it flew out from his head as he danced and made him look like his daddy during preachin' times.

In the kitchen the food people'd brought was spread out on the table for everyone, after the old people had their choice. That was one thing to look forward to about getting too old to dance — first turn at the food. Outside, the men dangled their legs from barrels or shared pieces of the parlor. Sometimes the dogs at their feet got into a scuffle (about whatever's important in a dog's life) and many nights there were more dogs then men hanging around outside.

Always a young fellow had to escort a young gal out back to the privy for "protection" and the men ignored the giggles they heard and the clothes that were turned about when the couple reappeared.

There was lots of talk outside about things like the vote for women and prohibition, doused with a good sprinkling of whatever was wandering around in a flask that night. Everyone knew Fred and Sarah Crismon were in favor of prohibition, so since it was their house and party, the neighbors respected this opinion and made certain flasks were out of sight if a Crismon appeared at the door.

And right there at his door, right inside, was a certificate on the wall. A governmental certificate of appreciation. Fred received this certificate from somebody in the government declaring him patriotic, and he tacked up that piece of paper on his wall by the front door. It was like he'd saved the whole damn country by modernizing. He was going to out-produce everybody else because he was so modern.

I want to go back to that certificate for a minute. Here's someone like my Dad or let's just take Clyde Blankenship. Clyde's grandpap came in here and cleared the land, by hand. Buried kids. By hand. Buried wives, same thing. Can you imagine that? Hands black from the cold dirt where you prepared a hole for that person you loved more than anything else? Every year his little patch of land got bigger and bigger. Every few years the flood came, took it all away, and he'd fight back to recover from that. Built the schoolhouse with the others. Everything's a fight, everything's a struggle.

Then suddenly we have men from off, getting neighbors like Clyde together and telling 'em how to manage their land, be more productive, not waste anything. Ha! Not waste anything. We used everything that farm produced, from cornhusks for the mattresses to pig's feet for the soup. I'm telling you now, they didn't know a thing what they was talking about, living in their towns. No, my dad had nothing to do with them and their damn deals. None of the old-timers did.

Then these same kinds of folks got on to using corn to make a bit of whiskey. Said that was wasting food. And who's saying this? Somebody in some city, driving a fancy carriage to his private club every night? And what about the soup Cook set out for supper? Didn't it go to waste because he didn't come home on time? Is Mr. Fat Face smokin' a big old cigar made from tobacco that could have been planted in something else to feed the troops? You bet your life he is.

My dad was home feeding his family and quite a few more, sending me and my brothers around with extras to homes that needed it. My dad just minded his own business and hired this guy or that who needed work to do something that really didn't have to be done, all just to help out his neighbor. And his business did well because of it. No, government from the big city was not welcome when it came to the older farmers.

But Fred now, he was younger and more open to things, and maybe he needed a little help, I don't know. But he was a different type in a lot of ways. Took some things more serious than us, like liquor, and didn't hold to the traditions like Dad did about some other things. Fred stood on one side of the little certificate, and Dad was on the other, and for a while, we was all friends.

If a man was lucky back then, he could buy land along the river to start a farm on the black, tillable river soil. By the early 1900s, these extensive bottom soils were the most productive farms in the county, with easy access to river transportation. Being near the river was convenient when it was time to load the harvest and send it along the highway of the times, for the Osage fed directly into the Missouri and then on to the Mississippi.

There was a dark side to river bottom life though. Part of the farm, the buildings and livestock, needed to be set away from the banks, so they wouldn't be washed away during floods. As quickly as the pioneers learned to gravitate toward the rivers for their farming, they learned something else about Miller County land. The black dirt they saw was not always the foundation for fertile growth they expected. Poorly drained terraces were called "buckshot or crawfish land." When the soil stayed wet, it became tough, plastic clay. When dry, it was hard as concrete. The locals called it "gumbo."

The winter of that year, January of nineteen hundred and twenty-two, we went fox hunting all the time it seemed. Many nights, beginning when the whippoorwills started their songs, we heard three toots of a horn from one ridge, then a few minutes later three more from another neighbor. Dad would call out his intentions as well and before you knew it, a hunt was on for that night.

None of this bunch hunted on horseback; they walked. Dad's hounds were often the best and led the pack. A fox knows all about the hunt and the dogs, and he's the only animal that will deliberately try to outhunt you. Sometimes I really think our fox enjoyed himself out there, judging by some of the things he did. I know the men sure did. They'd sit around the fire, talking and listening, saying things like, "That's my dog out in front now. I know the sound of 'er."

I went on my first all-night hunt that year. Herman Tellman was there to cook for us and keep the fire going. We had cold chicken and a jug, and Tellman brought his homemade sausages, of course. Dad laid a coat down on the ground, and I curled up with one dog next to me and another dog at my back. I insisted on sleeping with a dog ever since I laid down on Dad's coat one time and then said, "Dad. I think I feel something under here." Sure enough, I got up, they brought a lantern over, and underneath was a copperhead that soon was just copper — no head.

So that night, I think maybe somebody threw a blanket over the three of us. I was tired and wanted to sleep, but couldn't give up the talk and seeing the faces of the men shining gold in the firelight. They'd tell a few ghost stories just for my benefit. On a damp night the lichen on the rocks glowed in the firelight, and the men told me that was the Whoofenpoof's gold so I'd best be careful. By then I was old enough not to believe in the Whoofenpoof, but I enjoyed the teasing.

"Really? The Whoofenpoof's out here?"

"Oh yea, he's out there for sure, chasing his shadow in the dark, runnin' so fast even your Daddy's hounds can't catch 'im. Runnin' backwards, apickin' his tracks up so's you can't follow 'im."

I remember watching that fire, thrilled I got to be out there with the men. Then the black part:

"Grant, Les Leids been saying you knew about Crismon's gumbo."

"What's that?"

"Les told him you knew about it but didn't say nothing when he was fixing to buy the place."

"Leids? You mean Old No Land, No Muscle, All Mouth Leids? What does he know about farming?"

The friends joined in and took Dad's side: "How in hell's blue acre was anyone supposed to know about that?" "Professor more often let it go fallow than planted." "Leids always knows everything there is to know about another man's business. He should tend to his own."

Today, if you stand up on the bluff above the last bend before Thompson's farm, you can see where the Thompson farm began. The entire boundary on one side of the farm is the Osage River. It's obvious to even ungeological-type people like me that the river was originally much wider, filling the area between the present day bluffs on either side.

By the time Grant Thompson bought the farm where Hadley and his brothers were born, a much narrower river meandered from bank to bank as it made its way to join the Missouri. The family was particularly fortunate in this regard. The farm had a section where the ancient river left a terrace of fertile ground, safely above the newer river floor. It seems as though either there was a tremendous flood that deposited river bottom soil in a field up above the present foundation, or the river once changed course, leaving the good soil behind. Whatever the reason, Thompson planted in both areas: along the banks on the same plane with his neighbors, as well as in a field up the hill nearer to his house and barn. Both areas contained the prize soil of which there was never enough, and when the river did flood, the land on the upper level was often left untouched.

After a bit, everybody'd heard of the new lodge and knew it was called the Ku Klux Klan. By then folks had strong feelings for it, with a few against it. Dad's fox-hunting friends planned at one time to overtake the group during one of their meetings — just charge in there and rip off their hoods and expose them. I don't know if anything ever came of the talk.

That same year, we'd another newcomer in the neighborhood. Logan Hickey, a nephew to Mrs. Crismon, came to live with the Crismons, and we started seeing less of Leo since he had a pal at his house now. But we was still friends, and we hung around together at school. Just not so much afterwards.

Then one day an announcement was made that an open meeting would be held for folks interested in seeing what the Klan was all about. To go to this meeting, all you had to do was go with a member. They could invite you. Needless to say, Joe, Charley, Paul and me was there hiding in our usual spot, as we considered ourselves invited to anything we heard about.

First, everybody came in and said the pledge of allegiance and a prayer. Their favorite Bible reading was from Romans, where they picked out only certain parts and ignored the other. Of course I could recite it for you because we had to memorize Bible verses for Sunday school: "Dedicate your bodies as a living sacrifice, consecrated and acceptable to God; that is your cult, a spiritual rite, with a loathing for evil and a bent for what is good. Put affection into your love for the brotherhood; be forward to honor one another; never let your zeal flag."

Then we noticed Mr. Shorthair standing up by the back of the wagon like he always did. Next to that was a little stand, with a Bible on it, and a flag stuck in the ground and a table and two chairs. Most of the men sat on logs and benches they'd made. Someone said, "All rise!" Everyone stood up.

Some of the men was wearing white hoods and the men up in the front, the leaders, wore the whole shebang. Robe, hood, symbols sewn on the robe. And depending on the symbols, we could tell that man's place in the group. By the end Fred Crismon had a hell of a lot on his robe, and Les Leids too, so we knew they'd become big mucky-mucks. Many men was just dressed normal, no hoods or robes. After all, it was just The Klavern, same as The Moose, or The Goodfellows.

"All loyal Americans who have duly taken the oath of membership to the Ku Klux Klan may now sit down!" Most of the group sat, but some like the newcomers were left standing. I nudged whichever brother was lying next to me. "Look! Ain't that Otto down there?"

Down in the hollow Shorthair pointed to the group left standing. "Now, you men step forward and approach the front. Line up here. There now, that's fine." Smiling, always they was smiling. As friendly as could be. So the men left standing, Otto Thompson and the others, went up.

"Do you swear you are honest Americans, interested in the good of the country, acknowledging the love of God?"

Who's going to say "No" to that? No man's gonna sit down and say he ain't for America. Up in the front was a man with a big open book, and next to him was Mule's Teeth, hair long and oily like always.

"You will now be allowed to write your name in our membership book, as you have been spoken for and already voted in by this chapter. This entitles you to all the privileges of membership therein. With this honor, you will receive your copy of the Kloran, our sacred constitution, and your pin."

Not one of those men said, "Thank you kindly, but I think you're acting like a pace of jackasses." They just all moved in to sign the book.

After Otto signed his name, Shorthair nodded, smiled, and held out his hand, "That'll be ten dollars." Otto looked around, shook his head and held out his empty hands. He didn't have ten dollars with him. That was like carrying fifty or a hundred dollars with you today. But Fred Crismon stepped forward and said, "No, never mind Otto, I'll front you the money." Then dug in his pocket and paid. Paid for Otto like it was just chump change.

So here's my point: Crismon, Leids, they didn't grow up going to Post Oak School, so they never heard the Ponder stories and they didn't know Otto is half German. Otto is related to the most famous German Civil War vet in the county. He's a hyphenated American. They just initiated the enemy into their group. We boys didn't think about it then. All we knew is that Otto just joined something Dad was against.

I do remember one more thing that night. The speech was about the Declaration of Independence and the schools. The man who was talking was saying something like, "Remember our founding fathers. They owned slaves. They denied Indians political rights. Our schools have not been teaching history the way it happened."

I really do think I got most of that correct. We'd hear the same thing again and again, week in and week out. I can hear it like I can hear my Dad standing in our doorway in the morning saying, "Get out of bed. People die in bed."

Shortly after this time, the meetings changed. They started talking about people in the area and making plans. They talked about who they wanted to join, and who they wanted to change, and how to go about doing those things. First they worked on getting the sheriff to join, then they talked about Dad and not going to his blacksmith shop to give him business if he wasn't going to join.

*Fred Crismon was there every time we were, and we watched the night
he got a name, a title of some sort, in the group. I wish I knew more about this,
but we think we saw Otto go a few more times after that, but from then on,
the men wore their hoods and sometimes their gowns. Of course, when they
started going after us Otto weren't a part of it anymore. Since we weren't supposed to be there, we couldn't ask Otto about it, so I'm not sure why he went at
all. Maybe even Otto wanted to decide something on his own once in a while
without Dad's advice.*

Meetings with Hadley and Icel often involved discussions around religion. They were both active members of a local Baptist church. Although Hadley was open-minded about other denominations, Icel was
a bit firmer in her beliefs. She asked for specific details about my own
baptism and frequently pestered me about being baptized by total im-
mersion, "just to be sure." I was raised in a church that sprinkled the
baby's head during a christening ceremony, then asked participants for
confirmation when they were older. I said I felt it unlikely that my head
would be allowed into the holy kingdom while the rest would dangle
below for eternity. Hadley laughed, but Icel saw no humor in this.

After learning that Leo Crismon eventually became an ordained
Baptist minister, Hadley's idea of harassment based on conflicting denominations seemed less likely. Many people in Miller County were
raised in churches that were not firmly one denomination, due to their
dependence on available preachers. According to local newspapers of the
time, two subjects that received enormous public and private discussion
were man's belief in God and the use of alcohol.

The Volstead Act was passed in October 1919. It provided for enforcement of prohibition. This was the law Grant surely noticed. In
the past, both the Miller County sheriff and Judge Slade were frequent
visitors to the Thompson farm, where they often enjoyed a mason jar of
Grant's corn whiskey. But once again, changes took a while to appear
in Wilcox Bend, so it wasn't until spring in 1922 that prohibition truly
came to the neighborhood.

This was the moment when Grant had a chance to change the
Thompson family's fate. He could have picked up his family and left.
Professor Molls would have helped with the transition should they have
decided to move north toward the capital. Or they could have easily
returned to Brumley. With Uncle Lev at the bank, a farm that was a

proven success, the ability to do just about everything, and the money to pay for what he couldn't do, Grant had many options. Instead, he chose to stay the course. He'd paid for his farm, his grown sons lived nearby, and on the surface not much had changed.

Prohibition had gone into effect with the vast majority of the American population firmly against it. People living throughout Miller County continued to enjoy making stump water and home brew, but now it antagonized some of their neighbors. According to the Klan, such lawbreakers needed to be stopped. At first the sheriff was not very helpful, claiming he was too busy with other cases to patrol for prohibition lawbreakers. Why, it took him over half a day to make the ride to many of the citizens' homes. In truth, local authorities often hoped to avoid the issue and confrontations. In places where the law was spread thin, like Miller County, the Klan was there to enforce the law. Members of the Wilcox Bend Klan decided their help was needed.

According to documents provided by Crismon's grandson, Frederick P. Crismon was a sworn Justice of the Peace. If Hadley knew this, he either forgot it or chose not to tell me. After all, he also never told me he met his first wife while bootlegging liquor to sailors during his Navy leaves. But for some strange reason I have yet to explain, I never saw any reference to Frederick Crismon as Justice of the Peace in any of the newspapers or historical documents and so knew nothing about it until his grandson showed me his commission papers.

Perhaps it was not the Klan coming after Grant at all. Everyone knew the Crismons were against those refusing to cooperate with the law, but how irritating did Grant find teetotalers? Perhaps Grant harassed Frederick Crismon for his opposing views.

Driving to Hadley's brother Joe's farm in Leeton, Misouri one afternoon, we discussed this question. It was a warm and sunny day in September. As usual, I was driving with Hadley sitting next to me with Icel in the back seat. I remember the pear tree in Joe's front yard laden with huge pears.

I asked, "Do you think your dad made fun of people who didn't drink, or maybe bothered those who wanted prohibition?" Instantly I regretted asking this. I expected Hadley to leap to his father's defense, pelting me with a barrage of denials without considering this possibility. He didn't. He just said, "I'll have to think about that a bit. I've often wondered if Dad did something to start it all, like make a pass at Mrs. Crismon or something."

Grant Thompson was used to the two opinions, one for and one against alcohol, living side-by-side long before the Klan and prohibition arrived. Simon Cox didn't drink but Plez Moore did and they were both regular guests at Myrtle Thompson's diner table.

When I asked the same question to Joe Thompson that day, he was more direct with his answer. Joe was well over ninety by then and used two canes to walk, stooped over so far he was forced to look at the ground unless he made a concerted effort to raise his head. But his voice was plenty strong that day. "Hell no. 'Live and let live.' That's the way we was raised."

A story about Grant's son Otto suggests both sides of the alcohol question dwelled under the Thompson roof even when no guests were present. Otto was eleven when his mother, Emma Ponder Thompson, died. By the time he was sixteen, he was frequently drunk. He, like Tommy Alexander, liked to hang out at the Bagnell ferry landing on the south side, where they may have waited together in the evenings for the ferryboat to take them to over to the Bagnell tavern. One night when Otto was drunk, he passed out or fell asleep on the floor of the call bell's shed. In a dream his mother came to him, and after a nice talk, she asked him to promise never to drink again. He agreed.

Otto didn't drink, yet he often helped his dad make corn whiskey. The process required patience and observation, and like all good farmers, Grant had both. Three times he washed the corn, rinsed it in a round sieve, swished the water through the pan and rolled the fermenting corn 'round and 'round like a miner panning for gold. The weather helped determine when fermentation was complete. The warmer the weather, the quicker the grain ripened into whiskey. The more humid it was, the more likely fungus would grow and ruin the batch. A man had to pay close attention.

Grant was deliberate during the process for more reasons than wanting to create a finer tasting brew. Improperly distilled drink could produce fusil oil poisoning. Just a few ounces from a poisoned jug killed a man in five days. There was no cure. The doomed person suffered incomparable pain, thick, black lips, bulging and sometimes bursting eyeballs, blindness, and finally death. It was a terrible fate. The effects of a bad batch of liquor, well known at the time, helped convince many that drink was the devil's brew. They wouldn't touch it.

The boys knew about the possible poisoning as they also knew about

Otto's dream. They often heard Otto refer to the visit from his dead mother's ghost. There he was, drunker than a skunk, hanging around the ferry landing. Then there was his mother, standing over him asking for his promise to give up the drink. It was a promise his wife and children said he kept until the day he died. It did seem as though "live and let live" was at least part of the Thompson motto.

Leo Crismon went with Charley, Joe, and me that winter to work a trotline and rig traps. He was a freckle-faced kid, who always wore coveralls like the rest of us. Later when he became a preacher, my cousin Olive heard him preach at Rocky Mount.

For trapping, we boys liked to look for 'coons at the far end of Cotton Island, just a few miles down river from us. It was about even with Les Leids' place and he set traps on Cotton Island too. Every winter, we'd set traps between our farm and there for 'coons, muskrat, mink, and then we could sell their hides when the hide buyer came through in the spring. He'd pay five for a 'coon, three for muskrat, twenty for mink, and fifty dollars for a fox with a thick, red tail.

Trapping ain't as easy as it sounds. Where the river came over to the bluff was a bit of an overhang, and that was the best place in the world to set a trap, because that old 'coon was going to hunt right under there, not up on the bluff. Of course, they all liked to follow along the water, trying to catch crawfish, because everyone knows a 'coon likes to wash their food. Cotton Island had a lot of places like that.

One morning early we went to get our traps and we came up on the first one, and it had a 'coon in it and we thought, "We're not sure if this fellow is ours or Leids, but well, we guess he's ours." We took the 'coon and went to the next trap. Then we saw a big old 'coon in that one and wondered, "Well now, is this our 'coon or Old Man Leids? Golly, it must be ours." So this went on for a bit, and we did real well and got a lot of 'coons. We didn't realize we had set out so many traps but guessed we had.

By and by we got to thinking we've about as many as we can carry and maybe we should stop. We heard hollering. And more hollering. We're thinking, "Maybe Old Man Leids thinks that some of these 'coons of ours are really his." So we commence to run like hell, or as close as we could considering we was carrying a load of dead animals. We found a spot where we buried the whole bunch under some brush and ran home.

There's Mother. "Where've you boys been? I had to holler for dinner be-
cause you didn't come home."
    "Oh well, we were just busy getting our 'coons."
    "I didn't know you set that many traps."
    "Us either."
    After dinner Leo went back to Crismon's and Joe and I went back to get
the 'coons and skin them out there in the woods. The path went right past Les
Leid's place where he was working away in one of the outbuildings. He had
this grey hair that he combed straight back from his square-jawed face, but
while he was working it fell forward. It was usually perfectly combed back
with hair tonic of some sort. There was a nice bald spot back there.
    Leids saw us. "You boys mind helping me with a little job?"
    This is what he was doing: He'd made a trap door in his smoke house and
dug a big hole under that. We helped him carry the still from outside, back into
that hole. He'd a pretty nice set up. They'd started the enforcement for prohi-
bition in Wilcox Bend, something Dad said would never happen. Of course,
Leids didn't think we knew a thing about the Klan meetings and how he was
supposed to be destroying the still, not just hiding it.
    Then when we were fixing to go, he asked if we were on our way to check
the traps, and we said, "No, we already done that and didn't get a one." Then
we wished him more luck with his and off we went.
    Later that year, when the fur trader came through, he was surprised to see
our board after board of drying skins. He'd come from the Leids' home. "You
boys should tell your neighbor what your secret is. He got very few this year."

For a while, Miller County Kleagles must have worried their potential
new members were going to dry up. There weren't enough Jews, "Coloreds," or Catholics to present much of a need for vigilantism. Yet in
order to make money, new members were necessary, and the call for
membership needed to include a perceived threat. Once again, Hadley
was correct when he stated, "The KKK… were always about power and
greed."
    Perhaps during those early meetings Eldon members discussed
the problem of the Germans in Bagnell. Yes, what about those German-Americans? Shouldn't they be held responsible in some way for the
carnage produced by the war? After all, the U.S. suffered over 112,000
fatalities with twice as many wounded. Anti-German sentiment was often leveled at German-Americans and suspicions of them had yet to

dissipate. In many Missouri restaurants hamburgers were still referred to as freedom burgers and sauerkraut as liberty cabbage.

Herman and Missouri Tillman were Catholic German-Americans, but Herman was also one of the most financially-solvent citizens in Miller County and a leading citizen of Tuscumbia society long before the Klan came down river. Picking on old man Tillman did not look like a good idea.

There were some noticeable Germans-Americans in Bagnell, and Klan members believed they had no right to be so prosperous, for they were stealing opportunities from "real" Americans. In 1921, Clarence Lewis Diedriech became depot agent and wireless operator. Grandma Diedriech ran the Bagnell Hotel. Her baked goods were legendary: buns sprinkled with candied pineapple that sold for one cent apiece. Fritz Hohner ran a prosperous dry goods store. Others had good jobs with the railroad. Couldn't the Klan send night riders to harass some of those local Germans?

Interestingly enough, there was one club stronger and wealthier than the newly formed Klan lodges: the railroad. Men working for the railroad belonged to the largest fraternity in Miller County. They held coveted, cash-paying jobs, they watched out for one another, they were physically strong, and they could rely on "higher ups" if they needed additional help. After railroad men retired, they received pensions and actively supported those still working. In Bagnell, railroad workers protected their own, and their own were often of German as well as African descent. No, in Miller County, nobody wanted to start a fight with a railroad man.

Organizers needed a driving force and neither race nor ethnicity were useful in Wilcox Bend. So by 1922, "morals charges" became the leading issue. These charges included breaking the laws of prohibition as well as any behavior the local Klavern deemed lewd and immoral. This trend was seen in other areas of the country as well. The difference was that in Wilcox Bend, all that knowledge of bloodlines provided an easily identifiable enemy. If a man was immoral, all his family could be viewed with suspicion at best or as outlaws at worst.

So that year, his second year, Crismon went about getting ready to do it his way a second time, you know, everything he had in corn. And that spring Dad told him, "Fred, you'll only get one crop in three. I know what this river can

do." But Fred Crismon did what Fred Crismon wanted and with some of the modern equipment he had he was done sooner than anyone else. He pitched in to help the other neighbors with their planting and was a popular man.

In fairness I have to say, Grant Thompson did what Grant Thompson wanted as well. And that's the way it would have stayed had the KKK and Les Leids and Dad's fox-hunting friends not decided to get involved in everybody else's business. Every man got to do what they wanted with their own business. I believe that's the way it should be.

After the Crismons moved to Wilcox Bend, others came as well and soon there were quite a few new families in the neighborhood. Crismon was a man who understood the importance of order and the need to follow rules. He organized the neighborhood and these newcomers felt it was important to meet for church every Sunday, not just to depend on a preacher coming through.

It was so far to travel for the regular church, but talk started about developing a Sunday school at Post Oak School. We still didn't have a regular preacher, but we could have Sunday school on our own. When that happened we saw a bit more of the hill folk and river families during those Sunday meetings.

That summer, again like the summer before, we were want for nothing. Each week we had sun, cool nights, gentle rains and breezes. For months it went like this until the corn reached up like the year before.

Have you ever seen a perfect cornfield? That's what we had in the summer of nineteen and twenty-two. A person can't appreciate how beautiful it is unless he's seen one. There are three layers of color. First, down by the soil, is the dark green. If you stand up on the river bluffs, this part is so deep it looks black, because each stalk is thick and full and shades the others all day. Then in the middle where the ears start, is the perfect, strong green. The color God intended for the color green. Last, the top. The gold tassels from the ears feather out to form a golden quilt that Mother Nature tossed in the air and let float down on top of the field, covering her treasure. That was the sight we saw when we rode up and down the river.

So now it was midsummer and all was smooth and quiet. Gipsy was all set to be our teacher again next year when she got an offer at a school that'd pay her more. Up at Blue Springs. Dad told her to take it, but she said she'd think about it, because it meant she'd be away from family during the week. If she wasn't going to teach at our school, this suited Otto fine, because his first love was teaching, and he was ready to have another year of it. His farm had done so well the past two years, he had money in the bank. Dad and Jim could help tend his farm. Either way, we all knew a Thompson would be our teacher.

One day we'd driven the mule team to Bagnell, Mother, John, and me. Right off the ferry, even along with the river, were the boat yards and some grassy places. Behind that sat the town. It was pretty, in a gray sort of way, because it was built on a hillside, its buildings making steps going up toward the bluffs. Roads were mud or dust, nothing in between. Hand-painted signs.

There was about four hundred people lived there, and every one of them called the town "The Tie Capital of the World." Most days we'd see thousands of railroad ties waiting in stacks to be shipped out. There was even a real undertaker who made caskets for the townsfolk. This old guy, Old Man Phillips, he'd look us up and down and that drove everybody crazy thinking he was measuring them in his mind against the coffins he had stacked up in his shop.

But more than that, anything we wanted, we could get in Bagnell: prostitutes, taverns, tea weed, churches, sewing machines, and wagon parts. Anything a kid was dying to see and his parents was praying he wouldn't, he could find in Bagnell.

Get off the ferry and there was a drunk, curled up on his side at the edge of the hill. People strolled, ran, and dragged their goods to and from the ferry, and none of 'em gave that man a second glance. He was just a dog, sleeping in the sunshine.

If we kept walking up Ferry Street, in a minute or two we were at the crest of the hill and could look down on the other streets. Look there, who were those ladies standing outside the general store? No scrubbing floors and digging up carrots for those gloved hands. Even those from the White House had to buy groceries. Why am I telling you this? Because if the Klan really wanted to go after immoral ways, there were plenty of people around to pick on besides us farmers.

I drove the team up the short hill from the ferry and turned on the road where the mill was. Pulled the mules up under the trees at the side of the millhouse, alongside the teams already there. All the animals were dozing at their hitching posts. This was a good sign, lots of people there — a hint that there might be interesting news inside. Weren't nothing sacred at the mill, and we boys elbowed our way in front to be the one watching the slow stone wheels going 'round and 'round, all the while listening to the stories circling that room.

On that day, Mother and John walked on over to the stores along Oak Street, and I pulled the first bag from the back of the wagon. No matter how hot it was outside, stepping down the stairs and into the millhouse was like going into a cool autumn day. Darkness greeted me. A fine flour dusting covered the wide boards on the floor. The men looked over from the waiting bench and nodded when I entered, and I propped our sacks in line with those waiting to be ground. They moved over to make room for me on the bench when I was done unloading, and then I began the long but entertaining wait as the huge wheels ground the meal.

The mill house itself was shaded under sycamore umbrellas, and a row of windows opened out over the creek to let in the coolness of the water hurrying past. Tiny particles of newly ground flour hung in the shafts of sunlight coming in from the window. Sometimes the talk was as light as that side of the room, with its river breeze and rustling sycamore leaves:

"Dale, I got an old hound dog that'll eat grain faster than you're grinding it," a man called out to the miller. The miller, Dale somebody, was an even-natured sort who never smiled much, but never got mad neither. "How fast would that be now?"

"Till he starves to death." I laughed along with the men. The big man simply continued measuring ground meal with the deliberation of an old bull ox ambling into the fields for a day of plowing.

"Did you hear about the funeral up in Calloway County last week?" Another man from the bench asked his neighbor. We all shook our heads, "No."

"Well now, this old schoolmarm, it'd been her funeral a few years past. Yep, she'd already died, and they had them a service for her, and laid her body in the back of a wagon when it was over. But when they was abringin' her through the gates of the graveyard, the wagon wheel hit a post and jarred the wagon, body and all, and she done sat upright. Seems she weren't dead after all."

"Yep," was all the response his neighbor got, but I remembered to tell my brothers that one. We loved stories about things like people getting buried alive.

"Yes sir, so she lived another two years and then up and died again, and they sat with her all night and the next day was takin' her through that same gate when her old man said to the driver, "You be careful now. Don't you hit that post again!"

We all laughed.

One man, we called him Chicken Fat, sat over to one side on an upturned pail and leaned both hands on a stick. He had a lump on his back. We teased the younger kids to make them squeal and run because we swore he ate little children, which was what made the hump. Chicken Fat was a river man.

Perched on that little bucket, his bony knees looked like one pointed to the Confederacy and the other to the Union, and the veins and tendons in his hands stuck out like the roots of a tree along the riverbank. Sitting like that, with a bump at the base of his neck, he looked just like a turkey vulture. That day I thought there weren't an uglier individual on God's green earth.

I don't know where he lived when he wasn't poling a raft, but we'd see him down at the river fishing or in Bagnell hanging out at the mill. Long hair the color of muddy earth. Chicken Fat had the longest beard, and you never did see his lips. That beard just seemed to open up and a stream of tobacco spit would shoot out. I got to know him pretty well in a funny way, especially after the shootings. I'll tell you about that later. His talk was nothin' but a long slow drawl, for he was still the best storyteller of all.

"Estol Franks got a bit of a surprise last week." Chicken Fat's beard seemed to be doing the speaking and it took him a full minute to say that one sentence. He nodded just as slowly toward our line as he spoke. We leaned forward together, straining to hear his words, because he was prone to saying out loud what most people said only in their minds. He was also one of the reasons women wouldn't come down into the mill.

Chicken Fat went on to tell how this Estol, whoever the hell he was, had discovered his new wife (brought back after a trip to Kansas) was only four-teen instead of the seventeen her pop said she was, and had not yet seen her first moon. Estol owned quite a bit of land and folks speculated the bride's old man found that out and determined he was going to marry his daughter off regardless.

Chicken Fat gave a spit that sailed out the window and probably landed across the river.

"So folks, thinkin' the Lord's business was their own, said the marriage should be annulled, and th' little gal sent home to her pap." Honestly, you could fall asleep, take a nap, wake up and Chicken Fat would still be telling the same story.

"Now, Estol was happy with his new wife and wanted to let things be, but he consulted the preacher on account his neighbors was gonna do it fer him and he might as well hear the judgment first hand." He paused for effect. The ground meal fell from between the stones' middle in the same rhythmic pace as the miller's walk, the river continued on its way to find the Missouri and we sat there like none of us had a thing to do 'cept listen to what the preacher told Estol Franks.

"So Preacher asked, 'Gal? You take this man as kin?'" Another spat flew out the window.

"'Yes, Preacher,' she said. 'I take him mighty fine.'"

"And the preacher proclaimed the sin of lyin' done been committed, that she was too young to 'ave wed. But as the two were happy with the error in addition at that point, no sense in commitin' another sin. Because if'n ole Estol took the gal back to her pap, she done lost the only dowry she had livin' wit

ole Estol, so her chances o' weddin' another were slim to nothin'." Another spat sailed toward the river.

"So there you got it. Two sins don't take away sin." All the heads nodded together at the sense of it all.

Suddenly the mood got as dark as the musty air along the base of the deep stone walls. A man come down the stairs, a sack on each shoulder, probably seventy-five pounds each. It was Ty Sears. He stood there, looking over the lot of us sitting on the bench, not bothering to set his load down while he pointed his chin at me.

"That runt don't belong here," he said to the miller. "If'n you want my business to stay, he goes now." He was staring at me. I could feel my face get hot and thought maybe I should jump up and let him have my seat. Then I remembered when I saw Ty get whipped. That night I just figured the lashes didn't hurt that much, but after seeing him up close I realized that weren't so. It was because Ty was so tough. I just froze, because all I could see was that hard, unmoving face with those red streaks across his back.

Now here I'll tell you a story about Ty Sears as good as anything Chicken Fat could come up with. Ty's father lived in Tennessee where he both killed a man and lost his wife in the gun battle. So Mr. Sears took his baby and ran. But a lawman followed them and caught up with him hiding in a house with his baby son. Sears took the baby and held him up in the window, and of course the lawman did not shoot. Then Sears jerked his pistol from his belt and shot the lawman dead. The baby was Ty Sears, and he grew up as mean as his pap.

When Ty glared at me from the bottom of those stairs, I just sat there, not knowing what to do. Dad had told me to stay and look after the grain. I looked up at the miller. He hardly glanced at Sears while he continued doing his job, but said, "If'n you want that corn ground, take a seat with th'others or leave it be over that way." Seemed like the men on the bench were careful not to nod in agreement with the miller, even though they'd been kind to me. Nobody really liked Sears.

I said, "I'll come back in a bit," and scampered back up those stairs into the sunlight. I looked down the street and saw John sitting by himself with two girls standing in front of him. Mother had sent him out to the front step of the Bagnell grocery, where he was just minding his own business, watching the people go by.

By the time I walked across the street I could tell the girls were teasing him and making fun of him without him understanding. Suzzie Leids was one, a tall thing that resembled a swamp bird, and some friend of hers. I didn't hear what she said to him, but could tell by his screwed up face he was confused. Then I heard him say, "Dad told Joe not to talk to no trash gals."

Now normally we was the only ones that could understand what he said. But that day he spoke clear as a January sky. It wasn't a thoughtful thing to say, but I don't think John knew any better. He was in his twenties at the time, but remember now, he was always just a kid in his mind.

Well that girl pulled back her arm and let a slap streak across his face. He looked sad and said, "Go away now. I ain't gonna talk to no trash gals." Then Mother came out of the store and I came up too, and Suzzie and her dirty-legged friend scowled at us. Mother stood calmly in her good dress and hat and said, "Ladies?" I can still see her standing in the shade of the porch with her hands folded, crocheted purse over her arm. A blue plaid dress. But the girls didn't say nothing more. Just glared and stomped away.

We finished our other business, picked up the grain from the mill and before we left for the ferry went to Fritz Hohner's store. He sold ice cream for a nickel and was so honest he filled up the bottoms of the cones with a teaspoon.

CONFUSION (1923)

—Courtesy Missouri State Historical Library

American Civil Liberties Union pamphlet

Although Frederick P. Crismon's family was much younger than Grant's, the Thompsons and the Crismons quickly found their lives intertwined. Besides combining the chores of planting and harvest, the two women, living secluded in a man's world, enjoyed female companionship. The children walked to school together, and both families worshiped at the neighborhood schoolhouse.

Grant Thompson was furious with the accusation that he knew anything about the situation on Crismon's land, claiming Professor Molls was never a serious farmer who utilized all his land in the first place, so how was Grant to know such things? But Leids used Grant's benevolent offer to help get the land for a reduced price as proof: Grant Thompson made the offer because he knew the land wasn't worth the asked price.

Neighborhood gossip didn't end there. Frederick Crismon might have felt more than the usual amount of pressure from his father-in-law to succeed. Sarah Crismon was given a farm by her father before she married, as were her sisters. Crismon sold this farm then bought and sold another before they bought the Molls' place. Did he use the money from his wife's dowry for the purchase? Had he made or lost money with the transactions?

Frederick represented the newer generation of farmers. He shopped for one of the first tractors in Wilcox Bend and modernized in other ways. But we now know he was not earning much money from the Osage River farm. As well, corn prices were dropping.

After 1923, tensions between Frederick and Grant men started to grow. In the Thompson way of thinking, issues were settled with an argument or a fistfight. Then the quilting, burying, courting, and threshing brought folks back together again.

There's a time at the end of every summer when it's too soon for threshing and still too hot for butchering. Everything slows down. The river creeps. The grass don't grow. Cows and pigs lay around in whatever mud they can find. Dogs are lazy and horses stand in the pasture with their eyes closed. Count on summertime doing the same thing every year; there's a week or two of the doldrums.

During our doldrums of summer, church became even more of an all-day affair, even if we just went to the schoolhouse for Sunday school. After we met for the preachin' or Bible readin', we'd go outside to the wagons, spread quilts under the trees and then out come the picnic baskets. The men discussed butch-

ering, sorghum pressing and the upcoming school year. They'd decide who was going to be teacher, how many cords of wood every family'd bring in for the stove, whether or not the schoolhouse roof needed patching or if there needed to be more desks. Always there was something that needed plotting or planning, and talking was the only activity we felt like doing during the doldrums.

Our group did the same thing, year after year. On those slow Sunday afternoons, we'd all stay — babies, old folks, and teenagers of sparking age. We'd play horseshoes and nibble on chicken, pickles, cobbler, and gossip. One year a toddler was there, visiting Grandma and Grandpap, with just his mama because his pa couldn't come. And he had those soft, pudgy legs that make you want to squeeze them, with dimpled cheeks to match.

The baby was having just a swell time, chasing butterflies and jabbing his sticky little fingers in everybody's pies. His cheeks were so fat and round he hardly couldn't see out of his eyes when he smiled. His grandparents were so proud, because he was surely the handsomest, healthiest child. His grandma went off with his mama to do something, thinking grandpa had his eye on him, but Grandpa thought the boy was with the women.

Suddenly everyone's saying, "Where's Isaac?" jumping up from their quilts or pulling away from their conversations to answer that question. Then a horrible shout from down at the creek and we rushed there, hats flying, skirts held high. Then cries and sobbing. That loving, perfect child had run down to the creek, fell on a slippery rock and drowned before his grandparents saw he was gone. Who knew he could run as fast as that?

They brought him back up, his limp little body dangling over the arms that carried him, and everybody was crying out so. His grandpap vomited in the grass. It happened so fast, that child still had pink blushed cheeks. I'm sure there's never been a sadder day. Things like that happen to little ones and you have to wonder, why? Don't the Bible say Jesus looks after children?

And it was just another one of those friendly, warm Sundays when a cold chill fell between my family and some others. The topic that morning had been sin. That in itself was no surprise as it seemed to me sin was a major topic of my boyhood. I was either knee deep in it or looking for a way to jump in. But up until then, Sin was Simon Cox pushing a finger in your face shouting, right up there in front of God and everybody, "You're going to hell, Brother!" Personal salvation was a matter of public record. We was always noting who got saved, who oughta get saved, and who, like Tommy Alexander, staggered up to the front or down to the river to get saved every time there was food involved.

On Wilcox Bend, the good Lord spoke to folks through their crops. A good crop or a bad crop, there was always plenty of speculating as to what God was trying to tell a person. I always wondered how God spoke to men who were not farmers, but was never to find the answer to this as everyone at church lived pretty much like we did. Everything out in the open. No secrets. He's a drunk. He's a hard worker. He's a good neighbor. He's a lazy bum letting his family starve. Everybody saw the good as well as the sin.

In 1923, sin and alcohol were firmly entwined in the minds of many people. In general, prohibition's most ardent advocates were those who believed alcohol to be evil, and in an age where speakers were entertainment, men like Billy Sunday were in great demand. If a man discovered he had talent speaking to a crowd, he soon had a job and often would deliver talks on a variety of subjects. Billy Sunday's shift from baseball player to tent preacher was a lucrative one, for after he spoke, helpers in the red braces would help him bring in hundreds of dollars in donations from the enormous crowds. His "Booze Sermon" was said to be his most popular.

By the end of 1922 prohibition was in full force, and the Miller County newspapers featured a list of residents arrested for violating the law in every issue. The papers were also starting to show farms for sale, as the market experienced drastic lows in grain prices. Farmers were feeling the crunch, but by now the Thompsons had paid off their farm, thereby eliminating some of their financial strain.

Simon Cox preached against drunkenness, but otherwise appears to have stayed away from the topic of prohibition and other politics of the day. He preferred to stick to the basics of man, his soul, and acceptance of God's laws. But KKK promoters did not. They quickly jumped on the prohibition bandwagon and steadily maintained that those who made and drank alcohol were neither Christian, nor American, nor moral people. But like Les Leid's whisky still hidden under the smokehouse floor, Klan leaders continued to drink secretly in private. They often needed the help of alcohol to perform their most brazen acts.

Cox and Sunday had other differences besides their views on politics. Circuit riders like Simon Cox earned in a year what Billy Sunday may have collected in larger towns during just one night. Many rural preachers had farms or jobs during the week and preached on the weekends because in their areas it was impossible to live on the meager donations. This helps explain why Preacher Cox was often at gatherings involving food, and why the preacher was invited for noon and evening meals after preaching. Although he was friend as well as mentor, he was just as often in need of something to eat.

As surprising as it may seem, with religious figures like Thomas Dixon continuing to preach the hierarchy of the races, it wasn't unusual for ministers to join local Klaverns where they served as chaplain and gave biblical presentations at the meetings. Members were then encouraged to attend their church on Sundays as well.

Simon Cox disagreed with this practice.

One Saturday morning that same year, Paul went down to get something from Otto's, and went past where Noah and Moses were pastured. I was up getting water from the spring and here he come yelling up the ridge; we heard him before we seen him. Dad came out from working in the barn because he'd heard the same.

"What the devil, Paul?"

Now for some reason, I didn't go stick my nose in what was going on. Probably the first time in my life I didn't go check out something my brothers were up to. I don't know why. I'm glad to this day I never saw what happened. I just stood where I was.

What they found was this: someone had tortured Noah and Moses. Not just killed them quick and merciful like we butchered. Those handsome creatures only existed to help us humans. So why'd somebody do that? Well to torture us of course, and to torture Professor Molls, him being Catholic and against the Klan.

Moses'd been whipped so hard and for so long he'd fallen and was on the ground. He had a beautiful, soft, honey-colored hide. We think somebody'd hobbled him with a sickle on his right foreleg. Noah was half in harness and had tried to run away, only to charge into the barbed wire fence.

If a cow gets caught in the fence, often as not she'll just stand there until you come get her out or she starves to death. Not a horse. They'll thrash until they get loose or die. Well that harness got tangled up in those barbs and he'd pulled those fence posts out of the ground. He sliced up his legs and bled to death by the time Dad got there.

In my mind Noah is still as he always was: in a lush green pasture, swishing lazily at flies with a pitch black tail, or nudging my shoulder when I turn my back, or tossing his mane as he pulls the sleigh along a snowy path. And that's the way I'll always remember him.

How I wish I could forget seeing Paul, just a good kid who never hurt nobody, sobbing against Dad's shirt, and Dad soothing Paul's hair like Mother would, saying, "Shhhh now."

Before that day, nothing like that ever happened to livestock. Remember, we had free range and always watched out for our neighbor's stock. Why, up until the time Dad bought the farm they gave men twenty years in Jefferson City for horse thieving and rustling cattle. Before that they just hanged 'em. We knew it weren't nobody who knew the horses because they'd hitched Noah on the right.

Somehow Dad and Joe, some other neighbors too, got Moses up. Mother made a poultice and bandaged the leg. That was something they knew back then, what plant to press on a cut to numb the pain. Then they walked him back to our place so slow, slower than any funeral procession. I know they led him up as the sun was setting, shining gold and red on the roof, and we spent the night walking him so he couldn't lie down and colic. Mother made the poultice for him every morning and evening. She brought it herself down to the barn for us to put on and gave him precious sorghum on his grain to entice him to eat. That was one of the few times the four of us got along doing something — tending to Moses. We doctored him the best we could, but his trusting nature was gone.

Professor Molls came back and the men buried Noah on our farm near the sycamore. Professor didn't want him rendered despite the poor times. Professor stayed at our house for the night and sat at the kitchen table after supper telling Mother and Dad about the trouble the Klan was stirring up in Jefferson City. They'd kill livestock and give whippings for warnings, and if you were a member it was your job to go after others. Now they didn't just go after those they wanted to leave the area; Professor said they'd started going after their own as well. Members had more and more rules they was supposed to uphold.

When Plez came by season next, he'd already heard about it all. He went to where it all took place and examined the shelter and the old pasture with its one section of wire fence, and even what was left of the harnesses. He asked a lot of questions about who knew about horses in the neighborhood and who didn't. And I thought to myself, "We'll just wait now and give Plez time to figure it all out. He'll make things even."

The American melting pot started to boil during the 1920s. Historians blame changes in demographics and custom, brought on by the diverse groups living closer together in many areas than before. Riots, violence, lynching, and arson almost became commonplace. During World War I in St. Louis, Missouri, African Americans moved up from the south in response to new employment opportunities, inhabiting previously all-white areas. After the war, whites responded to these changes with rioting. In one instance, St. Louis whites rioted and killed thirty-nine African Americans. Especially gruesome were the World War I veterans, lynched while still in uniform. Frequently the person was burned alive, and then the remains were hanged.

Crismon had half of his corn cut and in shocks and half of it still on the stalk. My dad's corn was all shocked, but then he hadn't planted as much as Crismon. Dad did what he'd always done; there was no changing him. He held some back. The upper field was in corn and some wheat, with the river bottom only half planted. We had grain and hay from the season before and some money in the bank as well. Things had never been better as far as the farm was concerned, but the low prices at market made it somewhat harder.

Then, after all those months with beautiful weather, sunshine and gentle rain, it started to storm. It poured day in and day out. By the end of the day, our leather boots were soaked and had to spend the night in front of the kitchen stove with newspapers in them so they'd dry enough to wear again. We tried going barefoot from the barn to the house, but Mother rejected that idea after one day of all those muddy footprints. We went to sleep and woke up to the sound of the drumming on the roof.

Soon the road was nothing but a washboard. No way to stay dry. John fought to keep the fire going with wood always getting wet. Mother tried to dry clothes by hanging them inside the barn. Every day Dad went down to the river and watched the sycamore roots along the bank. First a foot was covered by water, then two. Then none of the roots showed. Then the tree trunks on both sides were even with the river. He also made a point to talk to both Jim and Otto about what was coming because they hadn't gone through something like that before. A flood was rough on those farmers, in ways many people don't think of.

Think of a farm more like a child than a hunk of land. A farmer easily spends nine months watching, working, and waiting for his crop. He never lets himself get too far from it. In his mind he's made those fields out of his muscles, blood, and sweat. He solves little problems along the way, every week. He's as protective as he can be, and he loves and hates Mother Nature depending on what she decides to do. It's more than losing the money the first time a flood takes the crops.

That's why Dad talked to my brothers, to prepare them for what they were going to feel, because there was absolutely nothing they could do but watch and wait. Patience is a virtue.

Sure enough, here come that old Osage River going right for our farm. Soon there were no banks left to stop it. Then it got from hill to hill. We lost all that we had in the river bottom. Even some of the upper field was lost, but not all. The flood done the same by all of us, up and down the Osage. We all suffered. But the old timers had followed the old rules: always keep something back. They had some hay in the loft, some grain in the silo, or money in the bank. And they didn't till all their topsoil, so the old roots held some in place. Trouble was, it'd been six years since a flood like that came through, and the newcomers didn't believe the river could change so.

There was little harvest for anyone that year, but the Osage was cruelest of all to Crismon. It took all his corn — laid it down flat — and what he had cut in shocks it washed down to the lower end of the place against the timber. He didn't really lose it in a sense, but in another sense he did because it was worthless for his cattle now, or to sell.

It was still raining early one evening when we were at our blacksmith's shop, almost a half mile down the road from our house, toward the river. Paul worked at the bellows for Dad while he hammered the hot steel on the anvil. Joe and Charley was there too. I stood on the threshold, muddy bare feet on worn wood. Dad used wood he found from an old squatter's cabin when he built that doorway. I can feel my toes curling over the edge, my hand stroking the door jam. The grain of the grey wood fell and rose in waves beneath my fingertips, smooth from wind, sun, and age.

Dad liked to work with the door open, even when it was storming out like it was that night. Through the sound of the rain hammering on the tin roof and the pounding inside on that anvil, came the sound of someone coming — a rider in the dark, galloping toward us.

Then in a lightening flash, I saw him, and in that instant, I saw the whole picture, frozen like a snapshot. As I can still feel the heat of the forge behind me, I can stare into the face of that mare, see her nose, nostrils flared, ears flattened against her head, hooves churning the mud. A man's hands are stretched forward on her neck, reins held in tight fists. Frederick Crismon's face a wet grimace and hair painted flat. Saddle and hat gone missing, leaving both man and beast looking unclothed. Then blackness. Just black.

In from the dark stumbled Crismon, crying like a baby. Of course none of us knew what was the matter and Dad said, "Well Fred, what in the world's wrong?"

He answered, "I'm ruint. I'm ruint!"

He'd sunk it all in the farm and left no reserve in the bank or in the field. I remember Dad telling him it was never as bad as it seems, but Frederick just went on, sobbing out his story. And then Dad said, "I don't know. Let's go up to the house and have something to eat and maybe we can figure out something." So they went to the house and while they talked that night, they came up with a plan. It involved all of us. When Crismon left he was in a better frame of mind. I swear it never occurred to me before this minute, but he broke a rule, didn't he? He was supposed to go to his Klansmen for help. He didn't. But I don't think they could've come up with the plan Dad did.

Still it rained. Then, when we knew it was never going to stop, it did. The sun came out. The mud dried up. After the river got back near its banks, we went to work. Fred and Dad and all us boys, we divided the work up as equally as we could. Dad went to Uncle Lev at the Bank of Brumley and got some money loaned. Part of the family was to buy every hog they could put their hands on. That was Dad, Charley, and I think Otto and Crismon went with them. That took more than a solid week. Hogs were going for about one and a half cents a pound.

Us boys, that was Joe, me, and Francis, and Paul helped too, we was to get us a roll of woven wire to make the fence. So we started to fence in Crismon's field. We ran the fence all the way down through Crismon's river bottom and up into the timber, wherever the corn had been. Leo Crismon helped too, of course. By this time the hogs started to come in and there were several hundred of them. People were bringing them in, driving them in, however they could. And those hogs started doin' what hogs do best — eat. They ate that sour mash and started to clean it all up. There's no better way to fatten a hog than on corn. We all know that.

Where there had been a cornfield was now a giant square of muddy slop. Big old hogs, pregnant sows, mama pigs with their piglets and some little ones just weaned, teenage hogs looking for their first breed, turned in with mud, corn stalks, more mud, river water, dead fish, leaves, branches and still more mud. All fenced in by us boys. And if all them animals weren't having enough of a heyday, soured corn, as everyone knows, is fermenting, and that meant those hogs got drunk on that stuff.

It was a swine dream come true. They'd chase each other 'round and 'round until they fell down, sides heaving, eyes glazed over. Fat little legs sticking straight out, pink snouts twitching. They'd snort and kick and pass out, snoring. Then after a while they'd wake up, eat some more, get drunk, stagger around a bit and sleep some more. It's a wonder none of them drowned in that slop. Maybe they did; I don't know. The whole neighborhood came by at one time or another to see it. But so far everything was going as planned, and if the hog market was good in the spring, we'd make enough to save the farm.

Then it was fall and time to head back to school. I walked home from school every day, of course, and could smell that pig party a mile away. I swear they got fatter and smellier by the day.

Hadley described his farm with the same diligence he chronicled his family. At first, my natural inclination to hurry up and write the story made his details of the land a tedious subject to listen to. And hurrying I always was. I'd have an hour or two for an interview before rushing off to my part-time job, picking up the kids at school, dashing to the grocery store, swinging by the dry cleaners, then home for dinner, dishes, laundry, and piano lessons.

Honestly, the only difference between me and any other housewife in mid-Missouri was that while I sat in the car waiting for the light to change, I often imagined a family I'd never met and never would, since most of them were dead. Well, there was one more difference: I was the human mother of two large, male, bird-hunting dogs that needed to run a few miles a day.

The old Thompson farm, officially referred to as the Herbert S. Hadley by Grant Thompson, now conveniently stood fallow and vacant, owned by a couple I knew. This land provided the perfect place to exercise the dogs and understand the layout of Hadley's story at the same time. The farm was intact in many aspects, and I could walk along the paths left by cattle, wagons, and later tractors and trucks, while I considered what I'd read and heard.

The more I hiked, the more I began to view the past differently. The life I left behind when we moved to the area started to fade from my memory. I no longer mourned the absence of exercise classes at a local gym. The cute, matching workout outfits were replaced by hunting pants with thorn-resistant front panels. Soon, I could distinguish between the clatter of the sycamore's leaves from the sound of the oaks. I could spot a tarantula against a black rock and morel mushrooms hidden in leaves on the ground.

I struggled up hills, slid down banks, and waded among mossy rocks, often not sure of where I was going. The love affair that started with an old man's tale and country ways continued with the sounds and sights of the hills. Before long, I started to hear the same sounds Hadley described: the river men singing their way down stream; the sound of a breakfast bell; wagon wheels on rocky dirt roads.

Did those sounds really exist? They were real to Hadley. When I listened, I heard them as well. But there was nothing to see besides trees rustling in the breeze. My dogs found nothing but a small creek, trickling through the hills of an Ozark farm.

One particularly lovely sunny day in July, I was in the area and decided to stop at the Herbert S. Hadley for a quick walk, sans dogs. I was about a mile from where the giant sycamore had been, coming up from where the creek joined the Osage River. For some reason, I had stopped and was standing quietly next to a tree. There was no background noise of traffic, so the step of even a squirrel rustling through the brush stood out. I listened carefully and heard the distinctive, rhythmic movement of a human. There was another trespasser on the opposite side of the ravine. Then I saw a man. I froze and waited, hoping the trees and bushes would shield me.

During the weeks before that day, I had occasionally glanced at a newspaper from the twenty-first century and read articles about drug dealers and meth labs in the area. As during Grant Thompson's childhood, outlaws sometimes enjoyed the remoteness of the Ozarks. We even had a city councilman arrested for his involvement with one such outfit. I thought of all the scenes Hadley had painted in my mind of boys hiding in the underbrush, listening and unseen. This was the whole reason they were able to attend the outdoor Klan meetings in the dark. They could crawl close enough to hear everything being said without being detected, mostly due to the denseness of the woods.

That was years ago. And it was night. That day it was sunny and bright, and I wasn't a kid sliding along the ground. I realized I was only a middle-aged woman out in the middle of nowhere with a stranger. I pictured my dear husband and sweet children looking down at my lifeless body murmuring through their grief, "What was Mom doing out there?"

I needn't have worried. As usual, Hadley was right. The dense undergrowth protected me, and even though I could hear him breathe as he trudged past, the stranger never saw me. Although I fought it in the beginning, something about those walks helped me understand the way Hadley told the tale. It followed the course of the Osage River. Sometimes they both moved slowly and at other times at an unsettling pace. I learned my lesson, however. I never went to the farm again without either a dog or a Thompson.

My memories of school always include the walks to and from the schoolhouse. I could walk one of two ways. I could stay up in the timber until I was almost above our farm, which is the way we went to the KKK meetings. Or, if there wasn't some extra chore waiting for me at home, I'd drop down by the river to see if I could find Old Man Sons or Chicken Fat and do a bit of fishing.

As I got older, I spent a lot of time with them, which Mother didn't take to too well. Sons was a refined man at one time, but when I knew him he'd given that all up to live in the woods whenever he could. He had those long yellow teeth and white hair going every which way. He laughed a lot and liked to camp out by the river with a smoke pit of green hickory going day and night for his catch. I stayed as long as I could with Sons, running home at the last minute with smoked fillets wrapped in newspaper stuffed into the front of my shirt to offer Mother. She might forgive me then for being late.

One day, I watched Fred Crismon down there, with a hound dog that always trotted at his heels. That dog was a darn good tracker, with fur about the same red as Crismon's hair. Thought I'd never forget his name, but I have. I watched him having a grand time, playing with a stick caught in a small whirlpool. Round and round it went, and the dog chased it, swam after it in the water like a dog chasing its tail. But then he caught scent of a 'coon in the woods, and he ran to the bank to chase it. Back out into the water jumped that 'coon, the dog right behind it, barking, and Crismon started yelling, "No! Come here!" because a 'coon can drown a dog.

Sure enough, as soon as the dog couldn't touch bottom, that 'coon turned and clawed its way onto the dog's head, sunk his teeth into an ear and hung on with all four feet until the dog drowned. All the time Crismon was screaming, "Let 'er alone! Let 'er alone!"

It was the walks in the autumn I remember the most, for when I returned home each day I'd notice one more piece missing from the land around our house. Our parents worked together during that time of year, and slowly cut, stripped, and picked the farm clean to get ready for winter.

All through September, the orchard was splattered with red, then one day after school there was only green. Every apple, with worm or without, on a tree or on the ground, was brought inside for use. At last, the oaks shed their leaves and the outdoors became naked as the cold days drew near, but the farm's buildings were fat and full. Bins brimmed with potatoes. Sawdust-filled barrels hid apples in the fruit cellar. Even the water in the springhouse cooled pickled fish and cider. Shelves were soon covered with the colors of the rainbow as Mother arranged hand-packed jars of red beets, orange carrots, applesauce, beans, peas, brown relish and yellow corn. A stocked root cellar is as pretty as the inside of a paint box.

Most of all I remember the smell. It made me breathe in deep and long every time I stepped outside and into smoldering hickory coming from the smokehouse. We smoked meat for some of our neighbors, and John kept the smokehouse stoked and busy for weeks. Rich and sugary, it's the best smell in the world on a cool day.

After supper, Mother and Dad strolled for a bit, looking over what they had done that day, explaining their work to each other. My father would stand, stroking his beard with one hand and pointing with the other at a field, pasture, or garden plot. Mother carefully watching his face while she listened, hands in her apron pockets. But when it was her turn to talk, her thin fingers fidgeted with the bun at the back of her neck. I always think of her hands when I imagine her. I see them making biscuits on the cutting table, sprinkling flour on the board, kneading the dough and patting it into circles all the same size. Perfect.

I usually called the Thompsons to see if it was all right to come for a visit. Most of the time it was Icel who answered the phone. "Well hello, baby," she'd say in her sweet-as-sorghum voice.

Then she'd holler over her shoulder as though she were calling in the pigs, "Hadley, it's Victoria."

Once Hadley was in the hospital for a long time. But when he got out he told me of plans he was making to drive to Colorado where he and his friends went elk and deer hunting. They'd spend nights in a shepherd's cabin, walk along the Continental Divide and pitch in to help folks looking for wayward cattle. Sometimes they hunted on land belonging to a woman Hadley said was almost ninety. They mended her fences while they were there. All this when Hadley was in his eighties: cross-country trips, sleeping on wood floors, big game hunts, mending fences.

I drove across the state one day to meet Hadley's cousin, Edith Emma. She was his sister Dessie Mae's daughter. Edith was eighty-five and worked as a restaurant hostess from 11:00 am until 8:00 pm. A few days later, I visited Otto's daughter Olive. She was ninety-one and lived with an enormous black dog alone on her farm. He must have had Newfoundland in him. Olive said somebody dumped him by the side of the road when he was a pup small enough for a shoebox. The dog was devoted to her but one day knocked Icel flat.

Hadley once said to me, "Sometimes in the morning I'll be lying in bed, thinking about how I need to get up and start doing things, and I'll hear Dad's voice, 'Do it now, Barney. Sometime ain't never time. Do it now.'" I was never around a Thompson without feeling a bit lazy compared to them.

Back on Crismon's farm it did just like Dad said. Them hogs got as fat as any in the county. Now, did he ever think for a minute what could have happened if they'd have got cholera? Nobody vaccinated back then. I wonder if Dad ever realized how much he stuck his neck out. If it had started raining again Dad could have lost the whole cotton pickin' works, just to help a friend. But throughout October and November the weather held. No more rains. Autumn became winter. Uneventful.

I don't remember how long it took them hogs to eat up that mess. Most of the winter anyway. By spring those hogs was plenty fat. We had almost a thousand of them and they'd gone up to three and a half cents a pound. Then we had to drive them up the river onto another man's farm, then to the ferryboat to be taken across the river, through the streets of Bagnell and finally shipped out in several rail cars. Ferryman gave us a deal because of all the trips. It took days to get them loaded and shipped out.

We got the hogs shipped to market and got the money back. Dad paid off the note at the bank and gave all the rest to Crismon. It was more than enough to save the farm. It seemed like a happy ending. To this day, not to my knowledge, have we ever been paid for anything, like the fencing wire and so forth.

Leo's journal recalls a much different story:

In the fall of November, 1919, my father allowed Grant Thompson and his son-in-law, Dell Popplewell, [married Dessie Mae Thompson] to put some hogs on fields of corn overflowed by the river. When they went to figure up the account and make payment, by breaking up the time into small periods and leaving out a day or two between periods, the amount figured by them was too small.

It was necessary for my father to call attention to the matter, and although they paid the exact amount, it was evident that the difference in figuring was not accidental and that they resented his catching it and calling it to attention. It has already been pointed out that father was appointed Justice of the Peace in Glaize Township. Dell Popplewell was being sued for a debt in his own township. Grant Thompson had him to get the case tried in Glaize Township before my father, at the same time trying to influence my father to make a decision in favor of Dell Popplewell. Because of the evidence presented in the case (I remember being present and hearing W.S. Stillwell, deceased in January 1953, present the case against Popplewell, I remember him addressing my father as "Your Honor) my father did not see fit to decide the case as Grant Thompson desired.

From that time Grant Thompson and members of his family began to try to drive us out of the community by various underhand methods and also by open antagonism. In passing by our house on the way to Bagnell or other places they carried guns and held them pointed towards the house. Also threatening and insulting gesticulations were performed by them as they passed the house.

Posted in the *Miller County Sentinel*, from Iberia, Missouri, are two small articles of interest. A 14 November 1919 column reads, "Fred Crismon, who bought the Moles farm of the Osage River near Bagnell about a year ago, suffered a heavy loss by the recent overflow. He lost about $2,000 worth of corn." The 21 November edition notes, "Grant Thompson of near Bagnell was here Thursday for the purpose of buying hogs. He and Fred Crismon are now feeding about 250 head and want about 100 more. They have a lot of corn damaged by the recent flood that must be fed at once." Both the newspaper accounts and Leo's recollections put the flood years earlier than Hadley recounted.

Then, once again, it was Decoration Day, nineteen and twenty-three. I was twelve, and Joe had decided to go to the Teachers Academy in Iberia. We start-

ed the same ritual as always. Up before dark, the giant sycamore stood and watched us getting ready to go, all black during the first rays of dawn, and then, by the time we drove the wagon past on the way to the cemetery, its flakey, white bark shone with dew in the morning sun.

When we drove along the road closer to the cemetery, we met up with other wagons, and the men pulled beside their pals to visit along the way. Nobody was in much of a hurry except the boys showing off on fast horses in front of the girls. This was the time there might be a new girl, a cousin or niece, visiting from off for the summer, and it was important to let her know, right then and there, who you were.

Old Man Sons rode up, tipped his hat and showed his yellow smile to Mother, who nodded back only as cordial as she had to be. Then he leaned over toward Dad,

"Looks like Estol'll be plowing up gumbo this year. Heard that little filly of his is about to pop." There it was again, God talking to us through our crops. Remarks like this were not fit for ladies' ears and one of the reasons Mother avoided Sons. He saved his manners for Sunday services, where they were fresh each week as they were rarely used in between.

There were no new girls there; the only new kid in the neighborhood was Logan Hickey and we'd already met him. We saw the new babies born over the winter, and a new grave was there from a death in March. We planted some bulbs Mother had brought for that. The widow, covered in pure black, couldn't even speak but in a whisper, and the women waited on her while she sat apart, under a tree. It was her first Decoration Day in forty years without her husband.

Mother asked me to fetch her some water. I got it right away, hoping that nothing else would prevent the women from announcing it was time to eat. When I set the pail down in front of her she asked,

"That Charley?"

I turned. There's old Charley. Big tough Charley, always first into the brush, always there to take up the slack, there's Charley helping some girls down from a wagon. But he's not just offering an elbow, like, "I'm doing what Dad says to do. Help the ladies and mind your manners around them." No Sir! Charley was offering that lopsided grin of his and those blue eyes that could charm a rattlesnake outta its rattles. Strong hands cupped the waist of the last girl while curls and flowered cotton swung up in a circle, until she settled, blushing, just a leaf on the ground. All like he was sayin', "Think I'll try what my brother Joe's been talking about all these years."

"Yep," I said. "That'd be Charley."

Before we ate, Cox asked that we gather around, up toward the fence, so he could talk to us a minute. He said he would be going away for a while. This was shocking news to us. It was like announcing the river would be changing course next week. Then he gave a talk about his "brothers" in Eldon, other preachers, who sold the souls of their flock to the devil. He meant giving names of congregation members to Klan organizers.

My sister Gipsy was there and announced she would not be teaching school come fall. We still had a few more weeks in our term, of course. So it looked like Otto would be my teacher next year. Always new announcements on Decoration Day.

Everything unfolded just like it always did, but still no Plez. And then? Ah, there they were… the sound of the even trot on a dirt road, hooves controlled and measured like a timepiece. Closer now, then quicker, full of life. A nice canter coming up the last hill and Plez was there, pulling up his horse at the last minute in a delicate bit of dust. His fine hands threw the reins my way and he was off to make the rounds like always.

I can see it all so clear in my mind. Over to the women first. "Stop whatever you're doing!" There he is, snitching a bite and getting a playful slap for his trouble. Giggles, snickers, and a pinch for Aunt Maggie that no one's supposed to see.

Then on to the kids. Give the lucky one a quarter. Then to the men. Paul and me, we hang around with his horse as a ploy so we can be nearer to him. Same as every other year, there's the flask and the jokes; this time he tells about One Tit Nellie. She's one of the women living at the White House in Bagnell and we boys freeze, listening, pressed against the warm flanks of the grazing horse, hoping none will see and shoo us away. They say the one Nellie has is larger than both a regular woman's and the men laugh. Paul and me, we're amazed our dad and them are talking about this like they was boys. Plez could charm thunder outta the clouds.

Then it goes to bloodlines, of course, and politics, and some talk about the Klan because the new president now, Harding, has supposedly joined as well. Then Plez catches sight of Charley chasing Anita Crismon. She's laughing, braids flying and carrying on, with something in her hand. Charley lets her stay just in front of him, because if he really catches her, her dad'll make sure the game's over. But Charley, he's learned a few things from Joe, and he gets some of the smaller children in on the game and then it's nice and innocent. Fred turns back to the group with Plez.

"Better be sure they know they's cousins." Plez winks at Fred and jerks his head at the game of kids chasing each other.

Fred Crismon just looks at Plez and doesn't say nothing, waiting for Plez to go on. He's not been laughing like the other men.

"No wonder you two get along so well," Plez says, looking at Dad and Fred.

Plez tries again, "You'uns don't know what I'm talkin' about?" Nothing but blank stares as Plez looks from Dad to Mr. Crismon, and they stare back at him.

"Sure. The Thompsons and the Crismons, kin. Emma Olive Ponder had a brother, Oscar F. Ponder."

"Yessir. I met Oscar," says Dad.

Plez picks up a stick and makes a E.O.P. and a O.F.P. in the dirt. Above that he writes Winslow P. March 30, 1881. Then he says, "Oscar Ponder married the daughter of Isaac Crismon and Sarah Rowden Crismon. Jennie Crismon. Sarah Rowden died real young." Plez draws lines that connect the J.C. to the O.F.P.

Dad says, "Oscar's wife was a Crismon? Only met them once, at the wedding."

Then Plez draws the lines down from the union of Jennie and Oscar. "Jennie's family was Liza, who married a Massey, Ann, who married William Clayton as his second wife, Asa, Carol and Rufe. Rufe was also married to a woman named Liza, and when he died, his widow married her father-in-law, Isaac Crismon, Jennie's father."

Plez takes his stick and to diagrams it all in the dirt, but we're kind of lost anyway.

We hear Fred Crismon say, "A Crismon never married a Ponder."

Plez shrugs and takes a swig from his flask and smiles at him with a perfect smile, all white and square. Later, it's time to eat and everybody's having a good time, like they always do. My sister Annie is there with her husband Neil Thompson and she's going to have a baby any day now. Neil tries to keep his hands off her, because even married folks should watch that kind of thing around others, but he gives Annie's backside a little pat as he passes next to her. She stops and keeps smiling at whoever's talking, but I see her take a step back and slide her fanny back against his palm.

There's Charley standing next to two men talking about a horse trader in the area. His back is to Anita, who in turn is facing her mother and friends. Then Charley sways a half a step back, until his shoulder presses Anita's long hair against her back. The clouds continue their travels across the sky while the earth rotates on its axis, yet Anita holds her ground until some other force of nature draws her right leg back toward my brother's. As loud as a slap in the morning air I can hear her skirt touch my brother's trouser leg. I doubt I'd notice such a thing today, but then, it might as well been an oak uprooting itself to fall across a table of food.

Mrs. Crismon frowns at Anita and says, "Sister, go help with the little ones." Anita goes, but not after staring straight at her mother with a small jilt of her chin.

Mrs. Hawkins has brought gooseberry cobbler. Gooseberries canned and saved from the summer before. That's the best news all day, because gooseberry cobbler is her pride and joy. Fred Crismon is in line next to Plez, and they're going down the table shoulder to shoulder. As we all could have predicted, the ladies let Plez just show up and eat.

Now here's the thing I whispered to my brothers in the dark that night. Fred and Plez are right across from me and between lips clenched in a smile, balancing a plate of fried chicken, spring lettuce and cobbler, Crismon leans over and says in Plez's ear, "I'll dang your dick in the dirt if I catch you tellin' that lie again."

Plez just flashes those beautiful teeth of his, looking right past Crismon's shoulder, and calls out, "Miz Blankenship! These are the finest biscuits I ever seen! Rode all the way from Arkansas for 'em!" Mrs. Blankenship shakes her head and scowls at him for flirting with her so. She's eighty if she's a day, but I can tell she likes it just the same. Everybody likes Plez.

According to both the *Miller County Autogram* and the *Eldon Advertiser*, local farmers had a hard time in 1923. First, there was a drop in cattle prices, followed by another drop in grain prices. Numerous foreclosures were announced by the sheriff for inability to pay tax debts. Farms were frequently for sale or at auction. One headline referring to Miller County at the end of the year read, "Assessment for 1923 Slumps Near A Million Dollars."

As a family, even the Thompsons were not exempt. Newspaper announcements show the bank of Crocker, Missouri vs. Grant's oldest daughter Dessie and husband Dell, for failure to pay taxes. After many such recordings throughout 1923, their farm, 170 acres southwest of Tuscumbia, was sold in a sheriff's sale. Eighty years later their daughter told me about the time Dessie and her children were cleaning out the attic after Dell's passing. They found a Klan robe and hood in a box. Dessie told her children not to tell anyone. Were Frederick Crismon and Dell members of the same Klavern? Leo's personal account states his father traded his Maxwell car to Dell for a mule because the car was unreliable. By now there were other active Klaverns in nearby areas within Miller County. From what we now know about repercussions against Klan members, two events are plausible. The group may have felt repercussions in order against Crismon for finding Klan member Dell Popplewell guilty in the previously mentioned lawsuit. As well, the Klavern may have pressured Dell to get his father-in-law Grant Thompson to join.

Despite the hardships of the times, in 1923 older brother Clyde Thompson was doing well enough to buy a new Ford while on a trip to Jefferson City. He had been proprietor of the Brumley Roller Mill for years.

Life was getting tougher than usual for some of our neighbors. It was hard times. But the Klan knew all the answers. They were going to blame rough times on somebody, and if you was against the Klan, you was the cause. Trouble started getting closer to us as well.

Some time in the early part of the summer, Mother, Dad, and my brother Paul went to Eldon. They went in that nineteen and seventeen Ford car that my dad bought a few years back, the one that was supposed to be bad luck. On the way home, they drove onto the ferryboat and after they pushed off from the bank in Bagnell side, Crismon walked up to Dad's side of the car. Suddenly there he was, bending his tall frame down to look in the window. Thin red hair falling into his face, squinting his eyes in Dad's face. He growled, "Listen you old forty-gallon Baptist you, I want that ninety-nine dollars you owe me on that hog deal, you son-of-a-bitch."

This really took my father by surprise, but he said, "Well Fred, I don't know about the ninety-nine dollars, but I've never taken a son-of-a-bitch from anyone in my life." And Dad started to get out. Crismon tried to draw a gun out of his coat pocket and the hammer evidently caught in the lining. The ferryboat man, Mr. Howser, saw something was wrong and grabbed the gun from Crismon. By then the ferry was at the south bank and Dad, Mother, and Paul drove off.

That evening Mother and Dad told us kids what happened. We were sitting out on the porch and the next thing you know, we look up and see a cloud of dust, rising from behind the ridge where the sycamore is, and we know strangers are coming down the road. Dad says, "Charley, get my gun off the wall." But before Charley even gets back outside, we know it's no matter, it's just a bunch of Dad's fox-hunting friends. They come on up, sit down, and start telling Dad what was going on with the KKK. Dad had been put on a blackball list. Folks was told they shouldn't bring their business to Dad's black-smithing shop or thresh together neither.

"How'd you know this?" Dad asked.

"It's the word around, is all."

Dad said he weren't paying Crismon nothing. Said nothing was owed, and that he'd never been paid for all the fence wire anyway. Seemed about the end of it. Crismon would calm down after a bit.

We still had a week or two left of school, and that was always the best time of year, if you can remember those days. The teacher's in a good mood, kids know school's almost out and suddenly they realize it weren't so bad after all. They start thinking how they're going to miss their teacher reading to them, or games at recess and things like that. The weather is warm and the door of the school is left open so fresh air can tempt everybody with the promise of summer.

Miss Gipsy had just come in for the morning. She'd already missed jab-bing herself in the head when she pinned up her hair. She'd taken off her tatted cuffs and laid them in the top drawer. We were opening our books to get ready for our studies and the little ones were lined up on the front bench for their lessons with the teacher. Suddenly, there were men in that room, coming up to the front. There weren't no place in that little room for any kind of a private conversation.

"Miss Gipsy, we are here representing the school board. We come to inform you that you have been relieved of your duties."

She just stared at them. Then, "But I haven't finished the term yet. We've still got two more weeks."

Les Leids, Elisha Stark, Mr. Gover, Pud Downs, Lester Vaughn. They all stood there looking like they owned the place while she was the one who was trespassing. Suddenly Gipsy looked very small. I thought, "Just do what you do to any bully, Miss Gipsy. Give it right back to 'em. Stand your ground." But she didn't, she just said,

"But why? If it's the money you're worried about, I'll finish for now and you can pay me next year."

"Ain't gonna be no next year for you. We've written to the superintendent and you are hereby absolved of any of your teaching duties from now on any-wheres in Miller County."

Then, meek as a field mouse, "But why? What have I done? I love these children. I don't want to leave them."

"It's not fit for these young'uns to hear."

She waited, so still, white-faced. Just looked at the men. None of us moved. I don't think we breathed, neither. She sat down, very primly in her chair. Back straight as hickory. Then finally, ah, there was the Gipsy we knew. The Gipsy with her bat and quick-thinking ways.

In a strong voice, "I've not done anything my students can't know about. Whatever your lies are, you might as well speak them now, because they'll hear them soon enough when they get home." We never been so quiet. Not one squirming bottom on those wood seats. Not one eye drifting to the window. Not one toe sneaking toward the door to be first outside.

I stared at the men and at their boots and knew I'd seen some of those boots out in the woods, in a ravine behind Kidwell's farm. I looked up at the front. It took five of those men to face one five-foot-nothin' woman? I knew then what coyotes they were. Couldn't they keep their business for the end of the day? Of course not. They had to shame her.

Les Leids sighed. He smirked. Ba-a-a-a. He glanced at all of us, then back to Miss Gipsy, sitting like an angel, hands folded in her lap. Leids was loving this. He was really the big shot now. All those times when people didn't pay no heed to him, now everything was different. He was the big man here, with his pack breathing behind him and a lone woman sitting in front of him.

He stared right at her. He waited. Took a breath, "All right then. You've been fired on moral charges. You've been seen out with your brother."

All he got was a bunch of blank stares.

Leids got irritated when he got no reaction. Then he said louder, "Courting! You and your brother, Jim Thompson." There were some gasps and murmurs throughout the room, and nobody was more surprised than I was. I looked over at Charley. We stared at each other. I could feel my face getting red and hot.

Gipsy jumped up, mad now. "That's a lie! And you've nothing but dirty, filthy minds to think such a thing. He's no relation you silly man."

"No? You Thompsons are a perverse bunch. Your sister Annie married a Thompson. Now they's expecting a kid and you know that ain't right."

"There's no relation there either!" But she never got to tell them that Jim was no relation by blood and that they'd never spent one night under the same roof in all their born days. Now I realize they knew all that, because everybody knew Maston Wornell; they just wanted to get rid of her. One man stepped in front facing all of us and said, "School dismissed for the year. Go to your

homes." The other two tried to take Miss Gipsy by the elbows out of the school, but she shook off their hands, for it was an insult that they would want to touch her like that. And that was the miserable end of the school year in 1923.

Then a few days later we heard it was time to vote on the schoolteacher for next year. All done by the men, same as usual. Women hadn't gotten the vote yet in Wilcox Bend. When Dad came home he was fit to be tied. Francis Crismon had been voted in as schoolteacher.

By 1923, the Wilcox Bend Klavern was predominately against those with loose morals: that alcohol drinking, non-church going, gambling, lewd dancing, and cousin-marrying group of people who were leading Miller County down the primrose path of destruction. Unfortunately for the Thompsons, their 'live and let live' philosophy and their wild ways put them right in the way of the Klan.

The illegitimate Gipsy was a big problem in the Klan's eyes, as her existence was an obvious byproduct of immorality. Thanks to Maston Wornell refusing to hide his daughter's baby, everyone knew Myrtle Thompson had the child out of wedlock. To make matters worse, this example of immorality became a model for youngsters when Gipsy became a teacher.

Gratefully, Frederick P. Crismon's grandson kept family information that he generously shared long after this story had unfolded. Both Hadley and the newspapers referred to Grant Thompson's standing in the community. Hadley noted any standing was well-earned. But Crismon family accounts describe how Thompson connections, particularly Uncle Lev's affiliation with the Bank of Brumley, gave the Thompsons unfair advantages on numerous occasions. Grant's mother had smuggled the family's gold into Missouri in a nail keg during the Civil War to start that bank. Clearly, this was an advantage to the family. But to the Thompsons it was an advantage they felt they earned.

The summer came and went. We threshed together that year, but things were all business with whispering and low talk and none of the relaxed happy times I remember from before. Then the weather turned cold for good. The days shortened along with the work times, and meals got longer.

The kitchen was the warmest place in the house. Mother would make a special pot of coffee for us after supper, and we boys would start in on the wooden bucket of peanut butter under the table. One of us would grab the leftover biscuits from the warming oven over the stove, and we'd eat peanut butter on biscuits, drink coffee, and talk. All of that was a real luxury, and we knew how lucky we were. Many nearby families didn't have near that much.

School started again and sure enough, Francis Crismon was our teacher. At school, he didn't pick on me like I was afraid he might. If you asked any kid that wasn't a Thompson, they'd tell you Francis wasn't a half-bad teacher. He was strict enough that the older boys didn't take over the room, but was nice to the little ones. He wasn't as fun as Miss Gipsy, but he weren't all that bad neither. Logan Hickey was still living with the Crismons and attending school at Post Oak. He and Leo were the pals, not us.

But if a Thompson asked to use the outhouse, the answer was always to hold it until the lesson was over. Or, if a Thompson needed a pencil, Francis didn't have one to loan. And if ten kids, three Thompsons and seven others, raised their hands, a Thompson wasn't the one that got called on. Probably nobody noticed this but us. Just like the water bucket during threshing.

Something else only I seemed to notice was about Charley. He was the oldest student, only one year younger than our teacher. He'd been pestering Mother to make sure he had clean clothes every morning, and he started wearing shoes. He never wanted to go down to the river to fish after school. He just wanted to walk home. Then I caught him walking with Anita Crismon, her hair hanging loose about her shoulders, and Charley was doing all the talking.

Girls had been eyeing him for years, giggling and trying to get his attention, but he never took much notice. Anita usually stayed by herself too, drawing pictures for the little ones and helping them with their schoolwork if they needed it. My brother Otto's daughter Olive was especially fond of her. Then all of a sudden, every time Anita was around, there was Charley, picking up something too heavy for anyone else, challenging somebody to arm wrestle or carrying Anita's books home from school.

Most of us boys took a gun to school so we could squirrel or rabbit hunt on the way home. I liked a little Winchester single shot .22. Charley preferred a .16 gauge L. C. Smith shotgun. We was supposed to leave our guns by the door and not shoot anything until we was out of the school yard, but Charley loved to shoot as much as he loved tobacco.

One day that fall there were ducks going over all day. Huge flocks of 'em, and during recess time old Charley just couldn't resist, so he grabbed his gun from where it leaned up against the building and Bamm! Bamm! He shot almost straight up, just as cool as a fifty-pound block of ice. Thud! Thud! Two ducks. Right there at his feet! Then he handed them to a skinny kid who never had much in his lunch pail to take home with him.

All the kids loved it and boy, what a racket! Not since the day Gipsy silenced Buster Leids had there been such delight at the schoolhouse. I know part of the reason he done it was to impress Anita and the other part was to madden Francis Crismon. And I have to say, nobody was better at both than a Thompson.

The plan backfired. Francis was furious. Now, I still to this day don't think Francis was a mean-spirited guy. I know there was that time with the bucket during threshing and all, but you got to remember, things were different. Just the week before, I hid up in a tree until some poor soul walked underneath, just so I could jump down and scare the living daylights outta somebody that never done nothin' to me. But right at this point, the Klan started to let some of the older boys, like Francis and Joe's age, join up as well. Maybe he joined, I don't know. But that group's kind of thinking took over like wildfire. Nothing was just for fun. Everything had to mean something serious.

So here's what happened next. We went inside and started the lesson on science. I remember him saying, "You marry your cousin, and it's been proven your kids won't be right. They might talk funny or have a queer-looking thumb." He was looking right at Anita, kinda like telling his sister this guy's no good and you don't want to get messed up with him. Then he kept talking, saying God gave out signs, warnings so people could see what was right and what wasn't, and he was looking right at Charley's bad thumb. The one that got caught up in the grinder.

So Charley just leans back in his chair, pulls out a big wad of tobacco from his pocket, shoves it in his mouth and commences to chew. Loudly. Charley'd drawn the first line in the dirt. Francis stepped over. Charley stepped closer. He coulda beat the tar outta Francis any day, but Francis was teacher. You was supposed to respect the teacher.

Charley couldn't just set there to let Francis insult him and his bloodlines, now could he? So many rules and they were all starting to clash. Finally, just in case there was one person in that room that didn't know he was chewin', Charley spit tobacco juice out the window. Thwat! Chicken Fat would've been proud.

Francis called Charley up to the front of the schoolhouse. He put Charley in a corner and drew a ring on the wall. Charley was barefoot that day. Francis told him to put his nose in the ring on the wall, and to do that Charley had to stand on his tip-toes. Then Francis had two girls to stand by him with hat pins. And what do you know, they were John's trash gals — Suzzie Leids and her friend.

Every time Charley's heels touched the floor, Francis told them to stick him with the pins. They done him that way until the end of the day. They stuck so many pins in him, I can still see the blood running down on the floor. Down poor old Charley's leg to his bare feet. But he didn't complain none. He took it. Couldn't show Francis he'd won. When we got home and told what happened that day, Dad was furious. He talked about that incident with a lot of people. Now both families seemed bent on destroying the other's reputation. And Anita? Didn't do no good what her brother done. She and Charley both started sneaking out so they could meet in the woods. Charley didn't go back to school after that. He was too old anyway.

The next thing we knew, my dad and mother and my brother Joe came back from town and had to pass by the Crismon house. That road went right by their place, maybe twenty-five yards from their front porch. Fred Crismon ran out with his wife and two sons, cursing my folks out, claiming he heard Dad and his friends had started a secret group. Had they? I don't know, but I don't think Dad was a part because we'd've known if he left the farm for meetings. I know Dad's friends talked about the idea though.

Anyway, no shots were fired that day. Mrs. Crismon was out there too, with a shotgun. We'd never heard of such a thing. My folks beat it out of there fast and came home. Everyone was pretty shook up. Now from this time out, for the next year and a half, anytime we passed the Crismon house, there was always some kind of trouble — sometimes pretty serious.

As Hadley's story journeyed from idyllic boyhood toward adversity, he would often stop, searching for the right words. "Even now, I get all emotional thinking about it," he'd shake his head and say. Although I knew the ending of the story after our first meeting together, our research and interviews jumped around in time and subject. That day, after knowing Hadley for two years, we were discussing the shootings more in depth. I started finding notices announcing Klan meetings in the newspapers and was excited to bring these over to the Thompsons thinking they would intrigue Hadley.

However, when I went back to the bright blue-green house on that day, he wasn't interested in any of those findings. Once again Hadley decided he didn't want to talk. "I just want to forget the whole thing," he said. "There's no justice. They're all dead now, so what's the point?"

But Icel told me not to worry; he was just tired. And sure enough, soon after this incident, Hadley went into the hospital for an ailment not curable by Icel's homemade cobbler. It was an extended stay. He was ill for months.

When Hadley was finally able to have visitors, I said to him, "If we get this story written and it gets published, you can have half of whatever it brings. Then you could do something with the money and in a small way, at least some good might come from it all."

"I want to give my half to the Salvation Army," he said.

I believe that Old Man Sons knew about us sneaking out because of the night with Tommy Alexander. I don't know where Sons lived when the weather turned really bad, but whenever I knew him, he was camping in the woods. Spring, summer, winter and fall, he'd stay down by the river with his smoke pit and a huge orange cat for weeks on end.

I'm going to tell you about a certain night. By that time the KKK had moved to the schoolhouse and they used that building for meetings from that year on, unless they was going to burn a cross or worse. We were still sneaking around in the night, spying on them and struggling out of bed the next morning for chores. Otto had stopped going. I think this might have been a problem for him, because once men were in with all the secrets and everything, they weren't supposed to leave the group.

When the Klan met at the schoolhouse, we'd crawl all the way up to the windows and stay underneath the windows to listen. This was much preferred to the meetings near Kidwell's ridge, because we were closer now and could hear better. The men inside always talked real fancy with their made-up words and little ceremonies. The end of the meeting was usually the best, with all sorts of rituals. We always had good warning about when they were finishing and could high tail it out of there and back down the path by the time the first man stepped outside. Sometimes other kids were there as well, watching with us.

This one time that year, I think it was Joe and me. There was a full moon, a yellow harvest moon, which everybody knows holds water. The perfect night to sneak out.

We were sitting in the shadows there, pressed alongside of the building, when we heard a wagon coming through the timber road. We swung around to the other side of the building, then waited in the brush and watched. It was

Les Leids driving with somebody in the back, somebody curled up, thrashing about and groaning. Once in a while the man cried out, holding his head one minute and his stomach the next. It was terrible. I'd never seen someone suffer so. And all this time, Joe and I are flattened in the shadows, hoping and praying nobody sees us. We can't believe nobody hears the man in the back of the wagon and comes out to help him. But they don't.

Leids acts like he doesn't even notice the body he just brought up. He just jumps down, ties up his team, and goes into the meeting. A few minutes go by. Nobody comes out to help the man. Nothing but the horse snorting and pawing at the ground a bit, more groaning, and the wagon creaking as the body rolls from one side to the other. Still just Joe and me.

The body in the wagon was still. Was he dead? Why wasn't anyone coming out to help him?

Then a loud groan. "Help me. Somebody help me. I cain't see nothin'. I'm dying."

Joe whispers, "Come on. Let's go."

Joe was the big brother and he called the shots. We left. We ran down the path and went to Sons's place along the bank and told him what we'd seen. He just shook his head and told us to be careful.

He never told us anything like, "You shouldn't be doing those things." Which brings me to why we never told Dad. I don't know. It was wrong of us. All we thought about was we shouldn't have been there; they were adults, we were kids, and we weren't supposed to be in their business.

Later, Joe told me the man in the wagon was Tommy Alexander, with fusil oil poisoning. Inside Leids was telling everyone that Tommy swore the liquor came from the McDowell's or Thompson's still. Well now, I know for a fact it didn't come from Dad's because we never saw Tommy at our farm. And anyway, wouldn't Dad or Jim gotten sick from the batch too?

And I don't think it came from McDowell's neither. From what I gather, Tommy was either poisoned deliberately, or by some fool who didn't really know what they was doing. Those old timers, they really knew how to make the stuff. They'd done it all their lives. They didn't rush things. One thing McDowell knew how to do was make a good batch of brew.

You know what I think? I think Leids poisoned him on purpose, just to get folks riled up. Why? Because he was a son-of-a-bitch. And because to him, Tommy was one of the lesser people. I remember how he acted when he pulled up. He never even checked on Tommy. No, I wouldn't put nothin' past Les Leids. And nobody else ever got sick from that stuff. Tommy was the only one.

What does that tell you? It tells you there never was no poisoned batch of whiskey. There was just a little bit, meant to do in two men: Tommy Alexander and Grant Thompson.

Remember now, Leid's still was hidden under that trap door, so as far as Crismon and the others was concerned, Les Leids was a teetotaler. Maybe he told everyone he reformed. Saw the evil in his ways. Gave up the devil's brew. No, I wouldn't put it past him to have done it on purpose.

Tommy died in that wagon. There wasn't anything they could have done to save him. Everybody knew that, but they could've at least given him a blanket for under his head.

Economic stress was now widespread in Wilcox Bend. With the unexpected popularity of the automobile, by the early 1920s the Missouri Pacific and Rock Island railroads reduced plans for expanding. Their requests for new ties diminished. Before 1920, when the railroad bought railroad ties from locals with cash, they believed hand-hewn ties would last longer, so those brought a higher price than the ones produced in a lumber yard. This was of great advantage to Wilcox Bend natives, who made their ties by hand. Now things were different.

By the mid 1920s, locals were left with one less way to make money, grain prices continued to stay down, and many farmers had to make a living elsewhere. For years the Thompsons enjoyed the status and privileges of having a teacher in the family. Teachers were paid in cash, and although a paltry sum, that salary was still a valuable commodity. Other work in the area relied heavily on trade, barter, or writing scrip. Teaching and selling railroad ties were the two exceptions. For almost fifteen years, someone from the Thompson family, JoAnna, Otto, or Gipsy, was the teacher. Now a Crismon was teacher. Grant might not have taken the change lightly.

Hadley had stated that a "big ruckus" occurred every year when the folks of Wilcox Bend decided who would be their teacher. Many historical accounts of voting for the schoolteacher in the Ozarks include threats, accusations, fistfights, and even shootings. Did Hadley's reference to ruckus mean flinging around fists or just words?

That year, Francis was elected teacher of Post Oak School Number Forty-Nine, when Otto Thompson clearly wanted the job. We know KKK chapters were encouraged to practice Klanishness, supporting KKK members to the exclusion of others. Was this an example of Klanishness or was Francis believed to be the better teacher?

It was 1923. Otto was thirty-three years old and married with three children. He also had years of teaching experience. He had a teaching degree from the teacher's college in Iberia, Missouri with additional college credits from Warrensburg, Missouri.

Francis Crismon was nineteen and according to the Crismon historians had attended the Iberia Teacher's Academy for one year. However, later newspaper accounts only mention the Eldon High School. As the newspapers would later report, he was also an active member of the Klan.

Other boys besides the Thompsons watched Klan meetings in the forest or through the schoolhouse windows. All of the ones I interviewed stated they recognized community leaders during those events; constables, other justices of the peace besides Frederick Crismon, and pastors other than Simon Cox.

"If they was wearing hoods, all we had to do was look at their feet. We could tell who they was by their walk, their boots, their horses, their voices. There weren't that many people around back then. We saw a preacher from the Elm Spring Church, and the justice of the peace from Bagnell," claimed a local resident.

Hadley stated,

> They had talked about getting our sheriff to join. It was very important to them, and they talked about that for a while. Then one night, there he was. He was the one who always came to visit Dad and share some whiskey. They announced somebody had paid his fee for him. They really wanted him in their group.

More formal research supports these trends. Klan committee minutes from a 1923 klavern in the state of Oregon describe ministers and their involvement in Klan organization. Their activities include giving sermons on the benefits of being protestant, planning St. Patrick's Day festivities, and declaring that the Klan originated during the days of Christ. Minutes throughout the year also note donations made to ministers of various churches.

The KKK has always claimed to be a Christian organization. There is bittersweet humor in the Oregon group's ignorance. They planned a St. Patrick's Day celebration, oblivious to its origins as a Catholic Saint's celebration. As well, Klansmen frequently referred to one of their favorite quotes from the book of Judges, when this is actually a book of Hebraic law. Ironic, considering their professed hatred of both Catholics and Jews.

The McDowells were good people. Simple folk. They'd been in the area since before the Civil War and had a few generations of twelve kids each. When a McDowell met another McDowell they didn't know, they'd ask, "Are you a Dog Creek or a Bear Creek McDowell?" There were so many of them in the area even they didn't know how they were related sometimes.

Quite a few McDowells didn't own land — they rented. And they hired themselves out to help others. The ones around us, they owned some land, but it wasn't real good. When it came to farming, for the most part they were just putting one foot in front of the other. McDowells tended to mind their own business and tried to get by.

There was Walter McDowell, over in Anderson Hollow, where folks could get anything they wanted. He made a nice batch of white lightening. Then there was Arthur, the one who got into trouble with the Klan. He sold minnows to make money. He was an uncle to Charlie, a pal of mine. There was a bunch of them. They fought amongst themselves sometimes, but never any gunplay I ever heard about.

The Klan claimed Arthur McDowell was with another woman besides his wife. They claimed they had proof he was making moonshine. They claimed they was better than the lot of us. Some of those men, the ones sitting on their makeshift benches, I know they done the same as all their claims, but Arthur was just an easy target.

So here's what happened the last time I attended a KKK rally. I'll never forget it. Everybody was back outside for this particular meeting. We'd scampered outdoors that night like we always did. Had to go see some of Joe's girls, and I think he proposed to three of 'em so we'd covered a few miles before we started up toward the ridge.

The moon was coming up as we got there. We crawled on our stomachs and elbows, dragging the rest of us along like lizards in the dust until we reached the crest over the ravine. They'd already started, so at first we was out on our side of the hollow, where we could hear the voices but not what they was saying. We was only half-buried under some bushes and if anyone'd come along, they'd have seen a row of dirty feet, sticking out from faded coveralls.

Fred Crismon and Les Leids, along with the henchmen Pud and Inky, were running the show now. Left on their own, I'm not sure Pud and Inky or even Fred Crismon would've caused the troubled they did. But they hooked up with Leids and when you wallow with pigs, you're bound to get dirty. The leaders was pointing to men sitting on the logs and making them stand up and then they'd sit down and the big wigs would say something else. But we couldn't figure out what that something was. So we crawled over to the other side of the ridge so we could hear.

"Irv Johnson. Is it true you've a Catholic deliverin' yer mail to yer house in Bagnell?"

"True enough, but what'm I to do about that?"

"Is the cost of a post office box dearer to you than your country?"

Irv sat down, hat in hand. Crismon and Leids peered at a list. I remember seeing Crismon's scalp shining in the moonlight through his thin hair when he leaned down to read. Leids was quite a bit shorter than him. Pud and Inky stood behind them. Pud could look over their shoulders, but old Inky couldn't hardly see nothin' with that belly of his always getting in the way.

"Herb Keller? You here?" one of 'em hollered.

Herb stood up, looking very uncertain.

"You were seen buying ice cream from that kraut Fritz Hohner in Bagnell. That so?"

Herb shrugged. "He's the only one who serves it. I promised my kids an ice cream cone."

"Is your love for your country something you don't teach your children?"

This went on for a while. Then they talked about the banks and that one bank, the Bank of Brumley, had Italians and a half-Indian as cashiers. So they was all supposed to take their money elsewhere. Then one man was told to stand up because he was a blacksmith and "closer to most of you than Grant Thompson." They reminded the group to take their work to him and not Dad.

Then Leids commanded everyone in the audience to bring in two new applications for members in the next two weeks and there would be a penalty if they didn't. Last, Klansmen were picked to be deputized to help the sheriff dispose of illegal stills.

Then the worst. Two members wearing hoods went into the brush and brought back a man, hands tied behind his wrists and a rag tied into his mouth. We couldn't tell who it was then, but later we saw. Then out came a cat-o-nine-tails. I didn't look but twice. They were tying him to a tree. I seen it was Arthur McDowell and I knew he didn't have the toughness Ty Sears had. I buried my face in the dirt and told Paul not to look, wrapping my arm around him and pulling him toward me. I heard the smile on Shorthair's face, and then a voice as cold as the grave said, "Let the lesson begin."

The second time I looked, the men were in a line, each taking one turn at the whipping. Arthur flinched with each stoke and quivered between them. We could hear him crying, even with the rag filling his mouth. Then we crawled back from there and ran faster than we'd ever run before. Down the path, though the brush in the moonlight, praying he wouldn't die and we wouldn't have to say we seen it all, vowing that was the last time we went into that snake pit. It was the last time. I saw enough to last a lifetime.

Arthur McDowell. They whipped him so hard that poor man, he just had the one set of coveralls. They shredded the back and he bled over all the rest. And how do I know that? Because the next thing I know, here come a stranger walking up our road and Dad ain't a bit surprised, nor is Mother. Arthur came to our house and Mother washed his clothes and mended them for him. I remember him sitting in the kitchen, wrapped in a horse blanket and seeing those coveralls hanging in the sun to dry. He didn't have nothing else. You can't believe they lived like that in those days, but they did. He'd been going around in them bloody, torn coveralls before he came to our house.

Some time after we quit going to the meetings, Mother was quilting. There were a few other ladies from the neighborhood there as well, and the talk came up about Arthur McDowell. Mother said how horrible it was, the whipping and all, and Mrs. Crismon said, "Yes, it is unfortunate, still and all, if someone's been warned and they are still going to break the law, you have to be stern with them or they won't stop what they are doing. We can't have people breaking laws."

There were plenty of people who didn't buy the KKK's insistence that they were a legitimate organization. Well-known orator William Allen White published a statement in the *New York World* stating, "The whole trouble with the Ku Klux Klan is that it is based upon such deep foolishness that it is bound to be a menace to good government in any community." There were other brave souls, like some of the people in Wilcox Bend, who tried to stand up and expose the group for what they were. One was Frank Burks, Democratic nominee for Miller Country Sheriff who in October of 1924 published this notarized statement in the *Eldon Advertiser:*

It is rumored that I am a member of an organization known as the Ku Klux Klan. I am not now nor ever was a member of such an organization and furthermore, I am not in sympathy with any such Klan or organization of the kind. In fact, I know very little about the matter of the Klan except what I see printed in the paper.

After paying their initiation fee, Klan members were strongly encouraged to start purchasing official KKK robes, hoods, and other regalia from the national chapter. These purchases provided even more money to the already wealthy national Klan organization. Although the Kleagles got their initiation money, stubborn Wilcox Bend natives often insisted on having their wives and daughters make their coverings from sheets to save money. Apparently other Americans were just as frugal, for there was a popular song during those times called, "Daddy Swiped the Last Clean Sheet."

Then something even more unbelievable happened. Joe and Dad went on into town and were shot at. I can hardly talk about it without getting emotional.

They had to go to Bagnell to get some cow feed and lumber, and some cement. They were driving a pretty feisty pair. Hyperactive horses, really, they were. You didn't just drive them any which way, they'd run away with you. But Joe could handle them. He was twenty and home from his studies at the Iberia Teacher's Academy.

So they had to ride past the Crismon house, of course. They got into town just fine, got the stuff and started back. The wagon bed held the cement and the feed, some hay, and a load of lumber in it too, I think. I don't know if you'll know what I'm talking about or not — you got a wagon with a seat across where you sit to drive — Dad and Joe were sitting on that seat. Like I said, Joe was driving. Just when they got by the Crismon house, here come Mr. Crismon, his wife, his two boys, and Logan Hickey. No words were passed. They came out shootin' and I mean shootin'. The same man we helped to save his farm.

Of course, the horses took off straight away because they got hit. Dad was thrown into the back of the wagon. He just got laid down. But anyway, Dad evidently stood up, probably just a reaction you know, because they shot at him and he got hit in the forearm and the chest and also in the forehead, but he threw up his arm and it saved his eyes.

Joe tried as hard as he could to control the horses and get the hell outta there. Which they did. My brother and father lived and the horses did too, and they all got home. But my brother Joe, he got hit in the shoulder, and to prove my point I can show you on my brother where he still carries number four shot in his back. When they got home, we picked forty, number thirteen shot out of Dad, in his arm, in his forehead, chest. But his eyes were saved. We picked

number four shot out of Joe as well. So two of the Crismons were aiming to
kill, because there were two different guns used.

Our farm had always been our refuge, but now she was becoming our
deathtrap.

The accounting of this scene was in the newspaper, as both the Tuscumbia and the Eldon newspapers started running frequent stories about the
feud as well as Klan activities. I read every word in those papers from
1923 through 1925. I found archival newspapers in two places, although
sometimes editions were missing. In addition, people often showed me
clippings they had saved, such as this description from an unknown
newspaper:

> Grant Thompson and son Joe were peppered with shot last Thursday
> by Fred Crismon near the home of the latter, about two miles east of
> Bagnell, as Mr. Thompson and son were returning home from Ba-
> gnell… Mr. Crismon was using a shot-gun loaded with No. 4 shot.
> Mr. Thompson was struck by thirteen shot and the son was struck by
> four.…

These articles as well as court records suggested Hadley's recollec-
tions were correct, although interestingly, Hadley told me not to believe
what the local papers said. He pronounced one editor as a Klan member and the other "scared of 'em." The papers had no record of Grant
Thompson ever being arrested or warned for violation of prohibition
laws, although many others were.

Leo Crismon's account written in the 1960s states:

> On one occasion (1923?) Grant Thompson was passing our place
> in his wagon. Otto was driving and Grant was down back of the seat
> protected by bags of grain or feed. He made threats against my mother
> who was in the barn yard. My father took a shot at him with a shotgun
> and one shot hit him in the face. My father, Francis and I were tried for
> this in the Miller Country Circuit Court at Tuscamia, before Judge
> Henry J. Westhues. Harry H. Kay of Eldon was Prosecuting Attorney
> and he was assisted by Barney Reed of Linn Creek. We were defended
> by W.S. Stillwell of Tuscumbia and Bill Irwin of Jefferson City. Judge
> Westhues dismissed the Charges against Francis and me before the

case went to the jury, and as I remember, the jury could not agree on a verdict because there seemed to be one man on it who was influenced by Lev Thompson, a brother of Grant Thompson.

During an interview with ninety-year-old Joe Thompson at his home, the subject of this shooting came up. Joe started struggling with his shirt, saying, "Look. Look here where they shot me." Despite my insistence that it was not necessary for me to view his naked torso, Hadley helped his brother off with his shirt and told me to feel Joe's shoulder. Under the skin on the right shoulder were indeed a group of obvious hard bumps. "I've carried that damn buckshot all my life," he growled. On the way home Hadley started to laugh. "I told you a shirt never suited Joe if there was a lady around!"

Judgement (1924)

—Courtesy Thompson Family

Miss Gipsy Warnell on the Tuscumbia Bridge

All right. Nineteen hundred and twenty-four.

The year started out in a way we never forgot. On January 2nd, the day after we'd tested our growth against the trunk of our giant sycamore, there was a freak storm. First there was snow, not bad at all. Then it started to sleet and rain. Thunder rolled up and down the river bottom like Mother Nature was caught between the hills and fighting to get out. The whole valley shook from the sound of it.

And the lightning. Oh my heavens, it almost hurt to look up at the sky, but we couldn't not do it. The light shot through the air, so close, reflecting off snow and water. Then, "Crack!" We knew we lost something to the storm and just hoped the livestock was safe.

Finally the weather lifted. We'd been waiting for this opportunity so we could take the wagon into town. Then we discovered soon enough the lightning's target: our sycamore was hit. Split in two, burned black by the bolt, it fell right across the road and we had to hitch up Moses to get it cleared away. You know, I still miss that darned tree. How can you mourn a tree? Answer me that one. Otto lost his draft horses, Bess and Banner, as well. Killed the minute the tree they was standing under was hit. Our Mother Nature did not play favorites.

Now I need to back up a bit and tell you that over near Brumley there were two men, and about this time Dad decided he'd play hot shot and get involved with them. Barney Reed, who owned a store in Ulman, was a big money man. Wolf Dawson was a big cattleman. And they had a cattle deal going from the stockyards in Kansas City, and Dad went in with this and bought twenty-three white-faced cattle and brought them down to the farm. Well, for those two other men, this wasn't that much of a gamble, but for Dad it was.

Dad had this herd for a while and all was fine, but one day early that year in 1924 he said to Mother, "Myrt, I got a funny feeling. I'm gonna sell the cattle." It's a good thing he did, because I'm telling you, it broke both Dawson and Reed. Bottom dropped out of the market, but Dad got out just in time. The money from that sale got us through the rest of the winter.

Spring was queer that year for there was only a mention of it. The dogwoods hardly bloomed and the ground was cold hard mud long past the normal time. Plowing was tough and men broke plows, very bad luck they thought, and it made them even more nervous than they usually were. It truly was bad luck and not just hill-country superstition, because they were forced to buy new plows quickly without any time to look for a good price.

This was the time of year men finished up on all the repairs needed for the season. Repairing harnesses, sharpening plows, fixing mangers, there was a long list awaiting each of them. In our family, Dad was usually real busy in his blacksmith shop with orders from neighbors during those months. But that year, besides a handful of old timers, there was nothing. Klanishness. The farm was paid for and we could support ourselves; Dad was concerned, but not panicked or anything like that. Thankfully, he had made some money on the cattle as well. Now it was time to work off the poll tax.

So that year, spring of nineteen and twenty-four, there was me, and Joe, Otto, and I believe Charley was with us, and Dad. I think there were four or five of us. We worked up the hill almost to where the Crismon barn was. And by God, here comes Fred Crismon and his two boys, and their nephew Logan, all armed with shotguns and one of the boys had a revolver. All we had was an axe, brush hook, shovel or fork of some kind. They started cussin' us to get out of there or they was going to shoot us. We got out of there pretty fast.

It was scary, yes, but the worst of it? This was the first time I saw my dad back down from anyone. I think now if it'd been just him, he'd have gone out swinging, swish, swish, swish and a few would never have walked the same again and Dad would've lost his life as well. But we were all there. Maybe it wasn't a hard decision for Dad, but it was still a real big one. Do you know what I mean? For him to back down like that.

Dad decided to turn Crismon in to the law. The sheriff had always been a friend. It was a county road and we were land-locked if we had to use a wagon or take Mother into town. Crismon's house was only a stone's throw from the road. So Dad filed charges for felonious assault, and he paid the poll tax with cash. That was in April of that year.

And what happened was nothing. The law was in the Klan. The Klan made up the juries. Same as what happened in a case come up involving Grandpa Blankenship and jury tampering. Nothing. Hung jury. Law couldn't do nothing.

The rule was, "Never corner something meaner than yourself." But now we were the ones getting cornered. They'd cornered us with Leids on one end and Crismon at the other. What I see now is that some on the other side, well now they was cornered too. They'd made a big commitment to live a certain way and let that group make their decisions for them. What happened if they didn't feel like going along with it all? What then?

Leo's account relates a different side:

> Again he pretended to be working on the road beside our barn one afternoon for an hour or two. My father, suspecting that there was some trick in it, called his bluff by walking from the house down towards the barn with his shotgun in his hands. My mother and Francis and I were behind him. When we approached the old man, Grant Thompson turned around and gave a signal and Otto and John, sons of his first wife, and Joe and Charley, sons of his second wife, came out from hiding with guns also. After making some threats he and his boys backed off and left.

Leo's accounts never refer to his family's affiliation with any Klan activities. So I asked his son Fred point blank if his father had ever mentioned the group. He responded,

> Funny you should ask. I was with Dad after my grandmother died, when we were cleaning out the attic and I found a rolled up certificate in a box. It was a membership order to the KKK with Leo Crismon's name on it. I said, 'Dad, what's this?' He mused, 'Well, well, well. I'd forgotten all about that. The group didn't really do much back then. Just harassed livestock and such.'

Increasing numbers of notices about Klan activities had already started to appear in the newspapers in 1924, such as this article about a town north of Eldon in Cole County.

Ku Klux Klan at Russellville

The rumor that there is an organization of the Ku Klux Klan at Russellville [in Miller County] seems borne out by the happenings of the past week. Last Friday night six Klansmen robed and hooded with the paraphernalia of the order visited the M.E. Church where a revival was in progress and made a substantial donation to the evangelist and singer. They walked quietly into the church and presented the donation together with a note commending the work of the pastors, and mysteriously retired, no one being able to tell from whence they came or where they went. Following this on Monday night it is reported that a large open air meeting was held in a field west of the town beneath a flaming cross — the emblem of the Klan. Entrances were said to have been strongly guarded and little is known of the meeting except rumors that it was attended by several hundred.

Newspaper coverage also described increasing cases claiming jury tampering in local courts, as Grandpa Blankenship had said, with no parties being found guilty.

Then finally it was May and time for Decoration Day again. The day was one of those first warm days in spring, when the sun feels hot enough to pull the buds right out of the ends of the twigs. We were at the cemetery after the work was done, waiting on supper. In four groups like always, with not much shifting in between. First the livestock: horses, wagons, a calf or two going to a new owner, all waiting under the trees. Second, the women, talking and laughing up by the church. Us kids were over by the pump. Last, the men, on the other side of the cemetery by some stakes set up for horseshoes.

The only thing new that day was a Kidwell cousin, come to be school-teacher at Blue Springs School until summer. Some of the older boys had run the last teacher off. The younger men, and I'm sure a few of the older ones as well, were looking her over like a filly at auction. She was nice enough look-ing, but not as pretty as Miss Gipsy. None of Crismon's group was there. They never came again.

Paul and me were listening for Plez Moore to come. We finished all the work and there was still no sign of him. We speculated if we'd ever had a Dec-oration Day without Plez. Then we heard a rider in the woods, coming at a gallop through the brush on the footpath, not on the road. Out burst Quincy Robinette, on his new, fine sorrel mare. He shouted, "Hey y'all!" and jumped down almost on top of three girls his age. He didn't have nice boots or even a saddle, but that mare was a beautiful sight with a coat he'd rubbed until it shone in the sun. There isn't anything better than regular linseed oil on an old wool sock to make a horse shine.

It wasn't hard to impress us boys, but even some of the men walked over to rub their hands along her withers and judge the brightness of her eyes. She held her head high and confident, assuming in her way that we were all put on this earth to admire her.

None of the Robinettes had come to work, but Quincy would want to eat just the same. Already some of the women were glaring at him, so I knew not to worry. They'd feed him but make him wait until all of us had eaten. I can see it all now, just like all the Decoration Days in my mind. There was every shade of green a person could imagine layered deep in those Ozark hills. The breeze would turn over leaves or wave the grass in the field aside, and another emerald layer, hidden a moment ago, would shine through.

There was always the shy boy standing a bit off from the others, his back closest to the women. He was afraid to get too far from his mother, but didn't want to make it look as though that were so. Wasn't so long ago one of us was that boy.

There were two girls, holding hands, laughing and sneaking into the outhouse, emerging a minute later wearing traded skirts and pleased smiles. They're so proud of their friendship. And there's one of my brothers whistling long and loud, because he just caught Bob Crockett and Ruby Clemons sneaking off into the dark of the woods, Bob's firm hand sliding around her waist as they disappear. Those were the scenes we always saw, and I could swear to you they happened that day and there'd be none to dispute it.

Plez missed that day. We didn't know it then, but he'd already had his last Decoration Day at the Hawkins Cemetery.

In the early 1920s, many newspapers and magazines throughout the country covered the story of the burgeoning Ku Klux Klan and its charismatic leaders. With the Klan's rapidly increasing wealth came political power. And with their political power came more wealth. There was a large rally at Missouri's capital. An article from a Jefferson City newspaper later noted:

> In February 1924, a large contingent of Klansmen held a formal gathering in the Hall of the House of Representatives of the Missouri State Capital… In an act of undisguised defiance, Klan members posted an announcement of their Capital meeting on the front door of St. Peter's Catholic Church, across the street from the statehouse.

At the end of this rally, Klan members donated $1,200 to The Salvation Army. I chose not to tell Hadley his favorite charity had once received money from the group that caused him so much pain. Now I wonder if maybe he would have found some solace in the thought.

Missourian Harry S. Truman had direct dealings with the Klan. Many of Truman's friends joined the organization and encouraged him to do the same. Biographers state he gave ten dollars to join the All-American Lodge and then demanded his money back when he determined what the group was really about. Truman's public clashes with the KKK began as early as 1922 and continued into 1924. Truman became a vocal foe, with some historians crediting the Klan's stand against Catholics as the reason.

A Klan organizer reportedly requested Truman's promise that he would not appoint Catholics to office, but he refused. Some newspapers (whose owners and editors were rumored to have been Klan members) denounced Truman as un-American during his campaign and he proclaimed the same about them.

None of this appeared in Miller County newspapers during the summer of 1924. Instead, editors noted that, "Miss Gipsy Wornell and James Thompson are visiting their parents, Mr. and Mrs. J. C. Thompson." Sandwiched between farm foreclosure notices and advice to grow watermelons because they cured appendicitis, was a short article entitled "Relative Advantages of Horse Power in Farming." This article described, "numerous reasons for the continued use of a good draft horse." Some of the modern equipment was proving to be an expensive and ineffective alternative.

Thinking about all this and what came first and all, I remember a time when I had the perfect chance to kill him. That's right. Before the feud, when we were still friends. I held Fred Crismon's temple in my sites one day. It was his right temple: that soft spot nestled beside the eye that curves in gently until it brushes against the cheek. Put your fingertips up there and feel the place. That's the perfect spot for a bullet.

I was in the underbrush, looking for a rabbit I seen go in there, but instead I saw Crismon, only twenty-five yards or so across Bear Creek. He was standing out in the river bed, and then he squatted down. So I did the same, squatted down to watch him and all. I don't know why I didn't just call out "hello" to him. He started easing jars out of the shoal there. Old Man Leids or someone else's whiskey, I suppose.

I knew better than to point a loaded gun at anything that shouldn't be dead. I raised the barrel up to my knee with my forefinger caressing the slope of the trigger. Then it came to me how similar those two places felt: my trigger and his temple. With nothing more than a squeeze, I could've drilled a hole in Fred Crismon's head, like he done in our lives. I was just messing around, being a stupid kid, because this was well before the trouble started and we knew him for the cutthroat he was.

Then the gun flew out of my hands and there I was, staring at Dad's boot and then up at his angry face. "That was a damned fool thing to do." There was a punishment of course. I cleaned out the hen house for the rest of the day and felt the barbs from the rooster up and down my legs, leaving welts to remind me of my sin. An eye for an eye, the Old Testament says. I could have taken both of his that day.

Then again in nineteen and twenty-four there was another confrontation. This time, I was with Dad. We tried to avoid it, but we still had to go past the Crismon property once in a while. If for mail or groceries, one of us boys would cut through the back way, up into the woods either on foot or horseback. But sometimes we just had to take the wagon. It still is the only road back there today.

On this occasion my dad and I rode our horses through the woods into town for groceries. We had a nice time in Bagnell, picked up what we needed and put the things in the saddlebags we brought. We were optimistic about avoiding trouble because we figured Crismon didn't know we'd gone into town, so he wouldn't be waiting for us to come back.

There were so many beautiful days in Wilcox Bend, especially in the spring and fall when the weather was mild and the trees full. And I think about those times now because Dad was never in a big hurry on those trips. On the farm he was always working on something. As a matter of fact, it occurs to me that I spent a great deal of my boyhood staring at his backside. He was bent over the anvil, the plow, a manger. He was always looking down, examining a hoof, the ground, seedlings.

But when Dad left the farm, he enjoyed his time away. I remember riding along at a gentle walk, our horses knowing the way and following the road or path without much effort on our part, and I was always looking up for great horned owl nests. We had saddlebreds, you know — easy on the rider with smooth gaits, backs like easy chairs and a trot you could sit. Missouri's always had prime saddlebreds.

Sometimes Dad would talk a bit, but most off he just looked and listened, and if I had something important to discuss with him, like a pocketknife I'd seen that I needed, this was a good time to bring the subject up.

On the way home we had to go right by Crismon's house, because we were to drop off some groceries at my brother Otto's. We got by the house without any trouble. Dad said, "I don't believe they're home." So we rode along quietly down the road about a quarter mile and were almost at Otto's when we ran into Crismon on horseback. He was carrying a double-barreled shotgun.

I thought for sure there would be killing. I know my dad was armed. I never learned if Dad was scared or not, but I know I was. I was only thirteen years old.

Before you knew it, Dad and Crismon both swung guns at each other and was yelling, "You lying son-of-a-bitch... you cheating faggot... this ain't your own personal road... I ought to kill you right here."

I started to cry and plead with Dad and Fred. And pray. Out loud. Boy, you would have thought I was paid to preach to the owls above I prayed so loud. I prayed the best I knew, "Christ God, help us please." And He surely did. They both backed down at the same time, and one of them told me to get the hell out of there. I kicked Goldie and galloped until we reached our farm, my heart about to burst from fear and guilt. I had left my father behind.

Then there was a horse cantering behind me, and I heard a single shot. I kept going and did not look back. Finally, I stopped. I waited at the entrance of our farm and wondered what to do next. I thought I'd faint off my horse I was so scared. But Dad made it home. He rode up at a gallop, the whites of his horse's eyes shining in the sun, and I could tell the horse sensed the fear. Dad's expression was frozen. I'll never forget the expression on his face. Frozen. Not a frown, not a smile, just frozen. The hollows in his cheeks carved in farther than they'd been ten minutes hence. And then it hit me: he was old. My dad was old.

He didn't say much, just asked if I was all right before we rode together the rest of the way, past the stump of the sycamore. I'd lost my tree and Professor's beautiful strong horses, and I could have lost my father as well. He could have easily shot Fred Crismon and then they would have taken him away and I'd have no one to protect me but Charley because Joe was gone too. That's what I was thinking. Just about me.

There'd never been a more selfish boy than there was at that minute. Sometime after it was over I looked down at my hands. I'd clenched down on my fingertips so hard, the nails dug into my palms leaving eight bloody moons. Then the nails turned black. They stayed that way for months.

Articles in the *Miller County Autogram* during the summer of 1924 frequently updated the community on the lives of the Thompsons, the Crismons, and the feud between the two:

> Grant Thompson and Fred Crismon were in court again this week, the result of a shooting affray between J. G. Thompson and Fred P. Crismon, both of near Bagnell, when Thompson was shot by Crismon. The jury was unable to reach an agreement.

As well, the usual local events were also recorded:

Three drowned when an auto plunged into the river off the ferry. Mrs. Henry Vineyard, Mrs. James Vineyard and her 2 year old child were going to visit F.P. Crismon. The child's body was recovered immediately. The body of Mrs. James Vineyard, wife of the driver, was recovered shortly thereafter, but the body of the mother, Mrs. Henry Vineyard, was later found floating by the Crismon farm. The brakes of Mr. Vineyard's car had not held. People on the ferry threw blocks under the wheels and others tried to catch the wheels, but the swift current quickly caught the automobile the minute it touched the water.

For the most part, our mother was as steady as they come. But all this commotion was hard on her, and she became very nervous. Dad decided she needed a trip to Brumley to see her family and spend some time in town. She didn't ride, so we had to take her in the wagon. I rode alongside the wagon with Dad, Joe, and Charley, and we were all armed. John and Paul rode with Mother in the wagon. We made sure the guns were in plain sight, not just because it was against the law to carry concealed weapons, but because we wanted to make it known we were outnumbering the Crismons should they decide to get ugly.

We came up to the Crismon place and there they were, sitting on their porch with their guns out on their laps. Fred, Leo, Francis, Logan Hickey, and Mrs. Crismon. Anita never played any part in all this. There was the same porch furniture we used to take out on the lawn during parties. Mrs. Crismon was there, honest to Pete, she had a shotgun across her knees. I know there are some that won't believe that's the truth, but it is the God's truth. Mother just clutched at her purse and looked straight ahead, but the rest of us stared at them — looked them right in the eye. So we just rode on by, all of us with our guns and the five of them with theirs, and I know the only reason they didn't start anything was because we outnumbered them.

That peace was short lived. Mother, John, Paul, and Dad stayed in Brumley and we rode home through the woods, hoping the Crismons wouldn't know what we was up to. I was back home in my bed sound asleep when all of a sudden Joe was shouting something, and I jumped out of bed, not knowing what the hell was going on. It was like the Keystone Cops in that bedroom.

The room was lit up with red and orange dancing lights. At first I was so confused I thought it was another lightning storm. Then fear really got a good hold on me, because I realized, it's the reflection of a burning cross, outside on our lawn. There's a huge burning cross out there because they know we've been at the meetings, and now they've surrounded us when Dad's not here. We know about Leids's moonshine still under the trap door, and the flasks outside the meetings, and the whippings of Ty and Arthur not done by night-riders at all.

But soon enough I realized it was much worse than that. Yes, the light was from a fire outside. But it weren't no cross; it was our barn burning down. We rushed outside and tried our best to throw water on it, Joe, Charley, and me, but soon knew it was hopeless. The silo burnt next. Joe said he saw two people running away through the fields when he first woke up. He thought they was either the two Crismon boys or one of them and Logan Hickey.

J. G. Thompson and son Joe of near Bagnell were business callers at the courthouse and Autogram office Saturday. Mr. Thompson had the misfortune to lose his barn and the contents by fire a few days ago. The building was insured for $900.00 with the clause allowing 2/3rds in case of fire, making the cash settlement $600.00. The barn contained 2 tons of hay, 100 bushels of corn, 4 sets of harness, saddle, bridles, etc. and the silo was about 1/3 full of silage. The contents were not insured and he estimates the loss to him at least $350. He states that the family was in Brumley when the building burned and the origin has not been determined.

June was a solemn month, and hot. It was the year of the thirteen-year cicadas when they crawled out of their hiding places in droves. Like the locusts in the Bible, those noisy creatures covered our earth and flew through the air. They were on everything in sight. And loud. Their sawing voices filled the air so we had to shout above them some days. This went on for a few weeks.

We worked hard to keep them from destroying all of Mother's garden, picking them off plants and tossing them into a barrel to burn. Their bodies crunched beneath our feet and even us tough boys couldn't stand their insides oozing between our toes for long. The cicadas forced us to squeeze our feet into shoes we usually didn't pull on until October.

Dad lost all the cushion he had against bad luck when the barn burned. He needed to have a good crop, and the price of grain needed to be high as well. The hollows of his cheeks seemed deeper by the day. Then, as if there wasn't enough of a test what with the shootings, the barn burning, and the locusts, there was a mid-summer flood and the bottom land was lost again. Some was salvaged in that we put hogs on it like we done for Crismons. We still had our upper fields, which actually did quite well.

Then some of our cattle was killed. We came out one day and three were on the ground. Throats been slashed. Then Nick, one of my dad's prize-winning fox hounds, disappeared. We never saw him again, but Nick was such a good tracker I know one thing: that dog didn't get lost.

I've no idea what happened to Crismon's fields that year, but it was a tight year for everyone. The tractor salesmen didn't waste their time coming around no more. The paper said there was over three hundred vacant homes in Miller County. Then one day that summer we had two strangers come up the road.

First one was the sheriff. Now, when I was a lot younger, he'd come up our way a few times a year to sit and talk, drink coffee or whiskey, and leave with something from Mother's kitchen. But we'd not seen much of him in the past few years. That day here he come cantering up, and I thought maybe finally everything was over. But he barely tipped his hat to Mother and didn't bother to get down. Nervous as a gentleman caller with Daddy holding a double-barrel.

"Les Leids's barn suffered a fire the other night," he said to Dad.

"Sorry to hear that," Dad said. "I wouldn't wish that on any man. Did he lose much?"

"His daughter caught it before it'd taken hold and they got it put out. She said she saw someone looking a whole lot like John running away." The sheriff stared at the faces looking up at him like he didn't even recognize any of them.

"John? Our John?" Dad laughed. "You know that's impossible. John don't leave Myrtle's side unless he's going to Otto's or Jim's."

"So you say, but I got an eye witness says otherwise."

"What the fire look like?" Dad said, just as belligerent now as the sheriff.

"What difference does that make?" he responded.

"What'd it look like? What was it made of? Where'd it start?"

"Suzzie Leids said it was some rubbish in the middle of the hall. A rubber tube, and some boards, some newspaper," the sheriff answered.

Dad laughed again, "Well, there. There's no way that boy started that fire. He don't build a fire like that, even if he ever did leave this farm and make his way to their place, that proves it. John's fires are all built the same way. He builds a square and then puts a triangle on top, and if the fire didn't look like that, he didn't set it."

Now I think the sheriff was a good man at one time. And I think he remembered that about John, so he reined in his horse to turn back to the road. But he threw a warning down on us before he left, "Your boys been running too free for a long time and it's finally caught up with 'em. Keep 'em at home if you know what's best." Dad turned his back on the man and started to walk away. The sheriff did the same. So then it was done. Everyone knew each turned his back on the other.

The next visitor was a hack pulled by a paint. It was a friend from Bagnell, and oh, we were glad to see him. He was a fox-hunting friend of Dad's and he brung pineapple buns and a new fox hound for Dad. He also had a newspaper with a notice he'd circled saying a man named Clergy Crismon now owned the Crismon farm. Fred Crismon had sold his farm to a relative.

We didn't have much that year, but we still had the farm, and Dad could pay Joe's tuition. Charley had decided to become a blacksmith. This was a perfect choice for him; he got stronger by the day. He was fixing to apprentice to a man in Tuscumbia as Dad said Charley had to work for someone else for a year before he came home to take over Dad's shop.

Sometime soon after that, in the middle of the summer, Dad and I was out at night following Diner as she chased a fox. It was just us that night; none of Dad's friends were around.

But anyway, somehow we had to cut back and come by the Crismon house. It was about midnight. We got past the house okay, but as we passed the barn Crismon stepped out from behind the barn gate with a double-barreled shotgun. I thought, "Oh God, he will kill us both and no one will ever know the difference."

Again I pleaded with Dad, and prayed, but the shots rang out, horses turned in the dust, I screamed and cried, but we got out of there alive. I know God had something to do with it. You may think not, especially after what happened later, but I think so. Some day, something will happen to you, and regardless of the outcome here on earth, you'll know what you felt and saw and heard. And you'll agree with me that something else is there with you.

Both Crismon and Dad were wounded that day.

The summer of 1924 was a glorious time for the Ku Klux Klan nationally. They had enlisted, bribed, and blackmailed so many politicians on so many levels that their national leader, H.W. Evans, was convinced he would be able to control the national elections in November. Evans was also convinced that he would be running for President in 1928.

In Miller County, *The Eldon Advertiser* ran a small announcement on the State vs. J.G. Thompson for felonious assault on 17 July 1924.

Then the 31 July edition of the *Miller County Autogram* stated "Jury fails to return verdict in Grant Thompson case… Dozens of witnesses were used in the case and the trial consumed more than a day and during which time the court room was packed beyond seating capacity." The same editions noted "An airplane passed over Tuscumbia" and "A boy was fatally stabbed at church by another boy."

The Klan was more out in the open than ever, and men like Grant Thompson were being declared outcasts. The 21 August 1924 *Eldon Advertiser* carried this article:

KNIGHTS OF KU KLUX KLAN HOLD OUTDOOR INITIATION

The Knights of the Ku Klux Klan held an open air initiation Thursday night in the Vanosdoll wheat field just east of Eldon Avenue and a large crowd was present for the ceremony. A large cross nearly twenty feet high was erected and at midnight flamed a bright glow that lighted up the entire east part of the city. Klansmen in their white regalia were shown on guard in groups, over the field. Fifty members were clad in the official regalia which is worn on three occasions only, it is claimed. For public parade, during initiation services and when charitable donations are made. A membership of over five hundred is claimed here and a class was initiated Thursday night.

Things were quiet for a few months between the two families. It was threshing time and harvest and for the first time ever, Wilcox Bend didn't thresh together. We was two groups and you can guess how we divided up. All the Thompsons and them that hadn't joined the Klan in one group. The Crismons and other joiners, I imagine, were the other. I really don't know. But there was no word from Simon Cox or the Professor, so it seemed to me the festivity was gone from the occasion. Maybe I'd just grown up and saw things differently, like what a lot of hard work it really was. I really was old enough to help out now, and Paul was the water boy.

Us boys saw the way Dad seemed beaten down. But that didn't worry Joe or Charley none, after all, they were young and strong — the age Dad was when he first started out. They knew they could handle things.

Then one day I was down at the blacksmith shop with Dad, and here come a rider, galloping into the yard, pulling up in a frenzy in front of the shop, throwing reins over the hitching post, running inside.

"We need your wagon, Grant, a drowning down at the ford." We ran for the harness, blankets. Mother threw together a basket of food. I got a bridle on Goldie and rode ahead bareback down to Brockman's Ford.

Here's what I seen: people looking down at their feet, talking softly, standing in a small group, much too quiet. A funeral wake at the edge of the river.

Off to one side a lone man. Grey hair slicked back, a goatee of a beard, hatless. Sitting up on a boulder at the edge of the river. At his feet a body, covered in a blanket. "He won't let us move the body," some man said, because now Dad had driven up in the wagon. Well, turns out Mrs. Leids was the woman in the blanket. Dad went over to Les and said something to console him and Leids turned to him, real slow, with the face of a coyote and in a low growl said,

"You did this. You killt her with your evil-lovin' ways. You touch her and so hep me God I'll kill you. You hear me? You hear me Grant Thompson?" Leids was shouting now, "You think you own this God damned river do you? I'd sooner shoot you than look at any of your kind."

A year before I think Dad would have hauled him off that rock, dead wife or no dead wife, and busted his face in. But Dad had changed. Everything had changed. Everything but the river. Dad just backed away. We never talked about it, but of course he told Mother that night in the kitchen. She told him talk was Mrs. Leids been seen at the river a few times with a German from Bagnell. Dad said he'd even fox hunted with the man a while ago.

Mrs. Leids never was much of a rider and must have gotten into trouble crossing at Brockman's. It always was tough to judge the river there. It was what she was doing down there that shocked the blazes outta us. We all thought that woman was as boring as spit.

In September of 1924, news of the upcoming election as well as Klan activities filled the local newspapers. On 18 September 1924, the *Tuscumbia Miller County Autogram* wrote a story about Republicans and Democrats denouncing the Klan in Jefferson City. Ostensibly, political parties may have denounced the Klan, but by now Klan membership had infiltrated both parties on state and national levels.

In September 1924, national leader and Imperial Wizard Evans read a speech at a Klonvocation in Kansas City. He stated, "There is danger that our heritage will be torn from us by men whose racial instincts, temperament and education unfit them for Americanism. The good are of American stock — native, white, Protestant." The event was well publicized.

Then, in October, a Miller County native wrote a response, illustrating how Klan members were becoming more and more vocal, and were following the urging of Klan national leadership to be active and visible in politics. The author vehemently supported the Klan and spoke out against the Knights of Columbus and foreign meddling. "Vigilance is truly the price of liberty," he argued.

Klan issues also infiltrated local elections and statements of opposition to this ran in the local papers. The Tuscumbia newspaper ran another article that same day about the feud, describing the State of Missouri vs. J. G. Thompson. "The altercation causing the trial was an argument between Francis Crismon and J. G. Thompson, which ended when Thompson struck Crismon."

There were a few days late in the fall of nineteen and twenty-four that marked the end of my boyhood. Most men can't tell you that — can't say, "Here I was a boy and here I became a man." But Charley and I can say that. If boyhood has to end sometime, that week was a hell of a way to say goodbye. Charley and I were together with nothing but our freedom. The memory of that week still runs through my head like a fever.

I don't recall how it come about, but Dad finally said Charley and I could do something we'd been wanting to do all year: cut us a load of railroad ties. At the time we thought it was kinda an early Christmas present, getting to take off like that. But now I think back and wonder, was Dad a little bit worried about going into the winter and figured it'd be good to have the cash on hand? I'll never know.

The plan was to ride to Grandpa Jake Anderson's place, where he'd surely let us cut timber off his land. Then at night we'd stay with Old Man Sons, camping out along the river where he'd been for a week or so, for he'd stay there until the weather got bad.

During breakfast, when I should've been thinking about getting ready for school, Dad told us to go ahead and get our things. I know it was a Tuesday because Mother was making pies. So we packed the wagon, hitched up the mules, and waited for those treasures to appear. Fresh pies right from the oven. You couldn't have paid us a million dollars each for them. We were planning on being gone for five days; Mother gave us six.

Then Dad helped us harness up Ned and Nell. He said, "You'll have to go past Crismon's, but they won't be expecting you and I don't believe he'll bother you if I'm not along." Besides, Charley had his shotgun, I had the .22 and we also had a little gun we just passed around. An Iver Johnson 38. We always had it stuck in a boot or a pocket but I couldn't even tell you where it came from. We believed Dad was right. We didn't believe the two of us would come across any problems going past Crismon's.

So with Diner running alongside the wagon, we waved goodbye and pretended to listen to all the last minute instructions. "Be sure to give Grandpa Jake the best pie," called Mother from the porch. I looked back over my shoulder to see her and Dad standing side-by-side watching us trot up to sycamore ridge. We still called it that, even with no sycamore. They waved goodbye, and I watched them until Charley drove the team over the crest and the house was out of sight.

Once again we started down the road toward the Bagnell Ferry. Past Otto's farm, brown and still. Then we seen the Crismon place. Anita and Francis would be in school, with Leo and Fred out working. It'd be just Mrs. inside. I was driving because if anything happened, we wanted Charley to have that gun ready to go.

I think about that morning and see now what foolish kids we were. We were just going to shoot anybody. We never thought what it'd be like to really kill somebody. To take a father or a mother from a child or a child from its parents for that matter.

We didn't say nothing. We just rolled on past that house, looking at the windows to see if a face appeared, and as we passed Charley turned and watched the door, his 16-gauge balanced on his knees. I knew he was covering my backside. But there was just quiet, so when we got to the ferry landing, we knew we'd made it and from then on was going to have a swell time.

Grandpa Anderson had lived in the same hollow since God was a boy, which he'd cleared himself with nothing but his axe and his ox. It was his animal I saw in Bagnell that night with Billy Sunday. Grandpa might've helped settle Miller County for all I know. You've got to stop and think about that a bit now: I mean he done cleared that land by hisself. Cut down every tree, burned out every stump, pulled out every stone until there was enough rock there to make a rock wall and enough dirt without rocks to plant a garden. And you wonder why men fought for their land?

He lived south of us, but there was no good road for the wagon so we had to cross at the Bagnell ferry, then travel along that road, and cross again at the Tuscumbia Bridge. It was going to take all day. A layer of ice covered the Osage, but it'd been mild and a thaw left shimmering pools on the surface that shown smooth and glassy as we rode by. And the quiet. The beautiful quiet of a winter day. Charley stopped in Bagnell to leave word we'd be bringing ties by in a day or two.

All my life before there'd been hundreds of ties stacked up in the railroad yard waiting to be shipped out. But the railroad was only buying ties for repairs now. Everybody was building roads for the automobiles. Used to be the tie buyer lived in Bagnell. Now he just came through once a month, so we left word with the railroad agent. We also stopped and bought lunch at the hotel like we was grown businessmen. Oh, we thought we was something special.

Along the way Charley and I got to talking, and our talk went to the hereafter. I said, "Charley, you recken there's a hereafter like Preacher Cox is always telling us?"

Now Charley was about eighteen then and not a kid like me. So he answered in an adult way, "That's one of those questions nobody gets to have answered until it's their time."

Well, I didn't like that thought much. I was thirteen and couldn't accept that there were some things you just can't do nothing about.

Then I said, "Well, I got an idea. This is how we'll figure out if there's a hereafter. We'll have a pact, and we'll take a sacred oath. Whoever goes first'll come back and give the other a sign. That way one of us will know."

Charley could really be a good sport. I mean he was practically grown, but he went along with it like we was still kids. He spit in his palm, I spit in mine, and we shook on it. There. Done. Now at least one of us would get to know ahead of time about heaven and hell.

So at the end of the day we got to Grandpa Anderson's place. His ox slept calmly in the long shadows. Both man and ox were too old to work the land by then, but every fence post was square and even, every row of barbed wire taut. We pulled up and he came out on his porch. Huge black bushy eyebrows danced while he talked. Old Jake told us to take any trees we wanted; he would've agreed to anything for one of Mother's pies. He gave us some hot cornbread in return with a bone for the dog.

He asked Charley, "Ya want a jug to keep yerself warm at night?" Charley took the brew for Sons.

Then on down to the river until we smelled the smoke of green hickory and found our friend. Chicken Fat was there too. We sat by the fire listening to Chicken Fat tell about the summer it was so hot the corn popped itself right there in the field and all the eggs in the hen house came out hard boiled. Yessir, the sap in them maple trees boiled and maple syrup poured right outta the tops of the trees and into the cups of people standing below.

I remember sitting there, on kind of a flat rock chair you'll find lots of times in the woods, staring at Chicken Fat and listening to his stories. I started seeing him different, and from that time on he wasn't so hideous to me. His hair, the color of muddy earth, was just strands of river grass. The purple veins standing up from the back of his hands were the roots of the river birches. And his bleary eyes? The eyes of a fish. He was just a river man. I'd like to meet another like him before I die.

Sons and Chicken Fat passed the jug back and forth. Diner and I fell asleep to the sound of the fire cracking and the "thwat" of Chicken Fat and Charley spitting tobacco into the brush. He called both Charley and me "Johnny." I figured he didn't know our names. He was gone when we woke up.

Sons fed us smoked fish and coffee for breakfast all that week. You haven't lived until you've eaten food cooked over a campfire. He made coffee in a tin pot, where he threw in the grounds, cracked an egg in with the eggshell, added some sorghum, and after it boiled a while it poured out as sweet as love and as black as Satan. I took my Winchester with me and every time I got tired of chopping at the ties I went after rabbits with Diner. I'd hand them over to Sons by the ears, and he'd cook us up fried rabbit with chopped onions and potatoes.

We seen a thirteen foot long black snake, his body thick as a stove pipe, and even though we knew he was harmless and good, really, we couldn't help being afraid of him. We jumped onto the wagon, then threw stones at him so he'd continue on his way and stay out of ours.

By the end of the week, we'd made a nice load of ties. We felt as fat as ticks, what between eating Son's food and Mother's pies all day and night. It was time to head back. This time we left before dawn because the mules were dragging quite a load now and moving slow. When we got to Bagnell we learned Chicken Fat left word that our load, "the ties of Masters Charley and Hadley Thompson" should be bought because he'd agreed to raft them farther down river where another line was looking to buy some replacements.

So we were very fortunate, because we were just two boys and others, grown men, had been forced to leave ties behind, branded with their mark, because they'd no buyer. It never occurred to us a man could work so hard at something and not make any money.

So we sold our wagonload, about ten ties, to a tie buyer by the name of Mr. Bone. He was also a barber. We had plans to take the money and buy six or seven sheep from Elliott Williams. (Mr. Williams married, just for the record, a niece of Jesse James.) As things ended up, we never spent the money on those sheep.

Passing Crismons again we saw the dog lift up its head from the porch and watch us roll by. Charley was ready though. And then right after we'd rounded a kink in the road and couldn't see their house, we heard shots fired.

That's all I know; don't know if they had anything to do with us or not. Of course, in those days you were always hearing shots and thought nothing of it.

That was the end of our week when two boys owned the world. Living in the woods, cutting timber all day, I learned two important lessons. First, fried onions taste good in just about everything. And one more thing. I learned if you share a jug with someone, they just might help you out down river.

Now that I'm at the end of my life, I'm glad I can go to that clearing by the water's edge and see Old Man Sons sitting by a campfire singing to hisself. He's taller than most, with a full head of white hair, and a grin of long, yellow teeth that shine in the light of the campfire like the eyes of his pal tom cat. I like to think about those times and feel the peace of those cool days and nights. Because that was the end of my boyhood. Within a month I was a man, and the next time I took the wagon to the ferry landing it was to take home the undertaker.

How'd we spend the money we'd earned from the ties? That went for his pay.

On 4 November 1924, another warrant was issued for the arrest of Grant Thompson, for yet another altercation with the Crismons. This time the nephew Logan Hickey was involved, who claimed Grant "did willfully disturb the peace of Logan Hickey, by then and there threatening, quarrelling at and challenging." Grant was to be kept in jail until the first Monday in December, when Circuit Court convened, but Otto put up the bond and he was released.

And then for a few weeks, life seems to have gone on as usual. In the newspapers, the big news seemed to be that Bagnell got street lights. Simon Cox was back and "filled the pulpit Saturday and Sunday night." Guy Godfrey, deputy game warden, was busy with violators fishing with traps and baskets, and for a month, somebody advertised that he'd lost his eyeglasses along the road outside of Bagnell. Oliver McDowell was going to have to defend himself against the State of Missouri for disturbing religious worship. A three-year-old girl got her hand stuck in the cogs of a washing machine and had to have her fingers amputated, and a ten-year-old died after being kicked in the chin by a horse.

On a state and national level, the Klan was a major factor during elections that November. Klan-backed politicians (of both political parties) won overwhelming victories. In State elections,

Missourians divided their votes in 1924 largely between Republicans and Democrats, giving Republicans more support but not enough to control the political system effectively. Sharp internal conflict prevented the democrats from moving forward from their gains in 1922. The Ku Klux Klan was one of the focal points of the conflict, the rural [pro-Klan] Democrats defeating an anti-Klan plank.

All of these notations were news to Hadley. If he ever did see them, he had long forgotten. One day I called to read the Thompsons some of the notices I had found as well as to ask Hadley some questions, with one of them being about the types of knives used to harvest the corn by hand. He responded, "They were a machete-type of knife, with a blade about 12-14 inches long. Did I tell you how tall corn grew back then?"

"Taller than a man on horseback," I correctly responded.

A laugh, "Who you been talking to?" I was no longer from off.

"You," I laughed back. "I gotta run. I love you both."

"We love you, too."

And that was the last time I spoke with him. Hadley died suddenly, a month later, of an inoperable brain tumor. His funeral was held on a windy, cold, rainy spring day. I sat on a pew by myself and cried all the way through the funeral. Afterward, there was a 21-gun salute from the local VFW chapter, most of whom didn't look much younger than Hadley had been. I was miserable and mourned his death for weeks, unable to explain to my friends and family how much he meant to me.

Without Hadley, my research continued. Other locals of his generation opened up after his death, including Icel. Some came across strongly for the Thompsons, others against. Some disagreed with what he had told me previously, but I no longer had Hadley to go back to. It was lonely. Current owners of the old Thompson farm were still kind enough to let me go there and run the dogs, and I felt closer to him when I was there. I didn't want to continue with the research, and without Hadley to urge me on, knew I could easily quit. But Hadley had died on my birthday. I took this as his final insistence I write his story down.

It was the last day of November, nineteen and twenty-four. Dad was in Bagnell that Saturday. Dad's old friend had been replaced by sheriff Charlie Williams. As I understand it, Crismon and Charlie were talking about us.

Although Fred had to sell the property, he was leasing it from Clergy. Now Fred had been going around saying that Dad and all the Thompsons never had fortunate luck and worked hard. We'd lied, cheated, and stole.

First, Crismon said Dad engineered that whole hog deal so that he made money on it so Fred never got what he was entitled to. Then he said Dad took more than his share during threshing, because some of the others used our silo to store their grain in. And he made money on the cattle when others lost it because somehow he knew cattle prices were going to drop and he sold out just in time. And why were Charley and my ties bought when others were still standing in the railroad yard waiting for a buyer? Maybe all this don't sound like much, but back then, with money being so scarce all a man had was his reputation.

So that day in Bagnell, here's what happened. Dad came around from between two stores; there was a little alley there and he'd cut through after leaving his horse out back at the livery. And as he came around the corner, he came across Fred Crismon, who was stopping people walking by. What was he doing? He was asking them if they'd be willing to state what a lying, cheating dog my father was.

It wasn't enough that the Crismons had harassed us in every way imaginable, now they had to get others to do the same. Dad told him to stop, and Fred said he'd do what he damn well pleased and started to reach for his pocket. Dad remembered what happened on the ferry and figured there was a pistol in there. He'd already been shot at and hit once and wasn't taking any chances.

"Oh no, Fred Crismon," he said. You won't be doing that to me again." Dad pulled out his own gun and started shooting. So Crismon ducked into the post office, and then Francis knocked Dad down and the constable took away Dad's gun. But Dad was still fighting mad. He cursed Crismon, who'd come out on the street again, and then Fred knocked Dad to the ground and proceeded to beat the living daylights outta him.

Dad had to go to the doctor for that. Early in December he got a change of venue for the trial, because there was no way a Thompson was going to get a fair trial in Miller County at that point. The trial date was set for January 4th, in Boonville and then they postponed it again until April 3rd and this time it was to be in Versailles.

GRANT THOMPSON SHOOTS FRED CRISMON
Old trouble showed itself again at Bagnell Saturday

Grant Thompson of near Bagnell has been arrested on a charge of felonious assault as a result of his attempt on the life of Fred Crismon at Bagnell Saturday morning. This is a sequel to the trouble that has been going on between the Thompson and Crismon families for some time.

Saturday's trouble came up very unexpectedly. It appears, from statements made by those standing near, that Crismon and Charlie Williams, deputy sheriff, were standing on the Bagnell post office porch talking about the subpoenaing of witnesses for use in the case of the State against Thompson, in which Crismon is the prosecuting witness.

Thompson came from the direction of the J.C. Calkin store and his presence was not noted by Crismon and Williams until Thompson was heard to remark, "Fred Crismon, you won't tell any more lies on me." Or words to that effect. Following this remark he opened fire on Crismon with a 38-caliber revolver. According to several witnesses, three shots were fired, one of them striking Crismon at the point of the left shoulder at the back and ranging toward the neck. The bullet struck the shoulder blade and glanced out, Crismon dodged into the post office and only one shot struck him. The wound is not serious, unless blood poison develops.

About this time, Francis, a son of Fred Crismon, threw Thompson to the ground, and other parties stepped in and took the gun away from Thompson. When Thompson was released, he continued to curse Crismon, whereupon Crismon struck him and knocked him to the ground. Fred Ridenhour, constable of Franklin Township, and Charlie Williams arrested Thompson and Williams brought him to Tuscumbia. Crismon's wound was dressed by Dr. Allee of Eldon and Thompson's injuries were dressed by Dr. Kouns.

Thompson is charged with felonious assault and Crismon was released. Owing to the nearness to circuit court, Thompson was held by Sheriff Kinder till Monday when Thompson was released on a bond of $5,000.00 to appear for trial at Tuscumbia December 18th at a special term of circuit court. Thompson was to be tried here this week on the first charges of felonious assault, but owing to his physical condition as a result of the trouble Saturday, he was given more time.

Leo's version states,

Soon after [the altercation at the Crismon house] Grant Thompson fired at my father at close range with a pistol at Bagnell, but by quick motion my father moved to such position that the bullet struck his collar bone and glanced out without any permanent injury. Grant Thompson was tried before a Justice of the Peace, Hendricks (I think) at Brumley and the case was scheduled for Circuit Court. Because of the influence of Lev Thompson, a brother of Grant, it was impossible to keep him in custody.

Times were tough at places other than our farm and the Crismon's. The Bagnell High School had to close, after two years of threatening to, because there wasn't enough money. On our farm nobody came to visit, nobody came to bring work for the blacksmith shop and we didn't go noplace. Dad was beat up and had his arm in a sling from getting into it with Fred.

There'd been terrible weather for at least a week — the blizzard of a century according to Mother and Dad. First rain, then it turned to sleet, then every day it didn't get above zero and a fog of snow went on for days. Then a steady downfall of sleet lasting three days and more cold. Day and night the sound of crashing timber surrounded us as the trees, covered in ice, lost their branches under the weight, Finally, it snowed a good ten inches. It stopped. The sun came out. But it was still cold.

I woke up to John cheerfully telling me it was twenty some odd degrees below zero. My brothers were just mounds of covers. Joe was home from the Academy and was sleeping with Paul. I was sharing a bed with Charley.

I didn't know why Dad hadn't rousted us out of bed like usual. Then I remembered it was Christmas Eve, so I guess that was why nobody told us to get up. Dad took care of the animals hisself that morning, even with his arm in a sling. I figured someplace, Chicken Fat was trying to stay warm and I knew he was saying, "It's so cold the milk is ice cream before it hits the bucket."

The river was frozen over; there was at least a foot of snow and ice. It had been such a bad month we hadn't been able to go to town to mail some packages to my brothers and sisters in Kansas City. So right after breakfast, Dad said they was going to go. Joe said, "I know where some traps are that'll need checking, and I seen the fox over there. Hadley and I can follow those fox tracks we seen over by the Riley bluffs and meet you all afterwards."

That was the plan. We decided that Charley and Dad would take the car and go by my brother's place and pick up Otto. They took a double-barreled shotgun with them and Dad and Otto would take the packages to Bagnell, then Charley was to come down the river on the north side and meet me and Joe at the Riley Bluffs. Joe and I was going to take the dogs. We was going to go down the river to Brockman's Ford, cross the river at the ford and come up the north side, hoping to jump this fox. And if we got the fox jumped (there's a crossing up there where fox always cross), Otto was going to meet us there, and we'd kill the fox.

Well, it didn't turn out that way. Joe and I go about, well, I'd say a mile, mile and a half from home, going down the river through the timber. Oh — it was beautiful. The most beautiful snow you ever seen in your life. Everything was so white and still. A bit before that, we heard some shooting, but we didn't pay too much attention to it. Somebody was just hunting like we was.

But after a while I heard somebody hollering. And I said, "Joe, I think they're hollering 'Old Joe!'" It was Otto, come to find us. Then what I remember was he was just suddenly there, in a clearing, by the river. Joe was standing next to me, on my left. We each had a gun in our right hands. The river was behind me and I could hear it running under the ice. And Otto is standing in front of me and he shouldn't be there. I mean, that wasn't the plan. I was thinking they'd already got the fox. Somehow, around the Bagnell Ferry, they killed the fox, and he'd come to tell me that. But you know what I heard? Stillness. That beautiful stillness only found on a winter's day in the woods.

"They've killed Dad," Otto said.

Where's Charley? Where's my brother Charley?

"They've got Charley," he said after that.

Well, we started running back to Otto's farm. The cold hurt my lungs so bad, and when we ran, we'd bust through layers of ice and the snow would be up to our knees. But we ran. And ran. "We got to go after Charley" was all we could think. It took a while to get back to our property, maybe an hour. We were out by Otto's barn and we started making preparations. What would we need? More guns? Rope?

Then about that time, here come poor Charley stumbling out of the woods. He was out of his mind. They'd hit him across the head and split his head open. His hands were frozen. I mean they were frozen solid. He couldn't move them or feel a thing. His coat and gloves were gone. It was below zero or just close to that. Frozen icicles of blood hung around his face. I can't tell you in enough detail how he suffered. We got him into Otto's wagon, hitched it up and went back to our place. Mother, Paul, and John still didn't know about anything. But I'm thinking, we got to go get the Crismons. We got to make them pay for what they done.

On that terrible day I learned many awful truths, and one was human blood has a distinct odor from the hog and fish and cow's blood I was used to. I am grateful God has spared me from being in a situation where I was forced to smell such blood again. Even though it has been over seventy years, I keep the memory of that smell. Not because I want to. When I enlisted, I joined the Navy in hopes that if I had to kill, I would be far enough away as to never smell human blood again. I needn't have bothered; I can smell that day as I can hear the river running along its course under the ice.

Up until that Christmas Eve, I'd spent my short life around blood and was never bothered by it. The pulse of our days was blood and always will be on a farm. We were in the fields all through calving season. I always volunteered to spend the night in the barn, burrowed in a mound of straw outside the stall, waiting for a mare to foal. I gutted the fish we caught and sliced them into fillets without thinking twice. And hog butchering meant meat for the winter and smelling the smokehouse for weeks. I loved the ritual before that day, but never again could I go and help during butchering day.

The minute the front door shut, Charley collapsed onto Joe and could not walk. He couldn't even stand. It took all of us to drag him away from behind the door, as he was determined to stay slumped on the floor. Somehow we told Mother what had happened. John was beside himself and not much help, just getting in the way and hanging on Mother. So we told him to never mind and hide under Mother and Dad's bed where he'd be safe. We told him nobody knew where the bed was, and he believed us. We could hear him in the other room throughout the hours that passed, whimpering like a lonely puppy under that bed.

Here's the story Charley told us, and I believe Charley like I'd believe my own eyes. Charley was driving the car and Dad was in the seat beside him. Packages heaped behind them. Just out the drive, of course, was Otto's, and he come out to go with them. Little Olive followed her daddy out to the car and asked, "Do you want me to take that gun?" Because Otto had slipped a pistol into his waistband. She never did like guns. But Otto said, "No" and kissed her goodbye.

Charley drove slow and careful down the road on account of the ice and snow. Soon they were at the Crismons. The front door was ajar just a bit, shutting softly as they pulled by. Charley broke out in a sweat and thought, "Why didn't I let Otto drive? I'm the better shot." But nobody came out. Just a shadow moving in the window,

They got over to the landing, and there was only a portion of the river not frozen with a place in the ice for the rowboats to run. They parked on top of the bank and walked down to the river, where there was already some people in the rowboat. They only had room for one more person. So they decided that Otto was to take that one place in the rowboat and mail the packages. The boat would come back after Dad and Charley.

Dad had this arm in a sling from being shot at and had part of his head wrapped up in a bandage with kind of a cap setting on it and he carried a cane in his left hand. Charley and Dad was setting there and Charley happened to look up and he said, "Dad, here come the Crismons and they're armed."

And Charley said Dad didn't even look up. So he said again, "Dad, here come the Crismons," and no sooner had he said that, there they were.

Crismon said, "Well, I guess we'll go across the river first."

And Charley said, "Well, I think that would be up to the ferryboat man."

Then Crismon said, "I guess I know who'll go across first."

About that time, Dad looked up. He was kind of squatting down on the bank, chipping at the ice on the river with a piece of ice. And evidently, Dad looked up. And Fred Crismon shot him right square in the face.

Of course he died. He was dead before he hit the ground. Dad was not armed. He was right-handed and that was the arm in the sling, from getting into it before in Bagnell.

So they started working on old Charley. They knocked his shotgun out of his hand, hit him across the head, but Charley was carrying that 38 in his boot. Us kids kind of all had a claim to it I think, you know, who was going to carry it. But this particular day, Charley happened to be carrying it. I'll try to remember what Charley told us. He sat on the floor in the parlor, talking like a crazy man. We were all crouched around him.

"I knew they were going to kill me. I knew that. But I thought I'd take one of them with me at least. I took that gun out. I stuck it in Fred Crismon's mouth."

He said, "Barney, I stuck that gun into Fred Crismon's mouth and I pulled the trigger as many times as I could."

Then he said he saw Francis Crismon stooping over to pick up the gun they'd knocked out of his hand. "I knew if they picked up that gun they'd kill me for sure." So he shot the guy that was picking up the gun, Francis Crismon. Then Charley broke and run.

Leo and Logan Hickey took out after him, and he run about a mile, mile and a half, trying to get home. But they caught him. I could show you exactly the route he took. They caught him at Will Brown's place. They took him to Elmer Kidwell's who was a sympathizer with Fred Crismon, and they put Charley up on the second story.

By now Charley was crying and, well, we all were. Joe was asking Charley to forgive him, because he begged off riding in the car. He was afraid of the Crismons after getting shot at and hit in the shoulder like he did. Mother was sobbing, saying she never should have let them go. And Charley, poor Charley.

THE ELDON ADVERTISER,
THE OFFICIAL PAPER FOR MILLER COUNTY
SPECIAL CHRISTMAS EDITION

GRANT THOMPSON KILLED
AT BAGNELL WEDNESDAY
GUN FIGHT OCCURRED ON BANK OF OSAGE RIVER

Grant Thompson and Fred Crismon Family Difficulty

Grant Thompson was shot and killed and Francis Crismon was badly wounded Wednesday morning on the Osage river bank across the river from Bagnell.

Mr. Thompson was out on bond for shooting and wounding Fred Crismon, the father of Francis Crismon, Nov. 29. The men of the two families met, it seems, on the bank of the river not far from the Crismon home. Reports are that Charles Thompson was also thought to have been wounded as it is reported he was seen leaving the scene of the fight limping as though he had been crippled.

The families of Fred Crismon and Grant Thompson, both farmers living across the river from Bagnell, have been having difficulties for two or three years, during which time several fights and two shootings have occurred. The situation was considered hazardous and Prosecuting Attorney Harry Kay, made the Thompson bond $25,000.00 but this was considered excessive by Judge Westhues, the Circuit Judge, who reduced the amount. Thompson had filled bonds for $8,000.00 and was released for appearance at a special term of court Dec. 29.

Francis Crismon was a student of Eldon High School, a fine young man. He was wounded in the back and reports are from those who came from Bagnell, that he told his younger brother he would not live.

Mother was shaking and told us she must go to Dad. Seems like it was only five minutes she was there and then she said she must go. It was two and a half miles from our farm and three from the house. Mother didn't own any winter boots. She pulled on her coat and Joe's over that and took a blanket for around her shoulders besides. It was as cold as the devil is cruel.

Do you know what a tow sack is? A tow sack's made out of hemp and is loosely woven. We got them from bran, or chopped oats or cracked corn. Mother fetched some and wrapped those tow sacks around her feet over her shoes and kept the sacks on by weaving around barbed wire, so she could walk those miles to the Bagnell Ferry where Dad lay on the bank. The barbed wire allowed her to walk in the snow and ice. She hoped the sacks would help keep her feet from freezing. So she prayed to God to please keep us safe, and she left in those homemade boots.

She went by herself. Said she must go by herself. In my head all I could think of was the song:

Oh mothers, let's go down, come on down, don't you want to go down?
Oh mothers let's go down, down to the river to pray.

We'd no real way to lock the door, so we propped a chair against it. Charley'd lost both guns, the rifle and the pistol. We had Dad's shotgun, still hanging on the wall, with Joe's and my rabbit guns. Not much at all.

Charley started to crawl across the floor to get behind the wood stove we had in the dining room, to hide. He refused to have his back to the door. I think he started to hallucinate again because he stopped talking and said nothing but "shhh...." His lips were blue, totally blue, and all around his mouth, too. We carried him into the hall, laid him on John's cot, and picked up the whole thing. Carried it into the kitchen to put him next to the stove. It was the only truly warm place in the house when it got that cold.

As Charley's frozen flesh started to thaw, he cried and thrashed. We found some liquor of some sort in the cupboard, and we tried to make him drink it, but he spit it out and screamed at us. My tough big brother. Nothing could console him. I knew he would die that day, while we all cried, Joe, Paul and me, to see him in such pain and what they had done to him. But you know, beside it all I was so proud of him. It took four of them to bring him down, and he still made it outta there alive.

Then he calmed a bit, and Joe held Charley's head on his lap and stroked his hair. That was one of those things we never talked about later, but I remember that. I tell you, we was all a sorry mess of bloody clothes; Joe trying to hold Charley's mangled hands in his, Paul and I shaking, trying to hold a gun, wondering who was going to bust through the door and get us next. We knew there was no law that would show up until it was all over.

Our minds were filled with the same terrible thoughts: What would we do without Dad? Would they kill Mother too? If Francis and Fred Crismon died, and if Charley lived, would he go to jail? I felt like John, like I just wanted to crawl under the bed and hide. I was whimpering inside if not outside I know. But showing who was scared or crying, none of that mattered that day.

Finally, Charley just went limp and numb to it all. We heated some water and used it to clean him up. Mother had been gone for such a long time at that point. Charley slept, or passed out, and we whispered, wondering if she would be the next to go. Joe thought one of us could take a horse and try to go get Uncle Lev in Brumley. We were talking about it; none of us wanted to split up, but we knew three boys, one half dead one, and John, weren't no match for anything the KKK might be sending.

The light was already down low in the hills when there was knocking at the door. It was Mother. Boy, were we glad to see her. Now, I know people knew by that time what was happening, but she saw nobody. Nobody offered to help her. Nobody even came out of their house or waved from a barnyard door. She walked there and back in that cold by herself, even though she had walked to so many of their homes, carrying food or what have you. Everybody just stayed away that day.

I crawled to every window and looked out, trying to see if I could see anything. And this is what I saw and I ain't seen it like that again. In the western sky, and spreading around to the north and the south sides of the house, a beautiful, even rose-colored sky. Just like the color of a dark pink rose. Deep and even, and it came from the horizon in the trees up and over the house. The black outline of every tree in the hills around our farm seemed etched into that red sky. Against it I could see even the smallest black twig sharp and clear. But there were no people.

Back inside, Mother sat on the floor, then John came out from under the bed and sat next to her. She wanted to unwind the barbed wire from her feet and take off her mittens, but her hands were too frozen and we had to help her. Then John said, "Don-Don do it" and pushed us away and we all watched quietly, sitting there on that old wood floor, with Charley asleep in the kitchen while John patiently unwound the wire and peeled the frozen mittens off. Neatly, placing the discarded rags carefully in a pile on the floor next to him. Folding them all in prim little squares.

Mother told us she prayed over Dad, that he was dead and that "they let me cover his body." She used the blanket she'd wrapped around her shoulders. I have no idea who else was there, but she had to use the blanket around her shoulders for Dad. Then those damn cowards, whoever they were, let her walk back wearing less than she brought.

When we got her hands free there was no water left to wash them properly. We had used it all on Charley and were afraid to go outside to get more, especially now that it was almost dark. There was not even enough water to make her a cup of tea. We had been very wasteful in trying to help Charley and hadn't thought about her needing something when she returned.

But even that day, we knew we must be practical and think of the live-stock. Dad had shown us that all the days he was our father. Despite what the day brought, there were still responsibilities that didn't go away. We were talking about what we should do, when John looked down and mumbled something into his shirt we couldn't understand. We had to prod him a bit to get out what he was telling us. Remember how I told you John always had to stay inside and help Mother? Well he snuck out that day, just before noon, and fed and watered the livestock. He'd just wanted to do what the other boys got to do when they was old enough. We laughed and hugged him. Good old John.

So that was all. We just sat in the kitchen together, Mother with Dad's blood on her front, the rest of us with Charley's. No supper for the first time in my life. And we cried through our first night without our father.

After Myrtle Thompson left Grant's body and started home, Elisha Stark, justice of the peace, subpoenaed witnesses for an inquest into the matter of Grant Thompson's death. He filled in the standard form, stating:

> Whereas information has been given to the subscriber, E. H. Stark, a justice of the peace of the county of Miller, Missouri, that the dead body of Grant Thompson, supposed to have come to his death by violence, has been found at Bagnell, Missouri on the south bank of the Osage River.
>
> You are therefore commanded to summon six good and lawful men, householders of said township to appear at 3 p.m. at the said place where the said body was found and is now laying, then and there to enquire and true presentment make as to the manner and by whom the said deceased came to his death. Hereof fail not, but of this writ and your service make due return. Given under my hand and seal, at Bagnell in said county, this 24th day of December, 1924.

The form was signed, "E.H. Stark, Justice of the Peace." On the lower half of the form it continues, "In obedience to the command of the within writ I have summoned W.H. Mead, Andy Bond, L.V. Vaughn, Harry Denny, John Kelsey, T. J. Houston, residents and citizens of said County of Miller to be and appear at the time and place within mentioned."

During the 1970s, Hadley had gotten copies of the proceedings along with all available court records concerning the feud. On this form, the men were asked the same questions at the beginning:

"Did you see a shooting affair on the south side of the river this morning?"

Their answers varied:

"Well, I looked up and saw a man fall and roll down the bank, other shots were fired." "I was on the opposite bank on the river up near the gravel and heard some shots fired, looked across the river and saw about half a dozen men and heard other shots fired." "I heard some shots fired, looked across the river and saw a man fall. Other shots were fired, and during the shooting two other men fell to the ground." "I heard someone shout, 'Put that up' or 'Put that down.' Looked up and saw two men scuffling. Just then shots were fired and one man dropped in the road. Immediately after, another man fell and rolled over the bank."

"Could you tell who the parties were?"

"No." "No." "No." "No." "No." "No."

Ridenauer, as constable, was asked some other questions. Among them,

"Did you search the clothing of Grant Thompson?"

"Yes, sir."

"Did you find any weapons of any kind?"

"Nothing except a pocket revolver in his pocket."

"What, if anything, was lying near his body?"

"A walking stick, or cane."

The conclusions were stated as:

> We, the jury, having been duly sworn and affirmed by E. H. Stark, a Justice of the Peace, of Miller County, Missouri, diligently to inquire and true presentment make, in what manner and by whom Grant Thompson by a wound caused by the discharge from a shotgun in the hands of a party unknown to this jury.

These statements took on more meaning for me when I stood on the riverbank in Bagnell and stared across the Osage. It is not a long distance. I believe I could recognize a great many people I know should they be on the landing on the south side. In a community with so few people, where folks owned but one coat and hat, it was difficult to believe that nobody recognized the people standing on the other side. Especially those with red hair.

When we were little, we used to get up early and watch for Santy Claus to come. My mother and Dad would go out somewheres and bring the stuff in — probably popcorn balls or something. No stuff like you get today, mostly something usable, maybe a shirt, a pair of coveralls, or taffy, something like that. Once or twice we had a Christmas tree. I don't remember if Mother and Dad gave each other any gift or not. The only present I remember giving was to Hilda Brandt. I gave her a little vanity case.

I'm sure there was not a worse Christmas for a boy than that one on 1924. The next day, Christmas, Charley told us the whole story again. I guess that was just some kind of hallucination, him shooting Fred Crismon in the mouth. He surely thought he did but his mind must have been playing tricks on him.

Later we filled in some of the pieces to the story. Charley said Crismon shot my father right in the face with a 19-gauge shotgun just about the time he looked up. Crismon was so close to my father that the hole in his face, just under the right eye, was about three inches across where the shot entered and about four inches across where it came out of the back of his head, just behind the right ear.

Then Crismon hit my brother Charley over the head with the same gun that he shot my father with. He hit my brother so hard that the gun barrel bent, and Charley was knocked to the ground and lost the shotgun he was carrying. Francis was picking up the gun so as to kill my brother Charley with his own gun, but Charley was able to get that pistol out of his boot and shoot him. Charley knew he had to shoot Francis or be killed himself. Charley then broke away and stated running for his life.

Crismon's nephew ran after him and shot at him. Then some others joined the chase. They ran him about a mile or maybe more before they caught him. Charley's hands were frozen and he was almost frozen from the loss of blood from the wound on his head. Anyway, they caught him and took him to a house where they held him prisoner on the second floor.

My brother could hear them planning while they talked downstairs, and they decided that if Francis died they would kill Charley. So in his mind he had only one choice. He jumped out of the second floor window and started to run away. He had gone about one-half mile when they caught him again. But just as they caught him, a neighbor, Joe Blankenship, was coming down the path on his way to town. He asked what was going on. I think he had a good idea. This neighbor finally talked them into letting my brother Charley go. And Charley started to come home. Still no coat and no gloves. I think Joe Blankenship must have feared for his life as well, knowing he might hear

*about it if he helped Charley any more than he did. But at least he helped him
get away from the Crismons.*

GRANT THOMPSON & FRANCIS CRISMON DIE FOLLOWING GUN BATTLE

*Family feud of two years brought fatal results
Wednesday of last week when they meet at Bagnell Ferry*

Grant Thompson was instantly killed and Francis Crismon fatally
wounded about eight o'clock Wednesday morning of last week in a
gun battle between the Thompson and Crismon families at the south
Bagnell Ferry landing.

This was the third time the families have had trouble when shooting took place. The first shooting was in front of the Crismon home
a year ago when Thompson was shot by Crismon with a shot-gun.
Crismon was tried by jury and acquitted in this case, both parties having exchanged shots in the first fight. Thompson was then arrested on
a charge of felonious assault and the trial at the July term of circuit
court resulted in the jury failing to agree. About three months ago
Thompson and Francis Crismon had trouble on the Bagnell Ferryboat. Thompson struck the Crismon boy and Thompson was fined
in justice court at Bagnell. Another charge had since been brought
against Thompson for disturbing the peace by members of the Crismon family. The feud again took on a very serious aspect the 28th of
November when Thompson made an attempt on the life of Fred Crismon at Bagnell and shot him in the shoulder. A charge of felonious
assault was brought against him for this shooting and the case was to
be taken to another county for trial.

Both families reside on the south side of the Osage River from
Bagnell. The Crismon family about two miles from Bagnell and the
Thompsons about a mile farther down the river. Both families realized
the seriousness of the trouble and Thompson had on several occasions
publicly stated that he would get Crismon at the first opportunity,
referring to Fred Crismon, the father of Francis.

It so happened that Mr. Crismon and his two sons, Francis and
Leo, and nephew Logan Hickey came upon Thompson and his son
Charles at the Bagnell Ferry Wednesday morning. The ferryboat being
on the north side of the river, they became engaged in a heated conversation. Crismon saw that Charley was armed with a shot-gun, and
demanded that he hand over the gun to them. Many different reports
are heard as to how the shooting began. However, during the melee

which followed, Thompson was shot and instantly killed by Crismon and Francis Crismon was shot twice by Charley Thompson who was armed with a pistol which he brought into action after pulling it from his pocket. One shot struck the Crismon boy in the arm and the other shot, which proved fatal, struck him in the spine.

The Thompson boy was then struck by Crismon with a shot-gun and knocked down. He jumped up and ran from the scene, going up the river chased by the Hickey boy, who overtook him south of Elmer Kidwell's. The Thompson boy abandoned his overcoat, overshoes and gloves and his hands were frozen. He was taken to the Kidwell home where he was thawed out. It is reported that his hands may require amputation.

The injured Crismon boy was paralyzed from the shot in his spine and his father took him home in the Thompson car, so it is reported. The Crismons had gone to town afoot, while the Thompsons had used their car.

The body of Thompson lay on the south bank of the river from eight o'clock in the morning till about three o'clock in the afternoon and an inquest was held by an order of the Prosecuting Attorney.

Friday the Crismon boy's condition became so serious it was decided to take him to the hospital in Jefferson City. An examination was made that evening when it was found that the bullet had struck the spine and that his condition was very grave. An operation was undertaken Saturday morning and the bullet was located in the marrow of the spine. He never survived the operation.

As the sun was rising, up drives a car. We are scared to death. We don't have cars driving up. But it's Matt Martin, his boys, and another. Matt's a mail carrier out of Brumley. The family is related to the Crismons and they've been sympathizers with the KKK and we know this. But Joe's a friend of Paul Martin and they've played on a team together, so we decide to send Joe out to see what they want. Next thing you know, he brings them in the house.

"We've come from a Klan meetin' in Eldon, where they voted to wipe the Thompson family out. But we're here, and we're here to stay."

So they come in, and they have some extra guns and some food Mrs. Martin sent. We have no water, but we pull down the bed from the wardrobe in the parlor and they sit there, right by the door, and wait.

We still don't have Dad's body, mind you. I heard from a lot of people they just let it lie there on the bank all day. I know the coroner pronounced him dead. Dead from what? Froze to death. That's what the first report said, and that was the KKK for you. But somebody must have stopped them from getting away with that.

That next morning it's a little bit warmer. We make our way out to the scale shed, where there's a space in the foundation to crawl under and we put Mother and John out there to hide. Mother's in the same clothes wearing Dad and Charley's blood. Charley's suffering something fierce in the kitchen. Joe has some whiskey he made from raisins with Paul, and he gets it, so Charley drinks it now. One shot of that and you could turn the world over. It seems to help, but we know we need to get Charley to the doctor soon.

Then more cars start coming. The first one, it's a big car, black. And then another one, bigger than the first, with running boards and all. We don't know these people and we've all got our guns out just wondering what the hell is happening. I'm only thirteen. A tough-looking character jumps out and opens the car door for another and quick as a cat out steps Cousin Happy, the number one bootlegger in all of Jefferson City. We learned later some hill folk watched the whole thing happen and went to send Happy the word. They were kin of the widow lady Mother and Dad sent food to.

Happy's real name was Elmer Wornell. He was my mother's brother's boy. He was a big guy — not the type you miss. He had a key to every door at the capital and delivered whatever they wanted when there was nobody there. They'd just pay up later. Remember, this was prohibition. And now he was coming through for us, pin-striped suits and all.

Out of the next car come men with machine guns, all in suits. They wouldn't come in. I don't remember them saying anything to any of us — they just stayed out in the yard, smoking, and waiting. They took their orders from Happy only. Joe was given a gun, a 45 with an automatic clip. He was supposed to hide in a big rose bush behind a boulder out in the yard. When the shooting started it was my job to keep the clip for that gun filled.

Paul asked, "Can you get us some water?" They did.

Well, this went on for a bit and nothing happened. Nobody else came. Then Mother, who seen it all from the scale shed, decides that her and John ain't going to be poor hosts. She came in from the back and changed her clothes and sent John out to build a fire in a barrel for the men in the yard to have some warmth. Paul decides he's gonna go get some more water, and you might think we shoulda never let him go, being the youngest, but there wasn't a rabbit quicker in the brush than Paul. So really, he was safer out there than in with us. Still, nobody else comes.

So here's Mother, not knowing where her dead husband is or what's coming next, but she's not going to be caught in an old soiled dress, and her guests, even if they are a bunch of hoodlums, are going to be properly fed.

By the time we have some plates ready to take out to the men, they've gotten pretty bored and are playing mumbly-peg. I'll never forget that sight either. Grown men, standing next to two burn barrels, one man with his legs spread wide, black and white shoes and thick-cuffed pants. Another throwing a knife between his buddy's feet and the rest laying out money on the hood of the car as the men bet on the outcome of the game.

Mother had hung out the wash on Christmas Eve morning, and it was frozen stiff as boards hanging there. Happy's men helped Mother by banging on the clothes with their machine guns, trying to see who could get the ice slivers to fly the farthest. Then one carried the clothes in to her. They didn't know what to do with themselves, Still, no Klan. Still, no war.

Finally, long after noon, another two cars. They stop at the sycamore ridge and wave a white handkerchief, then come on real slow. I'm sure everyone in the neighborhood knew when Happy's cars drove up, just as I'm sure everyone saw Mother walking to and from Dad's body by herself.

The only car we'd ever seen on our road before that day was our own, and now the farm was full of 'em. The first one coming up the drive is ours. We notice that right off. It's being driven by somebody we don't even know, and still to this day I can't remember who it was, but he tells us the undertaker already has a coffin that will fit Dad just fine. If we want, he'll send word back that he can come on.

The second vehicle is a flat bed truck, and they have a rolled up bundle in the back. We are all out there when it pulls up. Even John. Nobody says anything, but we know it's Dad.

FRANCIS CRISMAN DIES IN JEFFERSON CITY

Was Shot Last Wednesday By Charles Thompson

*Large Funeral Held at Baptist Church
Here Tuesday Under Auspices of K.K.K.*

Francis Crisman, 20 year old son of Fred Crisman, prominent farmer living just across the Osage river from Bagnell, died at St. Mary's Hospital in Jefferson City, about 5 o'clock Saturday afternoon, following an operation for the removal of a bullet from his spine. He was shot in the back by Charles Thompson, Wednesday, Dec. 24 and became paralyzed, the bullet lodging in the marrow of the spine.

The body of young Crisman was brought to Eldon Sunday morning and Monday one of the largest funerals was conducted at the First Baptist church by the pastor Rev. G. N. Magruder. An escort of over seventy members of the Ku Klux Klan, in full regalia, accompanied the body to the Eldon Cemetery where the regular order of service was conducted by officers of the Jefferson City Klan Realm of Missouri of the Invisible Empire of the Knights of the Ku Klux Klan. They took no part at the church except to form a line when the body was taken into the church and removed, but left the service entirely to the religious order of the church.

The bugle "taps" was one of the most impressive parts of the Klan program. At the grave the speaker read from the 12th chapter of Romans and said in the olden time when a Klansman's life was taken the prevailing idea was "An eye for an eye, a tooth for a tooth, and a life for a life." But the modern foundation of the Ku Klux Klan on the tenants of the true Christian religion put away this spirit of revenge and taught the higher ideals of life and Christian living.

The feud that existed between the Fred Crisman and Grant Thompson families was not a religious row or organization trouble as has been reported, but started two years ago when young Crisman and his neighbor, Charles Thompson, were candidates for the same school. Mr. Crisman securing the school over his opponent aroused a spirit of ill will.

Francis Crisman was born in Miller County, April 12, 1904. He united with the Eldon Baptist church during 1921. During his student life at the Eldon high school he was a favorite among his fellow students who liked him for his wholesome social disposition and life. Most the students attended the funeral services and expressed their regret for his untimely death.

Besides the father and mother Mr. and Mrs. Fred Crisman, he leaves one brother, Leo, and a sister, Miss Anita, both younger.

Hadley always said nobody could keep the boys straight, and this is evident in this transcript from a local paper which cites Charlie as the teacher in the family instead of Otto, as well as from Leo Crismon earlier stating that John was armed and shooting.

In the 1960s Leo also wrote his rendition of the occurrence:

Just before Christmas, December 24, 1924 Grant, Otto and Charley passed by our house going to Bagnell in their car. My father, Francis and I, with Logan Hickey, a cousin, walked through the fields to the ferry tower, on the opposite side of the River from Bagnell. Grant and Charley had shotguns. Otto had no gun as I remember. My father told Charley to drop his shotgun. He did, but as Francis approached him to take away the shotgun, Charley drew a pistol from his coat and shot Francis. [On the back of the page in Leo's handwriting it also says, 'Francis took the shotgun and turned to walk back up the incline to the ferry tower and Charley drew a pistol from the inside lining of his coat and shot Francis in the back.'] When Grant drew his gun my father shot him in the face and he fell dead on the ice. Charley then ran from the scene and Logan Hickey ran after him. And finally disarmed him. The pistol shot struck Francis in the back and went into his spine and paralyzed him. We took him home and called Dr. Shelton and Dr. Logan Allee of Eldon. The next day, Christmas Day, he was taken to St. Mary's Hospital in Jefferson City, where he died on December 27, 1924.

Francis had been attending High School at Eldon and had a rented room there. He was at home for the Christmas vacation period when he was killed.

Twenty years later Leo again wrote the story, with a few differences:

On Dec. 21 or 22, 1924, at the ferry landing on the east side of the Osage River at Bagnell, when my father shot Grant Thompson, both Grant and Charley were standing together on the ice when we arrived at the scene. The river was frozen out 30 to 50 feet from each bank and a row boat was used to cross the running water. My father order [sic] Charley to come on to the bank to try to unarm Charley. They both had double barrel shot guns. Charley passed by my father and father told him to drop the shot gun and Francis was to pick it up. As Charley dropped the gun and Francis stooped to pick it up Charley drew a pistol from an inside pocket and shot Francis. Logan Hickey was standing on the high bank and said he saw all the action.

It seems that my father had taken his eyes off of Charley when he dropped the gun and he did not see Charley draw the pistol. The pistol shot from Charley was the first shot fired. When my father heard that shot then he shot Grant Thompson in the head with his shot gun and he dropped to the ice and lay there until late in the afternoon. The pistol shot paralysed [sic] Francis and he fell to the ground. Charley held on to the pistol and started to run to the south, or up the river. My father told Logan to go after him and catch him. My father and I carried Francis to the Thompson car, a model T Ford touring car, with curtains up at that time. We drove back to our house with Francis and I drove the car back from our house to the ferry landing, where Grant

Thompson was lying and I walked home through the snow covered fields. As we were carrying Francis up the ferry road to the Thompson car, we heard him say "Father unto thy hands I commend my spirit".

Leo's son later added that when Leo heard him commend his soul to God, Leo knew his brother Francis was not going to live.

They say before a man dies his life passes before his eyes. All I know is when someone you love leaves you alone in the world, all you can think of are the good times, and they play in your mind like the scenes from a movie.

I could see my father sitting at the kitchen table on winter evenings, coffee mug in both rough hands, talking about the upcoming season and planning his crops. Then he was at the fireside, rocking and reading the Bible to us, then outside with his fox-hunting friends, smiling and laughing as he listened to their stories. Then he was working, and I could hear him grunt with the strain of a broad axe, stretching it high over his head before he let it fall, and I could see the sweat pressing his shirt against his body. Now he's swinging that sickle - swish, swish, swish. And there he is with Mother in the sled with Professor Molls, the three of them wrapped up in blankets, all waving and calling out "Goodbye" to those who're left behind. Then the jingle of the bells fading in the silence.

I saw my first motion picture after I left to join the Navy, and when I did, I thought the camera had captured the scenes that play in the mind after a death.

What did I really see? For seventy years I've had memories of my father lying in the bed I slept in with my brother Paul with half his head blowed off, and brains and skull bones all over his cap and clothes. It's not a very nice memory.

I'll share something I've discovered after years of living on this here earth. You know, I've lived through about every situation a man can find himself in. And in order to live, not just stay alive, but really live, a person's got to have rules to live by. Not somebody else's rules now, his own rules. He's got to figure out what his rules are and then he's got to really abide by them and when he does, that's when he'll know he's truly alive. And when he breaks his own rules, that's usually when he feels lost.

My Dad's main rule was, "Never be afraid. Fear'll never help you." And you know, even at the end there, I don't think he was afraid. Resigned maybe, but not afraid. He lived up to that saying until the end.

The newspapers and other surviving relatives helped paint a sketchy picture of events after the murders.

Otto's daughter Olive remembers being in school on December 24th. Her father appeared at the door and said, "Dismiss the children. They've killed my Dad." She also remembers going to the Thompson home before the funeral. After Grant was laid out on the boys' bed, an undertaker from Bagnell appeared. Otto came out to the parlor and announced to Mrytle, "They're gonna shave Dad." To which she replied, "Oh no they're not!"

The grandchildren all saw Grandfather Thompson laid out in the casket but they were taken someplace else during the funeral. Grant was buried at the Hawkins cemetery, with his first wife Emma, and the infants Gie Basel, Karma, and Web. Paul Thompson's widow told me that at the funeral a white dove came and landed on Myrtle Thompson's shoulder and then flew away. White doves are not commonly found in the Ozarks. Grant was buried with his full, scar-covering beard, the tip of a knife blade from his gambling days still imbedded in his head.

Charley was taken to Brumley and put under a doctor's care while he stayed at his grandfather Maston Wornell's house. His hands recovered without amputation.

For the next three months both the *Miller County Autogram* and the *Eldon Advertiser* kept the neighborhood up to date on proceedings surrounding the murders and legal events. But I never could find an obituary for Grant Thompson in any of the newspapers from the area.

On 8 January 1925, next to a story about an attempt by the Anti-prohibition Society in Missouri to repeal Dry Laws, was the following article. The Eldon newspaper chose to spell Charley's name differently than he did.

CHARLIE THOMPSON IS CHARGED WITH MURDER

Sheriff Frank Burks placed Charlie Thompson, age 17, under arrest last Thursday on a warrant charging him with first degree murder in connection with the death of Francis Crismon, who was shot in the spine by the Thompson boy the morning of December 24th.

The Thompson boy is now being cared for at the home of his grandfather, J. M. Wornell, at Brumley. The boy's hands are yet in a bad shape from being frozen the day of the shooting and on the advice of Dr. Dickson the boy was not taken from the home of his grandfather and his bond was filled without the customary procedure. The warrant and papers were drawn up the 1st day of the year by Pros. Atty Kay and by Pros. Atty-elect Stillwell, and the case will be presented by the latter.

A preliminary hearing is set for Friday, to be held at the court house before Squire G. T. Nichols, justice of the peace of Equality township.

Then on 15 January 1925, the *Miller County Autogram* ran two articles arranged exactly as printed here:

CHARLIE THOMPSON ABSOLVED FROM BLAME

Preliminary Hearing Friday Results in His Release

Charlie Thompson, who was charged with murder in connection with the death of Francis Crismon the day before Christmas, was released here Friday by order of Squire G. T. Nichols, justice of the peace of Equality township.

Only four witnesses were examined — Fred Crismon, Leo Crismon, Logan Hickey and Chat Lupardus. According to the statement of Fred Crismon, five shots were fired from a pistol by the Thompson boy, four at Francis and one at the witness. The court ruled in the boy's favor on the grounds of self-defense.

The testimony was taken in type-written form in case it should become a matter for grand jury investigation at a later date.

This case attracted much attention and the court room was well-filled by interested spectators from the time the court began at 10:30 a.m. 'till the decision was given at about 8:00 p.m.

KU KLUX KLAN MEETING

Regular meeting of Eldon Klan to be held at the regular place of meeting at Eldon, Missouri. Thursday evening, January 22nd. 1925. Important business to be transacted. All members urged to attend.

KLIGRAPP

Later editions of the same newspaper announced that Fred Crismon was in Bagnell Wednesday morning, and that Jim Thompson of near Bagnell brought his brothers Joe and Charles (Charley) to the home of J. M. Wornell. Joe was reportedly starting back to school and Charles was taking treatments from Dr. Dickson. The paper also reported Charles as spending a Thursday night with Perry Martin and family. Leo Crismon spent a few days at the Davis Hickey home.

Life went on as usual in Miller County. Hacks turned over on children, cars slid off icy roads, two boys got into a dispute at a play party and one got stabbed in the leg, there was an eclipse of the sun, and mothers were advised to give their sick children California Fig Syrup for their bowels.

On 7 February 1925, Charley filled out a sworn statement stating that Frederick Crismon did feloniously, willfully, deliberately, premeditatedly and with malice aforethought discharge and shoot off a shot gun at Grant Thompson which did strike, penetrate and inflict a mortal wound so inflicted as aforesaid the said Grant Thompson on the 24th day of December 1924, at the County of Miller aforesaid, did die.

According to the 13 Februray 1925 *Miller County Autogram*, on 12 February 1925 Frederick P. Crismon was charged with murder. According to this same edition, he moved his household goods to Eldon that Friday after being released on $2,000 bond, put up by Elmer Kidwell, Leo Crismon, and David Helton. The case was set for March term of the circuit court. A change of venue was requested. The case was to be tried on March 31st in Tuscumbia.

On 26 March, a preliminary hearing was held.

The first day of the first public hearing was held at the Miller County Court-house in Tuscumbia. They had long benches with backs on them, like pews, and along both sides of the courtroom were tall windows that went almost to the floor. They were needed in those days before air conditioning when the court was packed. The trial was on the third floor and from that room you could look over the treetops and see the river winding through the hills, wandering from bluff to bluff. That old building's still there.

Everybody was there. Old widows, Klansmen, friends of ours and the Crismons, salesmen. If a man left to spit somebody else slid into their seat. Folks waited four or five thick outside the door.

Outside, on the way to the toilets, were groups of people. Men in one group, women in the other. It could've been Decoration Day or threshing, but there weren't no laughter. No singing. No children or dogs. No flasks. Just quiet talk. Over by the outside pump were some men wearing suits and shoes made out of two shades of leather. Everybody speculated as to where they came from and why they were there.

Back upstairs it was hotter than Hell's hinges, and the hat on my lap left a circle of sweat on my pants. It was odd to be so hot so early in the year. Maybe it was just all those people in that room. The windows were pushed all the way up, but the breeze from the river was dead. The only thing that came into that room was the sweet smoke from a gypsy's fire pit. I was glad to see them there, like they was old friends come from out of town. They were selling catfish and squirrel and spiced apples. Dad couldn't catch me anymore buying their food, but I didn't go against his wishes anyway.

There were witnesses for the defense, who sat up in front on the witness stand sanding and varnishing the truth so long pretty soon it sounded like it's reasonable that a man using a cane and keeping his gun in his pocket somehow deserved to get his head blowed off.

In the audience, people fanned themselves with round paper fans that said, "Vote Wilson for Sheriff" on them. Nobody said nothing, or moved much neither. Uncle Lev sat through the whole trial, still as plump as his cigar, looking dressed up even in a pair of coveralls. He gave me some pocket money, probably to my brothers, too. But the real friends were some of Dad's fox-hunting friends, and these old guys were on the front row with the whole seat to themselves. This little blond-headed dude, he was sitting there with about fifty feet of coiled rope in his lap.

What were they going to do? Well, Klansmen weren't being found guilty anywheres during that time, and these men knew it. So when they brought Crismon in, if he wasn't going to be held for trial or found guilty, or whatever they were deciding that day, they were going to put that rope around his neck and throw him out the window. Hang him!

Then Mother got wind of it.

Mother felt she had to do whatever she could to stop the bloodshed. So she went to that hearing and when it was near the end, she went down the aisle to the front, then got down on her knees and started to pray out loud. The judge noticed and said she needed to go back to her seat. No. She would not.

She knelt in front of the first man, then walked on her knees to the second, until she had begged before every friend of my father's to stop and to let the law decide and then to abide by that. Finally two men got her to her feet and back to her seat.

Those friends of his, they knew the jury was stocked with KKK who would never convict Crismon. They felt torn I'm sure, between the two —

their loyalty to my father and their respect for my mother. I honestly don't know what Dad would've wanted us to do. Keep fighting, for sure; but my Mother had been through so much, and he wouldn't have wanted to make her life any worse than it already was. That's one of the hardest things to face, you know, trying to do what somebody would want when they ain't there to tell you themselves.

She talked to us about it I don't know how many times. "It don't take a very big person to carry a grudge," she'd tell us. "Fred and Sarah watched their son die. I know how that feels. There ain't more punishment than that, and if I was to lose one of you, after losing your father, I wouldn't be able to go on."

After Dad died, she took over talking to us like he would have. We were not to go after the Crismons. She made that plain as day. There were plenty who said they'd help us. There were plenty of plots and plans. But then there was Mother, a new person. Looking at our faces at the supper table saying to each of us, "I will not lose another child."

On Thursday, 3 April 1925, the *Miller County Autogram* issued this report:

THOMPSON-CRISMON DIFFERENCES SETTLED

Both Families Agreed To Drop Contentions
Which Resulted In Death In Each Family

A mutual agreement was reached here at the courthouse last week between the Grant Thompson and Fred Crismon families when all agreed to let bygones be bygones and drop their contentions and strife which resulted in the death of Grant Thompson and Francis Crismon, who were killed by gunshot wounds the day before Christmas, and scars from the feud carried by one member of each family.

This compromise was accomplished through the efforts of members of the grand jury who took the position that for the best interests of both families and the people in general the matter should be dropped by all parties rather than have the affair carried in court indefinitely and the trouble not being finally settled.

It is to be hoped that this will all work out for the best of everyone concerned, for the Bible says, "Blessed are the peacemakers."

After all that, we didn't even go into town much at all. If we did, we just left our grain at the mill and came back for it, and the talk stopped when we came in the door and didn't start up again until we left. We never went anywhere by ourselves and always were armed. Joe and me, we just weren't the type to sit back and let things take their course.

Joe spent a lot of time in Brumley at Grandpa Wornell's after he stopped going to the teacher's college. Les Leids was over there quite a bit as well, actin' like nothing had changed, slapping folks on the back like they was pals, calling out to others from across the street. As far as the law was concerned, Leids had nothing to do with the murders. But we knew he egged people on everywhere he went.

To this day I believe the Crismons were given an order to take care of the Thompsons. The Klan was the rope that either led you or hung you. Maybe Charley's mouth that morning at the landing had something to do with it, I don't know. Maybe he just wasn't going to let himself get tied up and whipped, I don't know. But I think the sheriff was trying to give us a warning the day he came to the farm.

Charley, Joe, and I helped Otto do everything that needed to be done. Mother insisted Paul go to school, but I never went to Post Oak again. Never even set foot in it, I don't believe. Did have part of a year at the Bagnell High School when they got enough money to get it started again.

We heard talk the Crismon farm was up for sale. Of course, Fred didn't own it but I guess a relative still did. We weren't afraid to go past his place anymore and welcomed it in a way, always ready to be the ones who would shoot first, just with the littlest come-on from them. But there was nothing. Everything as still as death when we went by. The Crismons had moved shortly after the shootings.

Then April was over and it truly was spring. 1925. You never saw the timber come up so fast. The day I'm going to tell you about must have been early because the dogwoods hadn't bloomed yet. The chokecherries and redbuds blossoms were out and the woodpeckers were busy claiming their territories for us all to hear. Rat-ta-tat-a-tat! Loud and clear from one hill. Then the rival answered just as quick, Rat-ta-tat-a-tat! Each proclaiming to anyone listening that they were the real owners of those hills.

I'd learned something just a few months before, back when I was a boy cutting ties with Charley: If a log is big enough, and the steep slope it lays on is cleared of trees, there's nothing that can stop that log's downward roll. Les Leids was like that log. He had cleared out all the obstacles standing in his way. He'd grown in community stature and was fat with power. Perhaps

206 Victoria Pope Hubbell

some men owed him. Perhaps they was worried he would fell them as well. But Les was as thick and solid as an oak trunk and nothing was going to get in his way as he rolled over everything in his path. Some would say he stirred up trouble. I say he was the trouble. He didn't loose a father or a son to slow him down none. He was still going strong.

Plez had come for a day or two, making puny attempts to cut firewood and help out around the place. We loved him, but that didn't stop him being in the way of our backswing every time we tried to get something done. Plez was really no help at all, but he played the organ for Mother and it was comforting to see him sitting on the porch drinking sassafras tea. That's one thing he could do very well. I also think he talked to Otto a great deal about all that had happened, but never in front of Mother.

Then Paul and me went to Brumley to hook up with Joe and come back with him. Of course, Mother and John were back at the farm. Maston was an old man now, his shoulders more bony than broad, but his mind still the likes of quicksilver.

We were on our way home, riding on the road north of Brumley. We'd already cut up the hill toward home when we heard the shot. Just one. We saw nothing then, and when we got to the top of the hill and turned back to look once more, we saw a log lying in the road near where we'd just left off.

We didn't pay much attention to that old log in the road until we noted a horse standing nearby, reins hanging on the ground while it grazed, sometimes stepping on them with a front hoof. So Joe said, "Hold up, Barney." And we looked closer down on the road and saw it weren't no log at all. It was a rider, fallen.

"Should we go on down there?" I asked. We couldn't see it was Les Leids lying face down with a bullet hole smack between his eyes, eyes wide open and covered with road dust.

"Hey now, what's that?" I pointed. Other riders were coming that way, hadn't gotten to the man and horse yet, still too far off for the horse to look up and wait. Of course, we didn't see Aunt Maggie come out of her house, her long hair pinned back, but falling to her waist. We couldn't hear Aunt Maggie tell everyone she'd seen a very tall, thin man in a red plaid shirt on a grey horse, appearing outta nowheres following Leids as he left town. We watched the riders until they went behind a clump of trees and we couldn't see none of them for a bit, but we knew they would be on the fallen rider in no time, so we just sat up there and waited. Breathed in the perfume of the cedar and sage.

No, all we saw was another figure on a black horse cresting a ridge and disappearing again, way over west. Nobody ever asked us, but if they had, we couldn't have told them who it was because we never saw his face. Just a black *horse. No, all we seen was the smooth, round rump of well-trained horseflesh, and the even, controlled canter of a gentleman. We sat up there on our horses and watched Plez ride out of our lives for the last time. He never said goodbye. When we found out the fallen log in the road had been Les Leids, Joe looked at me and whispered, "Stop whatever you're doing!"*

They never did find the culprit, but Plez did old Leids a favor. He didn't have to fall to his knees in front of another man. He got to die without beggin' or cryin' or clingin' to another man's boots. I believe Plez done what he could for Professor's horses and our dad.

The only person the law found fitting Aunt Maggie's description was an old farmer cutting back blackberry canes behind his barn. But his horse clearly hadn't been ridden all winter so they didn't even bother questioning the man. They found the gun tossed aside in the brush by the side of the road. It was just a regular old .32 Harrington Richards. Same as everybody and their dog carried. Weren't no sense for the sheriff even asking who had one because the answer was everybody.

And one more thing. When I was in Bagnell the next summer I saw something that made me smile. No, it made me laugh, and my brothers laughed when I told them. It was the first time I'd laughed since Charley and me went off to cut ties. We never told Mother, though.

There was Ty Sears, walking down Locust Street, just as mean and ornery as ever, and he saw me. I stared at him, and even though I knew I should pull my eyes away, I kept them on his face waiting for him to curse me. But he didn't. Ever so slightly, still with the frown that was frozen on his face, he tipped his hat at me and Mother.

As he passed, the sun caught a glimmer of something at his side. It flashed at me like a boy with a pocket mirror, issuing a come-on. I turned to follow it and sure enough, it was the handle of a pearl-handled .41 caliber Colt Lightening. I could've told you how long the barrel was because I'd stared at that gun so many times. That gun shot more dimes outta the sky than there were stars.

Life in Miller County resumed. The 9 April edition of the *Miller County Autogram* announced construction of the new hydroelectric dam. There was also a notice warning people about a rabid dog in the area, reminding me of a story Grant Thompson told the boys. When Grant was a boy he heard the screams of a man who had contracted rabies. Neighbors had locked him in an abandoned cabin and left him to die.

Other newspaper stories described a man falling under a freight train, a fourteen-year-old not being allowed to marry, violations of prohibition laws, and the marriage of Logan Hickey and Ruby Kidwell. During the next few months the paper reported on drownings, a fourteen-year-old boy killing a principal of a school, Hilda Brandt (Hadley's crush) visiting friends in Bagnell, and the continual advertisement of a man desiring to buy some false teeth.

In July, Myrtle Thompson was listed as executor of the estate of J. G. Thompson. The Missouri Hydro-Electric Company recorded the first deed in Miller County for the new dam, by purchasing 18.65 acres of river bottom for $550 from John W. Kehr. The first woman in Miller County was convicted of violating prohibition laws when Mrs. Josephine Wilbers, a widow, had her illegal still blown up by authorities. Her reported response was, "How will I make a living for the children?"

In August, Lee Thornsberry, the man whose name first caught my eye when he bought a pair of stretchy mules from Grant Thompson, opened his store at Dam Site, a newly developed area for the Bagnell Dam workers. A week later, preliminary construction of Bagnell Dam began. A meeting of the Eldon Klan was also announced.

Following the summer of 1925, the names Crismon and Thompson were noticeably absent from the newspaper. After following the families' whereabouts for years, I could not find mention of their names even though I continued reading newspaper issues through the end of 1925.

January, 2000

Why didn't Otto kill him? If I'd been in Otto's place I'da killed him. I'da killed the whole damn bunch. I tried it a few times after.

I'd go squirrel hunting where I'd know Crismon would be taking a wagon to gather corn on the river bottom. He'd come back to the area for that. And I was there in the brush once. I drew a bead at his head, the right side, same as where he shot my dad. My heart was beating like I just swam across the river and back, but instead I laid the gun across my knees for a minute and rocked back on my heels.

And then a soft voice from behind me said, "Walk away from that thought, boy. Yessir, crawl like lightening. Because only a blind man could make a shot like that." Then I heard a "Thwat!"

It was crazy. I was thinking about killing a man and the thought of old Chicken Fat opening up that beard and spitting tobacco juice with more accu-

racy than I could shoot made me want to laugh. Then he started to talk, takin'
all the time in the world and then some, in that easy drawl of his. I just sat
there and never looked behind me at the voice.

"The soul of men only got one soul. You kill a man, you kill yourself and
the folks you love, too." Finally, I turned to look at him. But there wasn't any-
thing there. I wonder now if I just imagined the whole thing,

Where is there justice? I looked for justice my whole life. Now I know jus-
tice is only fashioned by the hands of God. It is His business, same as birthing
and dying. I do not believe, as I once did, that I will see justice on this earth
anyway. No, I will not see it here.

All I see is that barefoot kid, standing in his Dad's field, the sun warm on
his face, and all God's good earth spread out around him. I can hear the crickets
rasping and the clatter of the sycamore leaves. I can feel the breeze off the river.
Look around — everything I need is in those hills. Water, sun, soil, fish, and
my brothers are there too. The part of me that's still a kid wants to forget all
the bad and just remember the good between those river bluffs and in those
hollows.

Icel tells me not to judge and that I got to forgive. The Bible says, "Judge
not, lest ye be judged." Well, I'm poor at the both of 'em. I can't forgive and I
can't forget. So I guess I'll be judged someday.

Yes, I will be judged.

2006.

Hadley's been gone for six years now. Without him as a guide, I
decide to take the dogs out to the old Thompson farm. It's fall and the
only green lies still and cold, covering the floor of the fields. The rest of
the farm is a hazy blur of gold and brown.

As I walk past the barn built by the boys after their father's death,
I stare at the rifle butt and pipe imbedded in the foundation. None of
the remaining relatives know why the items are there. Joe said, "They
weren't nothing, just a silly thing." I'm still suspicious and can't help but
shake my head and smile at the sight. Ah, those Thompsons.

I sit down on the ground and lean back along the hill where Hadley's nephew Phillip Thompson said the first homestead was. Someplace
behind me is an old cistern a boy once filled with snakes. But I don't
know where to stomp down the grass to find it. I just stare up at the sky
for a while and ponder important things and don't think about work that
needs to be done. Then I listen for the clang of the blacksmith's hammer.

It comes, of course. A song of one note, ringing through the cool silence, metal on metal. Then the soft drone of wagon wheels coming slowly down a rocky road. Hooves on stone and dirt, coming faster as the horses near the barn. Now the shouts and laughter of boys. They're picking apples for their mother, wasting the bruised and rotten ones by throwing them at each other, even though she's told them a million times she wants them for pies. She'll carefully cut out what is good and feed the rest to the hogs. I shut my eyes and let the sounds of the Thompson family surround me.

Much too soon the sun slips behind the hills and the chilled, damp ground makes me get up. I smell Myrtle's apple pies baking, because after all, it's Tuesday: baking day. It's October now, and John's fire in the smoke house fills the air with the luscious smell of smoking meat. It smells like cloves.

I need to get home to my small family. Like Myrtle Thompson, I'm the only female now in my house; both girls left Missouri to go to college. How Myrtle's heart must have ached when she lost children after such a short time. Some might think the pain dulls, because she didn't have them for that long, but I think not. Four years was only as long as I knew Hadley. It's curious how someone whose life crosses yours for just a piece of time can mean so much to you.

I call the dogs off whatever hole they've found and start to walk back to my car, when suddenly a flash of gray with just a shake of cinnamon darts in front of me. Then into the brush like a train to a tunnel. It's the fox, looking unkempt in his warm-weather coat. The rich, red of winter along his back is just starting. This farm belongs to him now.

Then right when I get to the sycamore's spot, I hear the shot and the horn. Hadley hollers over at me from the ridge, waving and pointing at the river to tell me one last thing he forgot to mention. He's worried I'll never get the story straight. He's right of course, but it's too late now. Our time together is just a memory. A memory I never want to cut loose.

EPILOGUE

—Courtesy Thompson Family

Hadley Thompson

Hadley did not finish the rest of his eighth grade year, but a few years later when the Bagnell High School had the money to start up again, Hadley enrolled. He quit at the end of October. For years, he told people it was because he "got drunk on plum wine, tore up a Halloween party and didn't want to face Thelma Osborn." He told me that same story early in our meetings. But later he recanted and said the real reason he joined the service at age seventeen is because he was so filled with "rage and frustration I just had to get out of there." Myrtle Thompson signed the papers verifying Hadley was eighteen. Hadley believed it to be the first lie she ever told.

Hadley met Anastasia "Annie" Furlong (18 January 1915 — 20 September 1992) while following in Cousin Happy's footsteps. While stationed at a Naval base in Philadelphia, Hadley rented a room from a man with property near the Wharf and used this room to sell bootlegged liquor to fellow servicemen. Annie was the man's daughter, and she loved to party. She also sang at nightclubs. Eventually her drinking became a problem and divorce ensued. She later told their daughter Patricia Anastasia Thompson (born in 1934), "He was the only man I ever loved. If I had stayed with him I would have ruined him." Hadley often gave public and private testimony that only when he met some Salvation Army representatives on a pier did his private life begin to turn around.

Hadley and Icel were married in 1937, by Judge Bert Rogers in Kansas City. Judge Rogers stated he was the father of Buddy Rogers, the husband of screen star Mary Pickford. Hadley told me many other bloodlines throughout the telling of this story, which were omitted because although usually fascinating, without Hadley's accompanied diagram sketched on a paper napkin, they were just too confusing.

Hadley's Navy career lasted thirty-eight years. During World War II, Hadley served as a Chief Commissary Steward, serving in both the North Atlantic and South Pacific. Hadley's veteran's records list him as Seaman 2nd Class Petty Officer, pay number 6-145, 5th Division, U.S. New Mexico, San Paulo, California, while photos suggest he was also an official photographer for the group.

After retiring from the Navy, Hadley worked for public services in Kansas City until 1955, when a doctor told him he only had about a year to live. Although the Thompson farm was no longer in the family, Hadley and Icel made the decision to return to the area of their childhoods. Soon Hadley became impatient waiting to die and decided he would clear out some brush on his property. The dying took far longer than he anticipated and in the meantime, he built and started Thompson's Resort on the Lake of the Ozarks. Hadley eventually lost all patience with the notion that death would visit anytime soon, so he and Icel owned and operated this resort for many years.

He took up carving local birds and animals, some of which can be seen at the Miller County Museum. Hadley also became active in city politics. He was never shy about voicing his opinion or standing up for something or someone and was responsible for building the public restrooms at the Bagnell Dam strip. I remember this every time I drive by, as I also think of him when I see the mounted eagles at the Lake Ozark Post Office. He and Joe had a guilty secret about the origins of the display.

Hadley died on 4 May 2000, at the age of eighty-eight. Years before, Hadley and Icel had planned on burial at a site other than the Hawkins Cemetery. But a few months before his death, Hadley changed his mind. Full military honors were given by VFW Post 2442, a group he had been active with for years. Even Hadley's obituary didn't quite get his family straight, as it left out two sisters and four brothers who preceded him in death.

Less than four years after Hadley died, Icel followed him to this quiet spot in the country, with all the Thompson relatives he knew so well, thanks to all the Decoration Days and lectures from Plez Moore and Aunt Maggie.

I drove past Hadley and Icel's house once, just to prove what I already knew in my heart; the new owners had painted it a respectable and modern color.

What became of Charley? According to Hadley, "Charley became kind of a recluse after all this. He married a Hendrix. I think her name was Netha? She was born and raised over there by Ulman and the Dog Creek School area. She had a cleft palate."

Charley drove an electric trolley car in Kansas City. Nephew Larry (Paul's son) recalls him reaching down and pulling Larry on to the trolley as a youngster. Charley had a son Robert Porter Thompson (Bobby) who married Peggy Ann Harris. The family believed Bobby died of a heart attack before the writing of this story. Genealogy records list their children as Marsha Ann, Lynn Ellen, and William Clayton, but I was unable to find any of them.

Charley was killed in a tornado near Kansas City in 1957. Hadley recounted,

> They came and told us that they thought it was Charley. And I went up there, and the only way I could tell it was him was his thumb. When I saw his thumb, I knew 'that's Charley.' He got beat up something terrible." [This reference was to the thumb maimed in a horse-powered grain grinder when he was a boy.] After he died his wife disowned us. I think it affected her mind, I don't know.

According to Hadley, Charley was in a motel room bed with a woman other than his wife when he was killed by the tornado. Half of the Thompson clan told me everybody knew about it so I might as well print it. The other half asked me not to write the whole story. But after Fred Crismon shared the KKK certificate and graveyard picture with Klan flowers with the world, it seemed as though it was fair to have honesty maintained on both sides.

After Charley's death, Hadley was walking around the old homestead one day. His mother and John had already moved to Leeton. Hadley remembered the pact he'd made with Charley and "hollered up to the clouds, 'Hey Charley! Tell me now, is there a hereafter or ain't there?'

"And then a big piece of corrugated tin rose up from the ground about a foot, turned over and then settled down, just as gently as you please. There wasn't a lick of breeze that day neither." Everyone in the family heard that story many times.

What about Joe? Joe gave up his dream of teaching and stepped into the role of family caretaker and farmer. On 10 September 1961, Joe was at the wheel after visiting Icel and Hadley. While traveling through Meads Flats, there was a head-on collision. Joe's wife Ruth died immediately at the scene and the others sustained major injuries. Later, Joe remarried and spent the majority of his life on the farm near Leeton, Missouri, where I interviewed him.

Directly following Hadley's funeral, one woman reported that Joe made a pass at her in the graveyard. Certainly, all the Thompson men had a good laugh over Joe's antics.

Old Joe was the last to leave. He died on 29 April 2004, just a month shy of his 100th birthday. He was buried at the Mineral Creek Cemetery, Leeton, Misouri, next to his mother and brother John.

And Paul? On 30 June 1934, Paul Thompson married LaVerne Burch in Lake Ozark, Missouri. Paul and LaVern's daughter died an untimely death at two and a half. She was buried in the Conway Cemetery with many of her mother's ancestors. However, some of her grandfather's enemies lie close to her as well.

As with his brother Hadley, Paul was in the Navy. Then he was employed as a credit manager for Sears Roebuck and Company, who transferred him to Colorado in 1969. He retired from Sears in 1975 and started a realty company, where the family credits him with starting the first timeshares in Vail, Colorado. He died on 22 September 2000 at the age of eighty-six.

During an interview in 2003, Mrs. LaVerne Thompson stated her husband felt they should leave Missouri and "do our own thing." Asked if her husband Paul ever said anything about the feud, she said he never did, and she never asked. The only statement she remembers him saying on numerous occasions was, "I remember more than they think I do." Indeed, Hadley and Joe made the statement on just as many occasions, "Paul was too young to remember much."

What happened to Myrtle Thompson and John? Grant Thompson's will designated the farm to go to his first family of children. Although she stayed on for a time, Myrtle left the Wilcox Bend area with John and Joe and moved to another farm. From there she continued to administer homemade polecat poultice to family members with colds, made by shooting a skunk, rendering the lard, then mixing in healing herbs and mint. (When asked if it worked, Joe responded, "Sure. We never complained of being sick.")

Every family member noted that until her death, Mrs. Thompson never let a visitor leave without sending home a jar of something she had canned or a loaf of bread. She would also send fresh cream for strawberries. John Winslow Thompson lived with her until he died at the age of 68. They were buried next to each other in Leeton, Missouri.

What became of Gipsy? Gipsy Wornell and Jim Thompson were married. Hadley said he "threw a Thompson fit" and wrote a letter he deeply regretted when he found out. Claimed he disowned the family. Later he told me even he didn't understand at the time how the two shared no common blood, as they all just thought of themselves as one family.

For a while Gipsy worked at Peck and Peck as a hairdresser in Kansas City. Gipsy and Jim remained active in the Thompson family and doted on the younger generation of Thompsons although they did not have any children of their own. Gipsy's last will and testament stated, "My grandfather on my mother's side was Maston Wornell. He was the only father I ever knew and I loved him."

What happened to Otto? On January 8, 1926, Harrison Otto Thompson married to Cleo Blankenship, died of Brights Disease at the age of thirty-seven. Knowledge of the disease is what caused him to return to Wilcox Bend to join his father in farming. He was blind when he died.

What about Plez Moore? As it turned out, not everybody loved Plez. He was shot and killed in St. Louis. During an interview at Joe's, Hadley asked, "Now what was Plez's relation to us?" Joe responded, "He was like family." Hadley persisted, "He had some connection to Aunt Maggie." At this point Old Joe laughed, shook his head, and laughed some more. Hadley just stared at him. With tears of laughter in his eyes Joe said, "He was sweet on her Hadley!" Ahh…no wonder the Klan hated those rowdy Thompsons.

What became of the Crismons after 1925? Census records and interviews with grandson Fred indicate the family relocated from Wilcox Bend to the Jefferson City area, as well as other places in mid-Missouri. Frederick worked as a postmaster and farmed throughout the years. Fred felt the murder of Francis had a huge emotional effect on both his grandparents. They are buried in a cemetery in Eldon, Missouri with Francis.

Leo Crismon became formally educated, attending seminary and producing many scholarly works for the Baptist church. He was a Baptist preacher for his entire life and fluent in many languages. He died in 1986.

Any previous romance between Anita Crismon and Charley Thompson died when the two men were killed. Anita Crismon became a nurse. Fred Crismon described his aunt as having a personality that made it difficult to be around.

What happened to the Klan following the trial? Although they didn't know it at the time, beginning in late 1923, the Klan started to receive the blows that eventually led to its downfall. First Philip Fox, the editor of the Klan publication *Imperial Night Hawk*, was sentenced to life for the murder of a national KKK official and attorney. In many of the states where the Klan was the most active, the base of immorality and hypocrisy became evident as the thin veneer of respectability started to erode away. Klan officials were caught in a variety of uncomplimentary positions, from embarrassing situations to grievous crimes, ruining their self-described reputation as law-abiding citizens with exemplary behavior.

At the national level, a young lady was tragically responsible for the final blow and eventual death of the national KKK when Grand Dragon David C. Stephenson abducted and assaulted her. Eventually she died as a result of her ordeal, but not before giving a deathbed testimony against Stephenson. The testimony not only described the frequent drunkenness of Klan members, it detailed her kidnapping, rape, and the entire physical and mental ordeal. She took poison hoping to get sick enough to be released, but died instead.

Stephenson had covered her body with bite marks, helping to validate her claim. When Stephenson did not receive a pardon from the then Klan-supported governor, which he had every reason to expect, he turned on many politicians. Stephenson had kept a file of letters signed by each politician acknowledging that in return for Klan support, they would vote according to the Klan agenda. Many letters also stated the amount of money they had been given for Klan support. Countless officials went to prison with Stephenson.

As well, the legislation finally passed as a result of senate hearings in the 1920s negatively affected their cause. Perhaps most importantly, the blatant failure of KKK leaders to live as they preached led to their demise. The rest of the country finally agreed with Grant Thompson's opinion: the group was not to be trusted. It distorted history, the Bible, hid stills under smokehouse floors, took money when no work had been done, and took advantage of the weak.

The Klan suffered internally from conflicting factions and competing egos. Although it continued to have a history in the United States and numerous resurgences, it never received the notoriety, mass membership, nor especially the openness it enjoyed from 1915 until 1925 and to this date has maintained a subversive and underground status.

What happened to the local community during the depression and shortly thereafter? On 19 March 1931, the town of Bagnell burned. They attempted to rebuild, however, because of more floods, fires, the depression, and the eventual demise of the railroad, Bagnell never thrived as it did before 1930.

In August 1931, Bagnell Dam was completed and the Osage River began to back up to form the new lake. Lake Benton, so named by the Missouri Legislature, was an unpopular name, so Missourians in the Ozarks simply ignored their legislator's decisions, and never used the name Lake Benton. To this day, the new lake is called Lake of the Ozarks. Bagnell Dam controlled the water on both sides. Downstream of the dam, the Osage was no longer the wild tributary to the Missouri it once was. Without natural movement and periodic flooding, river bottom farming in Miller County ceased to exist.

In 1933, W.C. Thompson, born in 1922 to JoAnna (Annie) and Neil Thompson, drowned in the Missouri River.

By 1935, much had changed in Wilcox Bend. People were busy trying to scratch out a living running fishing camps for tourists on the new lake or keeping their land despite the stresses of the depression. The railroad, the KKK, events in Bagnell, and the river no longer determined the outcome of their lives.

As automobiles flourished, people named the roadways but slowly forgot most of the names of fords, eddies, and bluffs along the river. Today there are people where the Thompsons and their neighbors once lived who do not know this land was once referred to as Wilcox Bend.

In May 1940, Dr. Preston Thompson, Uncle Lev's son, died at the age of fifty-three. He had always been close to his father, Eleven, and Uncle Lev could not be comforted. In April 1941, Uncle Lev died. His obituary read in part: "One of Brumley's well-known citizens, born November 11, 1857, died. He had been a member of the Baptist Church for 45 years. In 1890 he moved to Brumley and helped start the Bank of Brumley" [which, the reader will recall, later became part of Central Bank of Lake of the Ozarks].

Leo Crismon's Klan certificate

—Courtesy Crismon Family

The Thompson barn, built in Spring, 1925 by the Thompson boys

—Author's photo, 2010

NOTES

In an attempt to share some of the language that was such a part of life on Wilcox Bend in the 1920s, sections of this story are told in the first person using Hadley as the narrator. Although sometimes the text is an exact quotation, more often the narration has been edited for clarity and ease. Like most of us, Hadley occasionally changed his mind, remembered something at a later date, utilized another source for details, or repeated himself. Therefore, Hadley's first person narrative must be considered a composed voice, whose content is based on interviews with many other people as well as written texts. When important, these differentiations are clarified in the following notes.

INNOCENCE

p. 15 *same as a pointer* This phrase references a type of dog used for hunting game birds. Pointers characteristically bend up one front leg and point the tail parallel with the ground or upward.

p. 15 *Charley* Charley Thompson signed his name on court documents with this spelling although the newspapers used the spelling Charlie.

p. 17 *neighbor named Professor Molls* Goodspeed, *Miller County History*, p. 798. Other references for information about Professor Herbert L. Molls included interviews with Hadley and Joe Thompson and the local newspaper. The correct spelling of his name is Moles, al- though I used Hadley's spelling of Molls.

p. 17 *Hadley Herbert Thompson* Hadley was the namesake of Herbert Spencer Hadley, Missouri republican governor from 1908 to 1912. Grant Thompson also named the farm along the Osage where the story took place, "The Herbert S. Hadley."

p. 18 *Ever heard of the Thompson-Crismon* Hadley Thompson, interview with author, Lake Ozark, Missouri, 20 April 1996. This dialogue is a direct transcription.

p. 18 *I'm going to tell you... hurt me that bad* Hadley Thompson, tape recording, Osage Beach, Missouri, 3 October 1995. This section is a direct quotation from a tape Thompson recorded while recovering at Lake Regional Hospital.

p. 20 *Tommy Alexander* This fictional character's actions and subsequent treatment by the Klan are based on the life of two individuals usually referred to in interviews as "the town drunks." *Clyde Rogers and his wife* are also fictitious names given to actual people. The holy-hat saga was a favorite among Wilcox Bend natives although there was no consensus as to the names of the characters.

p. 20   *J.G. Thompson, one of our*   *Miller County Autogram,* 26 April 1917. n.p.

p. 21   *What can I...beating the hell outta me*   Hadley Thompson, interview with author, Lake Ozark, Missouri, 3 October 1995; 12 February 1998. This section is a direct quotation.

p. 21   *Two somber servicemen*   The following excerpt from 6 January 1919, *Miller County Autogram* illustrates Hadley's point:
The following telegram was sent by the Graves Registration Service from the Army Piers, New Jersey: to Mrs. Martha Roark, of near Capps Missouri:
'Remains of son, late Private Percy F. Roark, will be shipped to you. Await funeral arrangements. Private Roark died December, 1918 in France from the effects of influenza and bronchial pneumonia. It is probable that the local American Legion Post will act as escort for the body."

p. 21   *the scrip on our account*   This written notation of credit given to the customer was to be used at the store. It was handed out at the storekeeper's discretion and was also used when the proprietor didn't have correct change.

p. 24   *three different train stations*   Both the Rock Island and the Missouri Pacific line stopped in Bagnell before returning to Eldon. Then the Missouri Pacific continued on to Jefferson City and the Rock Island to Kansas City. However, it was common for other railroad companies to pay to hook up their cars to this line as well.

p. 25   *spur for the Missouri Pacific*   A railroad spur meant a dead end.

p. 26   *Black Bastard*   This dog in the Otto Thompson family, owned by son William "Noogie" Thompson, lived at a later date than this story states.

p. 27   *"The Klan weren't never about..."*   Hadley Thompson, interview with author, Lake Ozark, Missouri, 4 November 1997.

p. 28   *Billy Sunday was the biggest celebrity*   Torricelli, *In Our Own Words,* 61-63. This text served as inspiration for the flavor and words of Sunday's sermon.

p. 28   *ground his meal in a stump*   Until the 1800s brought the handy existence of mills, settlers hollowed out stumps of hardwood trees to create mortars. They then used a variety of instruments to create pestles to ground grain into meal by hand.

p. 29 *hair that wasn't pinned up* In the late 1800s and into the early 1900s, respectable women held their long hair in place with pins or under a bonnet or hat when in public places. The 1920s began to change this tradition.

p. 29 *Brother Kenneth's a son-of-a-bitch* George Peyton, interview with author, 5 April 2001, Lake Ozark, Missouri. This sentence is a direct quotation.

p. 30 *Bank of Brumley* Grant's brother, Eleven Coa Thompson, was a successful businessman according to two local newspapers and interviews. At the end of the 1900s, this bank was bought by Central Bank of Lake of the Ozarks.

p. 30 *outline of a flask or a pistol* It had already been illegal to carry concealed weapons in Missouri for decades.

ADVENTURE

p. 35 *Cousin Happy* This man was a relative from Myrtle Thompson's side of the family.

p. 36 *That Crismon boy* Icel quoted Hadley as saying, "That Hickey boy." As Logan Hickey, a nephew to Sarah Crismon, was not introduced into the story until much later, readers continually questioned who he was. Although he became a part of the feud, this confusion detracted from the story. The name was therefore changed while keeping Hadley's intent clear.

p. 38 *My half-sister Gipsy* Genealogical records spell her name this way as well as *Gypsy*. Newspapers and census records do the same.

p. 39 *Stop whatever you're doing* Although many of the Thompsons attribute this phrase to Plez Moore, Garrett references Elizabeth Mc- Combs as the author in *The Thompson Connection*, 205.

p. 39 *Tack* The bridle, harness, saddle, reins and other leather straps used to ride or drive a horse.

p. 40 *Granary* The Thompson's granary was a square building that housed grain after it was threshed or husked. They also had a silo.

p. 41 *a drummer* A term referencing a traveling salesman, so called because they "drummed up" business.

p. 43 *about nineteen and twenty* Hadley Thompson, interview with author, Eldon, Missouri, 5 March 1998. The first five paragraphs of this section are a direct quotation.

p. 44 *Sprouts* Farmers from the early 1900s often wrote about the thick underbrush in the area, which they called "sprouts," sometimes

swearing the regrowth was twice as thick as the original:
I have cut 'em and let goats eat 'em. I have beat 'em down with a club.
I have cussed 'em and finally just ignored 'em and they are still with
me. Truly, there is only one way to get rid of them, and that way is to
move off and leave them behind. (Lucus, in Jenkins, *History of Miller
County*, 28.)

p. 45   *the Billy Sunday crew*   This comment should not suggest that
Billy Sunday had anything to do with the KKK. Kleagles were often
recruited men who did not have steady jobs at the time, and these
two could have easily been recruited by the Klan after Sunday's visit.

p. 45   *Dr. Preston Thompson*   Uncle Lev's son was born 22 March 1887.

p. 47   *lodge pin*   This story about the man claiming his lodge pin was
a popular story at the time and attributed to many different individuals.

p. 50   *bird-dogged*   A colloquial phrase describing the boys following
him as a dog will do at the heels of his master.

p. 50   *"If there'd been a Mrs."*   According to Goodspeed's *Miller County
History*, p. 798, Professor was happily married. Mrs. Molls is also
listed as dying after her husband. However, she does not appear to
have spent much time, if any, in Wilcox Bend. None of the other
residents interviewed had any memory of her as well.

p. 51   *smelled of horehound drops*   A horehound drop is an old-fashioned cough drop with a distinctive gingery smell.

p. 52   *John was the oldest boy*   Hadley Thompson, interview with author, Eldon, Missouri, 10 September 1998. The following five paragraphs are direct quotations.

p. 52   *My sister Annie*   was Johanna Thompson, born in 1896 to Grant
Thompson's first wife. She was fifteen years older than Hadley. She
married Neil Thompson, and although he was not a blood relation,
Klan members labeled this union as immoral.

p. 52   *outbuildings*   These could include a smoke house, hen house,
spring house, granary, storage or scale shed. Most farms had at least
four or five such structures.

p. 53   *Prize-winning dog in Sedalia*   This is a reference to the Missouri State Fair, held annually in Sedalia, Missouri.

p. 54   *As far as I know*   Crismon, Fred, letter to author, Louisville,
Kentucky, 8 March 2008, p. 4.

p. 56   *My father has left a precious*   Crismon, Leo. T., personal journal,
1960s (believed), p. 1. Courtesy Fred Crismon.

p. 56   *Mr. Tellman was a foxhunting*   Additional facts about Missouri and Hellman Tellman are recorded in Goodspeed's *Miller County History*, pp. 817-818.

p. 60 *Ty Sears* The story of Ty's father is found in McNeil, W.K. *Ozark Country*, p. 15.

p. 61 *bald headed end of the broom* Complete lyrics in Randolph, *Ozark Folksongs*, vol. 3, p. 106.

p. 62 *Because Missouri experienced a civil war* Muraskin, *Missouri Politics*, p.18.

p. 63 *Grant Thompson was a nominal* Leo T. Crismon, personal journal, 1960s (believed), p.7. Courtesy Fred Crismon.

p. 63 *Les Leids was at the meetings* In the memories of Gaylord Strange, Hadley and Joe Thompson, and Robert Vaughn, the two Kleagles referred to as Mule's Teeth and Short Hair eventually left the area and turned over the administration of the meetings to three local men. Pud Downs, Inky O'Brien, and Les Leids are fictitious names given to the actions of the men they recalled. The actions of these characters are believed to be accurate although the actual names of the culprits were not recorded in this text. As these are totally fabricated names they should not be confused with any individuals who might have actually had these names.

p. 64 *stuck to Les like beggar lice* "Beggar lice" is a colloquial term given to a type of field burr, also referred to as "stick tights."

p. 65 *Remember history!* Excerpts of Mr. Shorthair's speech were taken from a speech of H.W. Evans, imperial wizard of the Ku Klux Klan during the 1920s. Evan, *The Klan of Tomorrow, 1924.*

p. 65 *Old Man Sons* was Oliver Son, the grandfather of Ruby Laurie. Hadley said about Ruby, "She's a tough old gal, like her granddad." Ruby in turn noted that Hadley had erroneously referred to Oliver as "Sons" instead of "Son" all of her life. She admonished me not to correct him. She also said her grandfather loved to attend fish-fries at the Thompsons and to play the fiddle while Mrs. Thompson played the organ. He always had marbles to give the children and was a big, tall man. Son married Mary Farris, who granddaughter Ruby remembered "had quite a tongue on her" causing Oliver to sometimes get out of the wagon and walk along beside it while she drove.

p. 67 *My mother, Myrtle Wornell* This paragraph was taken, nearly verbatim, from an interview with Joe Thompson, interview with author, Leeton, Missouri, 27 October 1999.

ALLIES

p. 75   *"creeping negroidism"*   Tom Dixon as quoted in Wade, *The Fiery Cross*, p. 122.

p. 75   *Abe-olitionists*   This term as well as "Black Republicans" was mentioned in a variety of texts, including histories of Miller County. The phrases were used in the mid-1800s and later to describe those in favor of the abolition of slavery.

p. 76   *For a thick-lipped*   Tom Dixon, *The Clansmen*, 1905, quoted in Wade, p. 123.

p. 81   *By 1925, close to five percent*   Klan membership is estimated to have risen to between 4,000,000 and 5,000,000 according to many sources. Half of these members lived in rural areas similar to the idyllic Wilcox Bend.

p. 82   *Dunk 'em again, Preacher*   This baptism story is attributed to many individuals and is likely part of Ozark lore of undetermined origin.

p. 83   *Threshing*   In the Ozarks, this word is pronounced "thrashing."

p. 86   *I was out in the country*   The full text to this song "The Widow's Old Broom" and others referenced in this section may be found in various sources as well as in Randolph, *Ozark Folksongs*, vol. 3, p. 107.

p. 88   *He warned that America risked*   Grant, *The Passing of the Great Race*, 1916, quoted in Wade, p. 148.

p. 93   *Any man who carries a hyphen*   Baker and Dodd, *Selected Literary and Political Papers*, p. 270.

p. 94   *Post Oak School Number Forty-Nine*   In reality, three Thompsons were schoolteachers: Annie, Gipsy, and Otto. All received attention from the Wilcox Bend Klavern. Events were combined to reduce confusion, with the events surrounding Annie and Gipsy told as involving just Gipsy. Mrs. Sarah Crismon attended the Iberia teachers academy as well. The bullfrog story is courtesy of Howard Ferris.

p. 96   *The Eldon Advertiser noted extraordinary*   1917 *Eldon Advertiser* clipping courtesy Gaylord Strange. n.p.

p. 97   *Citizens wanting to look over the farmers*   Community council cat-echism from the Mumford files, folder 18. 1917. Columbia, Missouri: Western Historical Manuscript Collection, State Historical Library.

p. 98   *"Man buried alive!"*   Clarence Lewis Diedriech, interview with author, 17 January 2002, Lake Ozark, Missouri.

p. 99   *One drew letters in the dirt*   The letters AYAK stood for, "Are you a Klansman?" while AKIA meant, "A Klansman am I."

p. 104   *That was the Woofenpoof's gold*   A more complete description of this folktale figure can be found in Young, *Ozark Tall Tales*, p. 76.

p. 106   *Someone said, "All rise!"*   This event was described by Willis Ezard, interview with author, 4 April 1997, Conway, Missouri.

p. 110   *could produce fusil oil poisoning*   At the time of this writing there was still no cure, with death being a certainty.

p. 112   *He'd made a trap door*   This event was described by Robert Vaughn about his uncle Les Vaughn's actions. Interview with author, Bagnell, Missouri, 5 July 1999.

p. 116   *Well now, this old schoolmarm*   A printed version of this story can be found in McNeil, *Ozark Country*, p. 81.

p. 117   *done lost the only dowry*   The girl's parents could not afford a wedding, so her only dowry was her virginity.

p. 123   *Sarah Crismon was given a farm*   This was originally stated by Olive Robinett (Otto Thompson's daughter), but later confirmed by Fred Crismon, interview by author, Lake Ozark, Missouri, 10 August 2009.

p. 127   *Professor didn't want him rendered*   Rendering is the act of processing the carcass into leather, tallow, fertilizer and so on.

p. 129   *Sure enough, here come that*   This section through the next two paragraphs is a direst quotation, Hadley Thompson, interview with author, Bagnell, Missouri, 4 November 1997.

p. 139   *A Crismon never married a Ponder*   Outlined in Garret, *The Thompson Connection*. Joe also said Plez had told the Thompsons of this relationship when the Crismons moved in.

p. 141   *Leo's personal account states*   Leo T. Crismon, personal journal, 1960s (believed), p. 3. Courtesy Fred Crismon.

p. 141   *Some time in the early*   The next three paragraphs direct quotation, Hadley Thompson, Eldon, Missouri, 4 November 1997.

p. 143   *"Courting! You and your brother*   The reader will remember Jim Thompson's parents were Emma Ponder and Grant Thompson, while Gipsy's were Myrtle Warnell and an unnamed man (later determined to be a Robinette.)

p. 145   *Girls had been eyeing him*   Olive Thompson Robinette, interview with author, 27 March 2001.

p. 145   *My brother Otto's daughter Olive*   Olive Thompson Robinette, interview with author, 27 March 2001.

p. 151   *If they was wearing hoods.*   Robert Vaughn, interview with author, Bagnell, Missouri, 5 July 1999.

p. 151   *Hadley stated, "They had talked*   Hadley Thompson, interview with author, Eldon, Missouri, 9 January, 1998.

p. 151   *More formal research supports these trends.*   From *Inside the Klavern; The Secret History of the Ku Klux Klan of the 1920s.* The events in this section are based on minutes from the LaGrange Oregon Klavern in 1923 found in this book.

p. 154   *The whole trouble with the Klan*   White, *Annals*, pp. 220-221.

p. 155   *Joe and Dad went on*   Hadley Thompson, interview with author, Eldon, Missouri, 20 July 1997. This direct quotation from Hadley begins here and continues to the end of the section where he states, "Now she was becoming our deathtrap."

p. 156   *Grant Thompson and son Joe*   Unknown local newspaper clipping courtesy Gaylord Strange.

p. 156   *On one occasion (1923?) Grant*   Leo T. Crismon, personal journal, 1960s (believed) p. 7. Courtesy Fred Crismon.

p. 156   *Look. Look here where they*   Joe Thompson, interview with author, Leeton, Missouri, 27 October 1999.

p. 161   *Now I need to back*   Hadley Thompson, interview with author, Eldon, Missouri, 4 November 1997. The text beginning with this phrase and continuing for the next five paragraphs is a direct quotation.

p. 162   *And what happened was nothing.*   This case was elaborated upon in the local papers. What had become a typical situation is described during the Medford trials, where three not-guilty verdicts were given to three Klansmen accused of "night-riding atrocities." A Klan-supported judge ruled that membership in the KKK was irrelevant in the selection of the jury, whose foreman also happened to be a cousin of the defendant. (Medford Files, State Historical Society Library, Columbia, Missouri.)

p. 163   *Leo's account relates a different*   Leo T. Crismon, personal journal, 1960s (believed), p. 7. Courtesy Fred Crismon.

p. 163   *Funny you should ask.*   Telephone Interview with Fred Crismon, 1 May 2008.

p. 163   *Ku Klux Klan at Russellville*   *Miller County Autogram*, 15 May 1924, vol. 4.

p. 165   *In February 1924, a large contingent*   Gary Kremer "History Matters," quoting a *Jefferson City Missouri News Tribune* article from

February 1924 in 4 November edition 2001, *Lake Sun Leader.*

p. 168 *Grant Thompson and Fred Crismon* *Miller County Autogram,* July, u.d. 1924. Courtesy Hadley Thompson.

p. 169 *Three drowned when an auto* Unknown source, 1924 hand written on clipping, Courtesy Fred Crismon.

p. 169 *she had a shotgun across her* Grandson Fred Crismon acknowledged this statement was likely true. Telephone interview with author, 10 August 2008.

p. 174 *In September 1924, national leader* Evans, *The Klan of Tomorrow.*

p. 175 *Vigilance is truly the price* *Miller County Autogram,* vol. 40, 23 October 1924.

p. 179 *On 4 November 1924, another warrant* Miller County Courthouse Records, Tuscumbia, Missouri. Courtesy Hadley Thompson.

p. 180 *Missourians divided their votes* Muraskin, *Missouri Politics, 18.*

p. 181 *Grant Thompson Shoots Fred Crismon* *Miller County Autogram,* 1 December 1924.

p. 182 *Soon after Grant Thompson fired* Leo Crismon, personal journal, 1960s (believed), p. 8.

p. 185 *Little Olive followed her daddy* Olive Thompson Robinette, interview with author, Eldon, Missouri, 27 March 2001.

p. 187 *The Eldon Advertiser, the Official* *Eldon Advertiser,* no. 26, 25 December 1924.

p. 190 *Whereas information had been given* This form was on record at the Miller County Courthouse, Miller County, Missouri, dated 1924. Courtesy Hadley Thompson.

p. 193 *Grant Thompson and Francis Crismon* Undated local newspaper clipping courtesy Hadley Thompson.

p. 196 *Francis Crismon dies in Jefferson* *Miller County Autogram,* vol. 40, 1 January 1925.

p. 197 *Just before Christmas, December 24* Leo Crismon, personal journal, 1960s (believed), p. 8. Courtesy Fred Crismon.

p. 198 *On Dec. 21 or 22, 1924* Leo Crismon, personal journal, 14 September 1982, p. 1. Courtesy Fred Crismon.

p. 200 *"Dismiss the children. They've killed* Olive Robinette, interview with author, Eldon, Missouri, 27 March 2001.

p. 200 *Paul Thompson's widow told me* LaVern Thompson, interview with author, Pueblo, Colorado, 7 July 2004.

p. 200   *Charlie Thompson is Charged with*   *Eldon Advertiser,* vol. 45,1, 8 January 1925.

p. 201   *Charley Thompson Absolved*   *Eldon Advertiser,* vol. 46, 8 January 1925.

p. 201   *Ku Klux Klan Meeting*   *Eldon Advertiser,* vol. 46, 8 January 1925.

p. 202   *On 7 February 1925, Charley filed*   County Record Book, Tuscumbia, Missouri.

p. 213   *He was the only man I ever*   Patricia Pfaff, interview with author, Mims, Florida, 20 September 2007.

BIBLIOGRAPHY
Interviews and Personal Communication

Arnold, Mae and Sylvia. Interview with author. Eldon, Missouri. 10 July 1995.

Brake, Harold. Telephone interview with author. Columbia, Missouri. 1 February 2007.

Coates, Bernice Thompson. Letter to author dated 18 November 2005.

Crismon, Fred. Letter to author dated 8 March 2008.

————, Fred. Email to author dated 12 March 2008.

————, Fred. Interview with author, Lake Ozark, Missouri, 10 August 2008.

Crismon, Leo T., Personal journal. 1960s (believed). Courtesy Fred Crismon.

————, Leo T., Personal journal. 14 September 1982. Courtesy Fred Crismon.

Diedriech, Clarence Lewis. Interview with author. Lake Ozark, Missouri, 17 January 2002, 18 February 2003.

Ezard, Willis. Interview with author. Carthage, Missouri, 4 April 1997.

Foster, "Doc" and Laura. Interview with author, ? November 1995, 5 October 1995, 10 October 1995.

Green, Eathel. Interview with author. Russelville, Missouri, 17 July 1996.

Hedges, Walter. Interview with author. Osage Beach, Missouri, 17 November 1995.

Hickman, John. Interview with author. Eldon, Missouri, 5 September 2001.

Howser, Burnam Edmond. Interview with author. Bagnell, Missouri, 26 January 2001.

Jeffries, Matilda. Interview with author. ? February 1995, ? August 1996.

Laurie, Ruby Son. Interview with author. Eldon, Missouri, 22 July 1996, 17 November 1999.

McDowell, Alma. Interview with author. Osage Beach, Missouri, 14 June 1995.

McDowell, Joyce. Interview with author. Osage Beach, Missouri, 7 July 2002.

McDowell, Ralph. Interview with author. Versailles, Missouri, 26 September 1995.

McKinley, Virginia. Letter to author. Versailles, Missouri, 11 November 2005.

234 Victoria Pope Hubbell

Pfaff, Patricia Thompson, Interview with author, Mims, Florida, 20 September 2007.

Popplewell, Edith Emma. Interview with author, Butler, Missouri, 31 October 2006.

——, Edith Emma. Interview with author, Butler, Missouri, 1 November 2006.

Robinett, Cornelia Olive Thompson. Interview with author, Eldon, Missouri, 27 March 2001.

Strange, Gaylord. Interview with author, Eldon, Missouri, 15 November 1995, 6 December 1996, 5 May 2000, 20 December 2006.

Thompson, Hadley. Audio taped dictation, Osage Beach, Missouri, 3 October 1995.

Thompson, Hadley and Icel. Interview with author, Eldon, Missouri, 20 April 1996, 1 May 1997, 9 January 1998, 5 March 1998.

Thompson, Hadley. Interview with author, Eldon, Missouri, 20 July 1997, 4 September 1997, 16 September 1997, 4 November 1997, 10 September 1998, 9 September 1999.

——, Hadley, Interview with author, Bagnell, Missouri, 6 October 1998, 12 February 1998, 9 September 1998, 31 December 1998.

Thompson, Joe. Interview with author, Leeton, Missouri, 27 October 1999, 5 December 1999.

Thompson, LaVern Burch. Interview with author, Pueblo, Colorado, 7 July 2004.

Thompson, Virginia Delight. Telephone interview with author, 1 November 2006.

Vaughn, Robert. Interview with author, Bagnell, Missouri, 4 December 1998.

Published Sources

The ABC of the Knights of the Ku Klux Klan, exhibit G in U.S. Congress, The Ku Klux Klan Hearings. 67 Congress. 1 Session — House Committee on Rules, 1921. p. 121.

Alexander, Charles C. "Kleagles and Cash: The Ku Klux Klan as a Business Organization, 1915-1930." *Business History Review* 39 (1965): 351- 353.

Arthur, George Clinton. *Bushwhacker; A True History of Bill Wilson, Missouri's Greatest Desperado.* Rolla, Missouri: Rolla Printing Company, 1938.

Baker, Ray Stannard and William E. Dodd. *Selected Literary and Political Papers and Addresses of Woodrow Wilson, 1916-1927.* New York: Grosset & Dunlap, 1925.

Bittersweet Magazine. Volume V, No 3, 1978 and Volume VII, No 2, 1979. Lebanon, Missouri: Bittersweet, Inc.

Christensen, L.O., Foley, W.E., Kremer, G.R., Winn, K.H., editors. *Dictionary of Missouri Biography.* Columbia: University of Missouri Press, 1999.

Community Council Catechism. Mumford files, folder 18. Missouri Historical Library, (originally Western Manuscript Collection) Columbia, Missouri. 1917.

County Court Record Book C. Miller County, Tuscumbia, Missouri. Courtesy Hadley Thompson.

Department of Commerce. Bureau of the census. 14th United States Census, 1920 and 15th United States Census, 1930.

Dixon, Thomas Jr. *The Fall of a Nation.* New York: D. Appleton & Co., 1916.

Evans, Hiram Wesley. *The Klan of Tomorrow And, the Klan Spiritual: Addresses.* Kansas City, Missouri: Knights of the Ku Klux Klan, 1924.

Furnas, J.C. *The Late Demon Rum.* New York: G.P. Putnam, 1965.

Garrett, Floyd Francis. *The Thompson Connection.* Conroe, Texas: Garrett Newspaper, 1984.

Goodspeed. *Miller County History.* Higginsville, Missouri: Hearthstone Legacy Publications, 1889.

Griffith, D.W., director. *Birth of a Nation.* 1915; New Jersey: Madacy Entertainment Group. Videocassette (VHS), 190 min.

Guy, Howard. *Walkin' Preacher of the Ozarks.* Topeka, Kansas: Capper Press, 1944.

Horowitz, David A., editor. *Inside the Klavern: The Secret History of a Ku Klux Klan of the 1920s.* Carbondale: Southern Illinois University Press, 1999.

Johnson, Paul. "The First International Nation, 1912-1929," in *A History of the American People.* New York: Harper Collins, 1986.

Lucas, Reverend S. Emmitt, Jr. [1889]. *History of Miller County Missouri.* [written, edited, illustrated and published by Clyde Lee Jenkins] Tuscumbia, Missouri, 1978.

Kirkendall, Richard S. *History of Missouri.* Volume 5, 1919 to 1953. Columbia, Missouri: University of Missouri Press, 1986.

McNeil, W.K. *Ozark Country*. Jackson: University Press of Mississippi, 1995.

Muraskin, Jack David. *Missouri Politics During the Progressive Era, 1896-1916*. Dissertation. Berkeley: University of California, 1969.

Murfner, Mary Noailles. *The Bushwhackers and Other Stories*. Chicago: H.S. Stone & Company, 1899.

Pederson, Lee. "Language, Culture and the American Heritage," in *The American Heritage Dictionary*, 2nd college edition. Boston: Houghton Mifflin Company, 1991.

Purvis, Thomas L. *A Dictionary of American History*. Massachusetts: Blackwell Publishers, 1997.

Randolph, Vance, editor. *Ozark Folksongs*, Volume 3. Columbia, Missouri: University of Missouri Press, 1980.

Schultz, Gerard. *A History of Miller County Missouri*. Missouri: Midland Printing Company, 1933.

Shoemaker, Floyd Colvin. *Missouri and Missourians*, Volume 2. Chicago: Lewis Publishing Company, 1943.

Tuck, Clyde Edwin. *The Bald-Knobbers; A Novel of the Ozarks*. Kansas City, Missouri: Burton Publishing, 1930.

Torricelli, Robert and Andrew Carroll, editors. "Evangelical preacher Billy Sunday excoriates alcohol as 'God's worst enemy' and Will Rogers skewers both the 'wets' and the 'drys' in the prohibition debate," in *In Our Own Words*. New York: Washington Square Press, 1999.

Wade, Wyn Craig. *The Fiery Cross - the Ku Klux Klan in America*. Oxford: Oxford University Press, 1987.

White, William Allen. Letter of September 17, 1921 to the editor of the *New York World. In Annals of America* Volume 14, 1916-1925. "Selected letters of William Allen White, 1899-1943." Walter Johnson, editor. New York: Encyclopedia Britannica, Inc. 1976.

Young, Richard and Judy Dockrey Young. *Ozark Tall Tales*. Little Rock: August House Inc., 1989.

Zinn, Howard. "The Socialist Challenge and War is the Health of the State." *A People's History of the United States, 1492-Present*. New York: Harper Collins, 1980.

Writer Victoria Hubbell, Ph.D. enjoys both conducting research and talking to people. As a result, she writes oral histories about fascinating people, places, and events.

Her most recent book *Blood River Rising* (Iris Press, October 2016) tells the story of two white families who become unwitting pawns of the Ku Klux Klan.

Hubbell's previous book *A Town on Two Rivers*, the history of a small town in the Ozarks, was based on over one hundred interviews combined with other historical texts. In 2015, Rowan and Littlefield published her chapter on storytelling and its effect on culture in their textbook *Jim Hensen and Philosophy*.

As a teacher, Dr. Hubbell has helped writers of all ages and at all stages of the writing process, although her favorite area is teaching composition at the college and adult levels. She is available for presentations to civic and educational groups, discussions for book clubs, and workshops at writers' conferences. Please visit her website at www.victoriaphubbell.com for details as well as to view additional pictures from the Thompson and Crismon families and possible questions for discussion.

In accordance with both Hadley Thompson and Fred Crismon's wishes and knowledge, half of Hubbell's net proceeds from the sale of this book will be donated to the Salvation Army in Missouri.

CPSIA information can be obtained
at www.ICGtesting.com
Printed in the USA
LVOW07s2129101116
512523LV00003B/4/P

9 781604 542349